# INTERWOVEN

# INTERWOVEN

Russell E. Ebersole
Nancy Goehring Ebersole

**Association of Baptists for World Evangelism**
P.O. Box 8585
Harrisburg, PA 17105–8585
(717) 774–7000
abwe@abwe.org

ABWE Canada
980 Adelaide St. South, Suite 34
London, Ontario N6E 1R3
(519) 690–1009
office@abwecanada.org

**ABWE**™ PUBLISHING®

# Dedication

With great affection and appreciation,
we dedicate this book to:

Our parents, all of whom are now with the Lord they
loved and served,
## RUSS and SUE EBERSOLE, SR.,
who throughout our years of ministry were great encouragers
and prayer partners. In their retirement years, when God took
Russ' first wife, Gene, to heaven, they provided a loving home
for Russ and his five children and were the children's main
caregivers for over four years.

*and*

## MILDRED GOODMAN,
who as a widow reared Nancy and her three siblings through
difficult and financially lean years and trained them to live and
serve the Lord. When Nancy's first husband, Harry, went to
heaven, she provided a loving home for Nancy and her three
children for four years.

*and*

## OUR CHILDREN
Russ, Cheri, Beth, Harold, Bruce, Susan, Joy, and Faith, who are
trophies of the grace of God and the prayers of many and who
have been a constant source of joy and thanksgiving to us.

Cover design is taken from cloth woven by
Igorot tribal women in northern Luzon.

INTERWOVEN
Copyright © 2002 by ABWE Publishing
Harrisburg, Pennsylvania 17105

First printing, July 2002
Second printing, January 2003
Third printing, May 2004
Fourth printing, March 2005

Library of Congress Cataloging-in-Publications Data
(application pending)

Ebersole, Russell E., 1927–
Ebersole, Nancy Goehring, 1937–

Interwoven
 Autobiographical, Non-fiction, Missionary
 ISBN 1-888796-29-4

Printed in the United States of America

# Table of Contents

# Foreword

*Interwoven* is a missionary classic! When you pick it up, you will not put it down until you have finished reading every word. The authors, Russell Ebersole and his wife, Nancy, have crafted an amazing story of vision, passion, and action under circumstances and happenings that boggle the mind. The prose is beautiful, the pathos most moving, and the purpose as clear as a cloudless sky—that purpose being to reach the world and preach the Word *"to them that sit in darkness and in the shadow of death"* (Luke 1:79). Tragedies and victories are blended in a gripping story that will challenge and change the life of every reader.

This is a story of lives surrendered, faith shared, and suffering endured—even unto death. We meet a present generation of men and women who, having heard the voice of God, respond to that call, saying, *"Lord, here am I; send me"* (Isaiah 6:8). How God directs their steps, interweaves their lives, and proves Himself faithful against incredible odds is extraordinary reading. Anyone considering a missionary career will "get the feel" of what is involved in serving the Lord today—especially in the developing countries of the world. Ample illustrations are given to show the relevance of the gospel *"to every nation, tribe, tongue, and people"* (Revelation 14:6, NKJV). Here we see the blessing and example of missions-minded grandparents whose godly influence extends to succeeding generations. It is also a chronicle of ABWE's work and the people involved in it, and how God opened new doors of opportunity for spreading the Good News. Be prepared to weep, to rejoice, to marvel, and to give thanks for the divine interweaving whereby *"the message of the Lord continues to spread and prove its glorious power"* (2 Thessalonians 3:1, Williams).

During my pastorate as senior minister of Calvary Baptist Church, New York City (1959–1973), it was my privilege, along with my wife, Heather, to know Russell and Gene Ebersole. They were missionary stalwarts—model servants of Christ—to whom young people could look as outstanding examples of faithfulness in modern missions. We thank God upon every remembrance of their lives and testimonies. During Gene's final illness, Heather was her close friend. They shared and prayed together through her ordeal of suffering until God took her home.

It is my prayer that God will use this book to challenge a new generation of young people to serve the present age, and do the Master's will.

Stephen F. Olford
Founder and Senior Lecturer
The Stephen Olford Center for Biblical Preaching
Memphis, Tennessee
May 2002

# Acknowledgments

With great gratitude, we acknowledge the important contribution Marjory Goldfinch Ward made in making this book a reality. Marjory was one of Gene's roommates at Wheaton College. She was deeply moved at Gene's death and, at the memorial service, Marjory shared with Russ her desire to write a book on Gene's life.

Much of the information concerning Gene's childhood in the Philippines came from Marjory's unpublished manuscript. The material covering the war years is stated as Marjory wrote it and is printed in this book with her permission.

Marjory, we can't thank you enough for your labor of love in writing as you did about Gene's life.

We want to express our deep appreciation to the director of ABWE Publishing, Jeannie Lockerbie Stephenson, who would not let us rest until we finished this book. Jeannie served with Harry and Nancy when they first arrived in East Pakistan (now Bangladesh) in 1963. We wish to thank her and Kristen Stagg, as they spent many hours editing the book. Russ' administrative assistant, Debbie Heritage, has been a constant source of encouragement to us as she has typed and retyped the manuscript. Thank you so much, Debbie.

Above all, we thank our loving Lord who has manifested His faithfulness to us in every circumstance of our lives.

# Part One

# The DeVRIES Family

> *"How beautiful upon the mountains are the*
> *feet of him that bringeth good tidings, that*
> *publisheth peace; that bringeth good tidings*
> *of good, that publisheth salvation; that saith*
> *unto Zion, Thy God reigneth!"*
>
> —Isaiah 52:7

1

# "That Hard Place"

Henry DeVries poured out his heart to his heavenly Father. "Lord, we don't have money to pay our medical bills, much less to pay for a trip to the cooler mountain climate of Baguio. We could never pay a doctor and a nurse to accompany us, even if we could find them."

It was 1924. Henry DeVries, pioneer missionary to the Philippines, had been warned by the doctor who had just delivered his first child that unless he took his wife, Gladys, to a cooler climate, she would not live. The DeVrieses had spent a few weeks awaiting this birth in the little city of Zamboanga in a remote corner of the Philippines. As they waited, they hoped God would lead them to "that hard place where no white man had ever been," a place they had prayed about since they felt called to missions. Instead, Gladys had gone into convulsions and almost died at the birth of their first son, David. Now the DeVrieses' faith was being tested as the doctor ordered them to leave the place where they expected to receive God's direction.

The next day's mail brought money to cover their expenses, and Henry had Gladys transferred from the hospital to a boat. As Gladys was carried on board, a fellow passenger asked, "Is that your wife, sir?" Surprised, Henry answered, "Yes. I'm taking her to Baguio. The doctor says it is her only chance."

"I am Dr. Valdez, chief of the Philippine Bureau of Health. These 11 men with me are also doctors on an inspection tour. We will be on this boat if you need us. Please call on us." Henry thanked them warmly and inwardly thanked God for taking care of Gladys' need for a doctor. He climbed onto the boat just as it prepared to weigh anchor. At that moment, he saw a *calesa* (horse-drawn cart) clattering up to the loading platform. The driver gestured wildly for the gangplank to be lowered. As the new passenger boarded, Henry recognized Gladys' favorite nurse from the hospital. Twelve doctors and a nurse. God met their needs. He spared the life of Gene's mother before Gene was even born.

Gladys regained her strength during those weeks in the cool mountain city of Baguio, and Henry attended a conference for school superintendents from all over the Philippine Islands. He asked the participants about the interior provinces of the island of Mindanao and met the superintendent from Malaybalay (pronounced Ma-lie-ba-lie), the capital of Bukidnon Province.

When the Filipino superintendent realized Henry's deep interest in that area of Mindanao, he encouraged Henry to settle in Malaybalay. He assured Henry that no missionary had ever gone to that region. Hearing of the DeVrieses' interest in Bukidnon, people warned Henry that the interior tribes did not trust any outsider, and he would find it impossible to win their confidence. As Henry and Gladys continued to pray, they had a certain assurance God had directed them to Malaybalay, that hard place where no missionary had ever been.

They journeyed back from Baguio to the city of Cagayan de Oro, in Mindanao, where friends assisted them as they prepared to go into the interior. Gathering their few pieces of furniture and a small kerosene stove, Henry hired a Model-T Ford truck to haul these meager possessions up the perilous road from Cagayan to Malaybalay. As they said goodbye to their friends and ventured into the unknown, Henry's excitement mounted almost beyond endurance. At last they were on their way to the place and people God had chosen for them.

Henry and Gladys soon left the seacoast behind as they ascended the twisting road. The Model-T carrying the excited young couple and their baby bounced through one canyon after another on the narrow track. They crossed and re-crossed swift mountain streams. They climbed to the brink of a precipice, only to wind down the other side on one hairpin curve after another. During that 12-hour spine-tingling journey, the ancient truck tipped over, dumping some of their belongings. But they managed to get the truck righted and continued on their way. They were only able to get as far as the town of Tangkulan with the truck. From there on, the trip was by horseback. At last they arrived in Malaybalay, slipping and sliding down the muddy street.

The DeVrieses' first home in Malaybalay was two cramped rooms over a rickety store. Soon after their arrival, the lower level was made into a noisy *cabarat* (dance hall), which made sleeping almost impossible. Yet at that time it was the only place available to them in the village. The Bukidnon people were afraid of the strangers and their new religion. This kept Henry and Gladys isolated from the very people they longed to reach with the gospel of Christ. They wondered how to bridge the gap to these suspicious people. Gladys, a nurse, made a limited start in showing the compassion of Christ by offering medical assistance. When the people of the town learned that she could help their children, they began bringing them to her for care.

One night around 10:00, the chief of police, who lived across the road from their tiny apartment, begged Gladys to help his little son, Pinto, who seemed to be dying. With a kerosene lantern to guide the way, Henry led his wife over to examine the comatose child. After careful questioning, Gladys decided he probably had food poisoning from spoiled fish he had eaten. She gave him an emetic and other medicine. The next day she returned to treat him again. The father was deeply grateful. "How can I repay you?" he asked. "You don't need to pay me," Gladys replied. "When little Pinto is well, that will be our pay." Three days later, the little boy was playing out in the yard. His grateful father came again to thank Gladys. "With your help and the help of the God you worship, my little boy didn't die," he told her.

A day or two later, the same chief of police sent men to help Henry finish repairs on a little nipa palm house that he had been able to rent outside the town. It was a three-room hut built high off the ground with split bamboo walls and floor, and a galvanized tin roof. The house was really little more than a shack, but every window framed a gorgeous, ever-changing panorama of lights and shadows playing over the surrounding mountains.

The DeVrieses were thankful to move away from the noise in the town to this little nipa hut. Gladys started a small clinic on the tiny veranda of their home, which God used to begin breaking down barriers. This clinic was the humble beginning of what later became the Bethel Baptist Hospital of Malaybalay, a ministry carried on for many years by ABWE missionaries Dr. Link and Lenore Nelson and many Filipino medical workers. The hospital continues to this day under the capable direction of Filipino Christian medical personnel and is still being used of God to reach Bukidnons for Christ.

As often as Henry could, he strapped a pack on his back and, with an interpreter, explored the narrow trails through the dense encircling mountain forest. One trip could take three weeks of hiking or horseback riding from village to village. Everywhere he went, Henry found those who were hungry to listen to words from the Bible. He discovered he was the first white man to enter many of the interior districts; the first white man many of the tribal people had ever seen.

Deep within the dense forest, halfway up the side of the mountain, Henry came to the house of Malamundo. As a young man, the chief offered human sacrifices to evil spirits. He had once offered a man's liver torn from his freshly killed body. Repeatedly, Malamundo's hands were covered with human blood from killings that were not wanton murders born of rage or haste, but deliberate and purposeful tribal executions. He wore the *Bagani* shirt that, according to tribal custom, could be worn only by a chief who had killed many people.

When Henry DeVries first met Malamundo, the chief was in his early fifties. He listened courteously to the white man and offered the hospitality of his house for the night. Henry laid down to sleep, blanketed in the thick tropical darkness of the deep forest. Then, from several places at once, he heard a strange choking wail, a sound that accompanied pagan ceremonies. The fearful muttering continued until the sun filtered through the towering treetops and a new day dawned. It was a sound Henry was to hear often in the jungle night, but he never heard it without fresh shock at the rawness of heathen terror.

After Henry made several visits to Malamundo, the attitude of the chief began to change. On one visit, he listened intently to every word the missionary said. Finally he spoke. "I have heard you before, but this time I listened." From that time on Malamundo's one topic of conversation was his Lord who saved him from the terrible fear he had known.

Years later, Henry returned to the same area of Bukidnon Province after a prolonged absence during World War II. Again, he lay down in the darkness to sleep. From the houses scattered all around the chief's house, Henry heard a low voice begin to sing "What A Friend We Have In Jesus." Other voices picked up the melody until the missionary was encircled by the sound of singing and the murmur of voices quoting verses from the Bible. Finally he heard the old chief begin to pray, thanking the great God for all the good things He had made: the trees, the sunshine, the stars, and the tall cogan grass for the roof of his house. For two hours Henry listened, tears of joy rolling down his cheeks as the chief interrupted his prayer with singing, making up the words of praise as he went along.

Again, Henry could not sleep through a long, dark night. But this time, he could not sleep because of the great joy that flooded his heart and mind. God had gone before and made the crooked places straight. He had shattered the doors of bronze and cut through their iron bars. Those suspicious people, those Bukidnons, had come to know Jesus Christ as Savior.

# Chapter Two

# A Life Spared

Two years after the DeVrieses' arrival in Malaybalay, Gladys was expecting her second child. Malaybalay was 74 miles over punishing roads from a mission hospital in Cagayan de Oro. The physician there, Dr. Smith, advised Gladys to arrive at the hospital at least six weeks before her baby was due. Due to the complications she experienced with the birth of her first child, Gladys dared not risk having her second child in Malaybalay without adequate medical attention.

But the rainy season set in early that year. For two weeks the twisting road to the coast became impassable. Not even the mail truck could get through to Malaybalay with the DeVrieses' support money. Henry had ordered a car from Cagayan. The night before the car finally came through, the mail truck splashed down the hill into the village, bringing a letter to the missionaries with enough money to pay for their trip to the coast.

The DeVrieses left at dawn in the Model-A touring car they had hired. Ahead lay a day's journey down a twisting, canyon-split road. In places the gravel surface had completely washed away, exposing rocks up to the size of a football for the Ford to bounce over. Gladys held on to the supporting bar across the top of the car and braced her feet against the back of the front seat, trying awkwardly to lift her heavy body away from the worst of the bumps. She prayed desperately she would make it to the coast before the baby was born. Occasionally she glanced over the side of the road and caught her breath at the sheer drop over the edge.

On the wide plateaus, the sturdy little car sank up to its running boards in mud.

After 14 exhausting hours, the DeVries family pulled into a darkened mission compound in Cagayan de Oro. Knowing the trip they had just come through, the doctor examined Gladys immediately and found both her and the baby apparently in good condition.

On November 1, 1926, Gene DeVries was born. She was the first child to be born in the mission hospital in Cagayan, two days before the new facility officially opened. In December, Henry took his family back to Malaybalay to reopen their house and resume the work they had begun. Little by little, the people of the village began to trust the missionaries. In increasing numbers they came for medical attention. Some returned on Sundays for Bible class and a preaching service. As often as possible, Henry continued to hike up mountain trails to reach into new areas.

By the fall of 1927, Henry and Gladys knew they must return to the United States for a badly needed rest. Henry took his family to accommodations at the hospital. Then he returned to Malaybalay to dispose of their few pieces of furniture and close the house for the year they would be away. On November 1, Gene's first birthday, Henry caught a ride on a hemp truck back to the coast. Arriving in Cagayan, he began to notice with mounting horror a series of funeral processions moving slowly through the streets. He counted 12 small coffins. Rushing to the hospital, Henry ran to the room where he had left his family well and happy only three days before.

He saw Gladys bent over Gene's bed. The little girl was so ill that Henry recognized her only by the silky blonde hair spread on her pillow. She had been struck down by a sudden epidemic of cholera. Patients, most of them children, were crowded into the small hospital. During the crucial days that followed, the most desperately sick children died. In fact, only Gene survived.

When Gene was strong enough, Henry booked passage on a ship to Manila, the first stage of the family's trip back to the United States. Word spread quickly that the ship would be carrying a sick American baby. The captain welcomed the missionary family aboard, escorting them to his own roomy cabin on the main deck. He moved in with the first officer to make a place for the sick child.

The boat reached Cebu before 7:00 in the morning. Henry went ashore at once and telephoned a missionary friend, Mr. Dunlap, requesting he send a doctor to the ship. He replied reassuringly, "We have a fine Christian doctor here who attends our church. He is the United States Health and Customs officer for Cebu." Shortly afterwards, the doctor came and examined Gene carefully. As he stood up, the doctor wiped his eyes and called Henry aside from the cabin. "Your little girl is critically ill and badly dehydrated," he said. "I will do what I can, but you must get her to Manila as soon as possible."

The family arrived in Manila to discover all the hospitals were badly overcrowded. A young Jewish pediatrician boarded the ship to examine Gene. He had her taken from the ship to a small hotel not far from his office and began treatment immediately. Under his expert care, Gene began to show improvement. Within a month, she gained enough strength to travel. When they found room on a ship, a most grateful family of four set sail from Manila Bay, past Corregidor Island and into the China Sea, homeward bound. God's mighty hand had intervened to spare the life of Gene DeVries; not only bringing her safely into the world, but helping her recover from cholera when few others did.

*Chapter Three*

# Bethel Mission

The DeVries family headed back to the Philippines in the spring of 1929. Upon their arrival in the country, they went directly to Baguio City to wait for the birth of a third child, Henry Junior. Nicknamed Buddy, he would complete their family. In Baguio, the delightfully cool summer capital of the Philippines, an American military doctor at a government hospital attended Gladys.

In spite of all the skilled medical attention, Gladys again almost lost her life in childbirth. Throughout the night, two doctors and three nurses tried everything they knew to save her. Around 4:00 a.m., one of the doctors fell exhausted into a chair and said, "I'm sorry, Reverend DeVries. That is all we can do."

Henry went out into the hall and stood at the window facing the lovely Santo Tomas mountain as the moonlight flooded the valley. He dropped to his knees with his eyes wide open facing God's majestic creation and called out to God. "Lord, for the sake of the Bukidnon babies who need her, and the Bukidnon people, and for our own children, if it please Thee, heal Gladys."

He rose from his knees, his desperation replaced by a deep and settled peace. Three hours later, Gladys opened her eyes and smiled at her husband. Within a few weeks she was well enough to return to Bukidnon. God had again intervened and spared the life of Gene's mother.

The village people of Malaybalay welcomed back the DeVries family. Once again they came for medical help, saying, "Ma'am, you were very good to us. You love our children. While

13

you were away many of our children died. If you had been here, perhaps they would not have died." Most of the people no longer feared the outsiders or their new religion; they had become accustomed to the presence of the missionaries. The foreigners' children also broke down barriers.

Not long after the family's return, Henry built a dormitory to house a small boarding school. Two young women came from the United States. Nurse Rhoda Little helped in the medical work, and Beatrice Kuer helped teach the Bible and was a house-mother for the girls who boarded at the school.

Henry and Gladys held a Sunday school in their small living room until the class outgrew it. Henry then built a larger house, high off the ground. Underneath the house, he laid planks on boxes to seat more than 100 for the first service held in the new meeting place. The DeVries children were included in every-thing that went on: the clinic, the dormitory, and the small church, in what was now called Bethel Mission.

As they watched the development of the work that meant so much to their parents and the other missionaries, David, Gene, and Bud began to think of their own spiritual needs. Gene trusted Christ as her Savior while a small child. During the first class that instructed believers in the fundamentals of the faith, Gene asked that she be allowed to join the group to be baptized. Rhoda Little went over the lessons carefully with the child to satisfy her parents that Gene fully understood. One tiny blonde girl then accompanied the group of 20 dark-haired believers who were baptized in the Suaga River 500 yards behind the mis-sion compound.

Gene loved to watch her mother and Rhoda Little treat the babies who were brought to the clinic. In time, she began help-ing. She cleaned sores and applied ointment and bandages. She also accompanied the dormitory girls as they conducted Sunday school in the surrounding villages. From these centers developed the second and third churches in Bukidnon.

If her father had meetings close enough to return before dark, Gene pleaded to go along. As he preached to the adults in one group, she gathered the small children and taught them Bible verses.

Gladys taught her children using the Calvert correspondence courses. She often had to send over to the dormitory to get Gene when it was time for school. Gladys expected her children to sit up straight and behave themselves as they would in any class-room. Always pressed for time, Gladys also seized natural oppor-tunities to teach the children. When vendors came to the door selling vegetables, the children learned how to handle money and manage simple arithmetic.

Even though the children learned a great deal in that infor-mal structure, Gladys and Henry decided to enroll them for at least one year in a village school before they entered public school in the United States during their next furlough year.

Gene and her older brother, David, enjoyed the village school and liked their classmates, many of whom were friends from Sunday school. There were some, though, who tried to make things hard for the little *Americanos,* taunting and threaten-ing them. Only once did this ugliness break out into a physical attack against Gene. That day, a group surrounded her in the school ground, knocked her down and began to spit on her and kick her, tearing her dress when she tried to get away. She ran home as soon as she could escape her tormentors. Large bruises covered her face and body. Her hair was dirty and disheveled. Her dress was torn. She was covered with spit and grass.

Gladys took in at a glance what had happened and began to clean her daughter and treat her wounds. In the midst of this, Henry walked in, clenching his fist as he fought to control his surging anger, saying, "This has to stop. I am going down to do something about it."

Gene left her mother and put her hands over Henry's clenched fists, pleading, "Daddy, please don't; please don't. They did this because they don't know Jesus. They didn't mean to hurt me." Even at this young age, Gene's heart was tender and sensitive to God's prompting.

In the spring of 1937, after a seven-and-a-half-year term in the Philippines, the DeVries family returned to the United States for their second furlough. For some time, Henry and Gladys had desired to affiliate with a Baptist mission agency that shared their doctrinal convictions and practiced methodology compatible with their own missionary philosophy. They found such a board in the Association of Baptists for World Evangelism (ABWE). The DeVrieses were accepted as ABWE missionaries on January 12, 1938.

# Chapter Four

# WAR!

After the DeVrieses' furlough, David stayed in Manila to attend high school. The rest of the family returned to Malaybalay, where Gene and Bud soon noticed their father's prolonged absences and air of preoccupation. Late in 1941, Henry began work as a chaplain for the armed forces—mostly Filipinos—scattered throughout Mindanao. Henry did not tell his family, though, when he took on the additional responsibility of ferreting out information vital to military strategies. Roaming through the mountains, climbing familiar trails, Henry discovered the location and strength of hidden fighting units. Drawing on his knowledge of the terrain, he filled in valuable information about places of concealment for later guerilla warfare.

On Monday, December 8, 1941, 12-year-old Bud went as usual to the village school. (The calendar in the Far East is one day ahead of the United States.) Work had scarcely begun when a Filipino soldier burst into the schoolroom, ran up to the girl sitting next to Bud, and blurted out, "Your brother has been killed! The Japanese have bombed the camp in Davao!"

In the confusion, Bud ran home to discover the Japanese were bombing Filipino army installations throughout the islands. American forces could not retaliate. The United States government had made a commitment not to attack any Japanese plane or ship that had not first attacked an American target. Antiaircraft guns did not even shoot at planes seen flying on a bombing mission straight toward Clark Field, the large U.S. Air Force base north of Manila. The first shots were fired by Americans only after bombs began raining down on Clark Field at the same time Pearl Harbor exploded under a surprise attack.

Hastily, and far too late for the DeVries family to get away, the Red Cross ordered all Americans to evacuate the islands at once. By the time the message came, Henry had plunged into frantic arrangements to get 42 dormitory girls to their homes. Many of them lived on the coast, 70 tortuous miles away, down an exposed military road in clear view of Japanese strafing planes. Snatching a truck large enough to hold the girls, Henry crowded them in quickly, covering their huddled forms with blankets in a desperate attempt to conceal their presence from the low-flying planes.

Praying for God's protection, Henry drove to the coast, delivered the terrified girls to their parents, and drove back to Malaybalay. It was better for his peace of mind that he did not know then how few of those girls would survive to see the end of the war.

While watching for a chance to escape from the country, the missionaries kept at their work, hoping their isolated location offered a degree of protection until the "brief flare-up" could be resolved. Americans felt supremely confident that the vastly superior power of their forces would quickly crush the Japanese attack.

Just before Christmas, Bethel Mission began to feel the effects of the heavy bombing of a Philippine-American army camp just across the Suaga River, behind the mission compound. The missionaries knew they must withdraw into the interior if they were to survive.

No word had come from David. His parents hoped and prayed that he was safe with friends in Manila. In the middle of December, Henry was informed that David planned to leave Manila on the ship *Corregidor*, heading for Mindanao and the family home. A few days later, Henry caught a news broadcast that was interrupted with a special bulletin: "The *Corregidor*, leaving the harbor of Manila, struck a mine and sank. There are a few survivors. As the names are received we will inform you."

Frantic with fear, Henry kept the news to himself and clung to the radio, hoping for news of survivors. David's name was not mentioned on any list of dead or surviving passengers. After three interminable days, a telegram finally arrived from a friend in Manila. The message stated: "David with the saints."

Nearly out of his mind with worry, Henry dared not mention the telegram to the rest of the family. Was David dead? Did "with the saints" mean he was in heaven? There was no way to find out. The distraught father, desperately wishing his Christian friend had used plain English, tried to spare David's mother the anguish of his own uncertainty.

Making plans to evacuate the family, Henry had no real hope that they could be protected for any length of time. He knew only too well the military conditions on Mindanao. On one of his investigative trips, he had received a painful reminder of the island's limited defense against invasion. Traveling to a remote ranch to check on a supply of horses, Henry passed a group of men on a *patag* (a flat piece of land) surrounded by small bush-like trees. Stopping to greet the men, Henry found a group of 48 American pilots, navigators, and mechanics who had escaped the Japanese attack on Clark Field. With two lieutenants and 46 sergeants "equipped" with two rifles, no ammunition, and 14 shovels for digging foxholes, the unit had joined the resistance army on Mindanao.

When Henry identified himself as both chaplain and missionary, the men asked curiously, "Where are you headed?"

He explained his mission. After a silence, one man asked hesitantly, "Sir, would you tell us something from the Bible?" Another man added, "We go to church when we're at home."

Henry reached into his knapsack for his Bible. After a brief message, he suggested, "Perhaps some of you have questions." Until nearly midnight the men plied him with questions and shared with Henry something of their own desperate situation. Their food had to be brought after dark when the Japanese planes ceased strafing the area. They had no idea how long they were to stay there, nor what they were expected to do.

When Henry arose to leave, the men asked eagerly, "Are you by any chance coming back this way?" When he indicated that he would return in a few days, they insisted, "Will you come early enough to tell us more about the Bible?"

Deeply moved, Henry promised to come back as soon as possible. He thought of David, recognizing that some of the men in the group were scarcely older than his own son.

Several days later, Henry broke camp early enough to hike to the *patag* before dawn. He arrived before sunrise to find the area deserted. Moving cautiously to a headquarters site, he asked a guard, "Can you tell me what happened to those men out there on the *patag*?"

The young corporal turned in surprise. "Haven't you heard? Two transports of Japanese troops landed at Taglawan (about six miles away). Those men were sent down to hold them off."

Not wanting to believe what he heard, Henry asked, "Were they issued guns?" The soldier turned away, answering tersely, "No, sir, just whatever they had with them."

Sickened, Henry guessed the truth. The Japanese landed in force—and with three machine gun bursts wiped out 48 weaponless men. To his increasing horror, the missionary found this tragedy was not unusual.

Christmas arrived and still no word about David. The Filipino church insisted on its regular Christmas program. The missionaries gave in reluctantly, knowing that any large gathering increased their danger. During the program, Henry heard the approach of Japanese planes. Looking out the window of the church, he saw 24 bombers approaching, flying quite low. A little girl had just quoted the Christmas story from Luke chapter 2, first in English, then in the Bukidnon dialect. Interrupting the narrative of "peace on earth," Henry commanded abruptly, "Scatter quickly; the children to the dugout, the adults to whatever shelter you can find."

Within seconds the congregation scattered under the house, under the trees, or in the dugout Henry had made under a mango tree near the house. Their hasty conclusion to the Christmas program effectively prevented casualties.

Early in January, the Japanese bombed the Philippine–American army camp across the Suaga River, using a thorough "box bombing" with 24 planes, six from each direction. Gladys, Bud, and Gene ran to the dugout and peeped out to see the commotion, but Henry stood outside with a movie camera, taking pictures that had to be left behind only a few days later. He jumped for the dugout as the bombs began to fall all around the compound.

Soon after dawn on January 10, 1942, the DeVries family loaded their car and closed up the mission buildings. Christian friends at a secluded ranch offered shelter to the family. Unaware of the extent of their danger, the children enjoyed the month at the isolated Cudal ranch. Except for the sound of planes, they could forget about danger. Several times Henry ventured back to the mission, camouflaging his car with smears of red clay, retrieving what his family needed or checking on events in the village.

In February, Henry moved the family again, from the ranch to an empty house at an abandoned forestry station higher up in the mountains. From a vegetable garden nearby and with supplies sent by friends, the family managed to get enough food and make themselves fairly comfortable. They slept on the floor and cooked over an open fire outside the house.

Gene and Bud were not unduly alarmed about their situation. Since they had never known what most people consider safety, they could adjust to increasing uncertainty. Together they roamed the forest trails with Bud's pony, Panky, and the family German shepherd, Trixie.

On his last trip to Malaybalay, Henry heard that General Fort, commanding officer of the American forces in the area, insisted all missionaries cross over into Lanao Province to wait for evacuation. Lanao Province, which adjoined Bukidnon Province, offered a regular supply of food and a degree of official protection, but the missionaries felt grave qualms about going there. The area was the stronghold of the fierce Moros, notorious haters of "Christians," by which they meant anybody not a Moro. The missionaries feared the Moros far more than the Japanese. So far, the Americans had not experienced the force of Japanese hatred; they did know the Moros' reputation for brute savagery. Henry considered it far safer for the family to fall into the hands of a high-ranking Japanese officer in an official surrender than to meet up with a reckless group of Moros or a band of marauding Japanese.

Reluctantly, the missionaries left their mountain hideout and began their trip toward Lanao Province. On their way, they stopped at Malaybalay to load down the car with everything that could be crammed inside. Even Gene and Bud realized sadly that Panky and Trixie must be left behind in the care of Filipino friends.

Pulling away from Bethel Mission, the family kept to themselves the obvious question, "Will we ever see any of this again?" Each one felt confident the Americans would land momentarily to take over Mindanao. None of them had any clear conception of all it would cost for the Americans to regain control of the Philippine Islands.

Thousands of American civilians were trapped in the Philippines by the suddenness of the Japanese attack and subsequent invasion of the islands. Although they did what they could, the harassed military authorities were helpless in their attempts to evacuate civilians. A few Americans managed to get out, but the heavy concentration of Japanese planes and submarines in the area effectively thwarted most rescue attempts.

The DeVries family had pulled up stakes and left home so often that they had become accustomed to moving. The confusion added excitement; the parents kept their fears to themselves, providing as normal a life as possible in every situation. This attitude prepared them well for what lay ahead.

When they came to Cagayan, the town had been evacuated, the deep silence broken only by the barking of an abandoned dog. Just beyond Cagayan, approaching the first bridge, Henry sensed something wrong. He stopped the car three feet before the road dipped down to meet the narrow bridge. Moving cautiously forward on foot, he stopped abruptly, aghast at their narrow escape. The bridge had disappeared. Henry assumed it had been bombed.

In a low voice, he called out, "Anybody here?"

Out of the darkness came a lantern with a red bandana around it. A voice answered him, "Hello, Reverend! What are you doing here?"

Henry recognized a friend who drove a regular bus schedule from Malaybalay to Cagayan. Henry asked him, "What happened here?"

"Didn't you hear? A flood washed out every bridge between here and Iligan."

"Any idea when they'll be rebuilt?" Immediately he knew the question was foolish.

"No, no. The troops have evacuated. They expect big Japanese landings all along the coast any minute."

Henry turned the car around and headed back to the Bukidnon plateau. Dawn broke as they turned into the Gearhart ranch, where they could get a little sleep. Later in the day they continued on toward Lanao Province.

It was 1942. Gene was 15 years old. When her father looked at her slender frame and winsome beauty, his throat ached with loving pride and a hollow fear. Though he felt he could face death a thousand times to keep Gene from being scarred in body or in spirit, Henry knew an agonizing frustration at his own helplessness. Hoping desperately for David's survival, he clung to Bud and Gene, praying for their protection and that the family could stay together.

# Chapter Five

# With the Moros

Moving into Lánao Province was a futile grasp at straws of hope. The offer of protective custody had come, unfortunately, from a Moro sultan who promised to provide shelter in return for a "gift" of 100 rifles from the American general. Henry did not relish the idea of accepting "protection" from a Moro. Wrapped in insolence, wearing a look of proud derision, sure of his destiny and of his duty, the Moro warrior intended to kill Christians and infidels, thus earning his place in Allah's heaven, where his victims would be compelled to serve him as slaves. The Moro believed the more Christians he killed, the higher would be his place on the steps of the throne of heaven.

Believed to be of Persian stock, the Moros had been driven from Spain during various wars between Muslim groups. For at least 500 years, the Moros had been a part of Philippine life, yet they had maintained their distinctive racial and religious characteristics. The very name "Moro" roused terror in the hearts of Filipino tribespeople, and with good reason. Murderous in his implacable hatreds, the Moro, on occasion, went completely berserk in a fanatically religious determination to commit suicide by slaughtering Christians. A Moro with a bent to suicide had been known to stay on his feet, swinging his wavy-bladed sword, even after his own body had been pierced through in a mortal wound.

Henry had never forgotten the chilling calm of the Moro who told him, "You are an infidel dog. All your people are infidel dogs. You have no right to live and pollute the earth."

The missionaries faced a choice of virtual captivity in Moro custody or capture by the Japanese. Henry felt that he should keep his family away from the Japanese as long as they could cling to the hope of evacuation. Holding their heavily loaded 1937 Chevy to the sunbaked road, listening for the shouts of Bud, who was posted on the running board as a lookout for Japanese planes, Henry headed into the village of Salaman, praying the Moros would honor the wishes of the sultan, whose name was Kakidiron, and who felt some obligation to shelter the Americans.

A sultan served as spiritual leader, or *hadji,* for his particular group of Moros. Fearing Allah's wrath, the Moro usually did not dare violate the orders of his *hadji.* Years before, missionary Dr. Frank Laubach had won the friendship of the sultan in Salaman by teaching some of the Moros to read. In gratitude, the sultan gave his solemn word that he would protect any missionaries who came into Lanao Province. It was to be hoped the other Moros in the area would not touch the Americans, whom the *hadji* chose to shelter.

Near the village, the *hadji* lived in a huge barn of a house built 20 feet off the ground, with a high bamboo ladder leading up to its only door. Reaching this temporary and uninviting refuge, the DeVries family joined a group of tired, frightened, and bedraggled Americans. Responding to the sultan's shouted invitation, the refugees climbed wearily up the ladder into the one huge room of the house.

To their dismay, the Americans found they had to share the house with the sultan's 12 wives and innumerable children. For a little privacy, they screened off makeshift partitions with blankets and sheets scrounged from their jumbled belongings. Even this privacy proved an illusion, for the sultan's ever-present children delighted in peeking in at the visitors.

The DeVries family piled their knapsacks in their small section of the room and tried to make themselves as comfortable as possible. Gladys fashioned sleeping pallets on the floor made of split bamboo loosely laid across heavy floor joists.

Any group of Americans presented an irresistible temptation to the Moros. Known to be accomplished thieves, the Moros considered Americans fair game. The sultan's guests were an overpowering temptation.

Soon after the Americans settled in, Moros from outside Kakidiron's tribe began to converge on the scene. As Henry watched, he saw Captain Wyatt, a military friend, approaching. Reassured, he remembered the Moros held Captain Wyatt in respect because he showed no fear of them. Shortly after the captain had come to the Philippines, he received word that his wife and two children had been killed in an automobile accident. Not caring whether he lived or died, he took on himself the responsibility to face the Moros and kill as many of them as he could in order to protect Americans and their Filipino supporters.

Passing by on patrol, Captain Wyatt sensed the missionaries' danger and moved in immediately to help. Accompanied by four friendly Moros armed to the teeth, the officer approached the group, encircling the house, loudly challenging any ten of them to step forward and fight him with their choice of weapons.

No Moro dared accept the challenge. As they backed away, Wyatt ordered them to leave the area; he then waited with the Americans until the group had dispersed. Immediately after Captain Wyatt left, 200 Moros returned to swarm around the house, seeking to gain entrance. The split bamboo floor 20 feet off the ground could be reached by a high bamboo ladder. A constant stream of Moros climbed up and down the ladder, wandering through the house and picking up anything that proved attractive: scissors, clothing, odds and ends of salvaged possessions.

The old *hadji* stood the invasion as long as he could. Finally he stepped out on the high, narrow veranda of his home. Raising his arms in command, he held out his cane that supposedly had acquired magical powers on his trip to Mecca. Then he shouted out an anathema, the punishment of Allah himself, if the Moros harmed the Americans under his sworn protection. His threat frightened the Moros enough to chase them away for a few hours. The next day an even larger group returned to harass the refugees. Inside the house, the Americans tried desperately to achieve a semblance of normality. Gladys and Gene worked with the other women to provide food and drinking water for the group, a nearly impossible task.

Water had to be carried in buckets from the lake below the house. The lake, unfortunately, also served as the toilet facility for the Moros, who refused to build toilets on land they considered sacred. The *hadji's* house stood between a mosque and a cemetery, both preserved as sacred land that was not to be contaminated with human excrement.

Not surprisingly, a violent epidemic of dysentery had raged through the Moro tribes. It was absolutely essential that the refugees boil all drinking water and dishwater. Without such precautions, they had no hope of avoiding dysentery.

Gladys knew the water must boil hard for 20 minutes. To her horror, she discovered the filthy water never even came to a full boil. And since there was scarcely enough boiled water for drinking, the dishwater came directly from the polluted river.

Crowded together in the hot, stifling house, the refugees in their terrible thirst snatched swallows of the nauseating liquid before it even had a chance to cool. The improvised water cans, placed on the open fire and loosely covered with banana leaves, could not keep out the smoke. The filthy water took on an acrid, smoky taste.

Futilely, Gladys tried to wipe off their few dishes after they had been "washed." The confusion in the house mounted. Herded together so tightly they could scarcely move, none of the group dared go outside for fear of attack. To add to their misery, incessant, heavy rain fell on the slanted roof.

One by one, the Americans fell sick. Gene grew violently ill.

Hiding her anxiety, Gladys tried to make her daughter as comfortable as possible in the tiny space they occupied. When she left her home in Malaybalay, Gene weighed 120 pounds, a normal weight for a 15-year-old girl of average height. Under the onslaught of illness, Gene wasted away to a distressing thinness.

Early one morning, the missionaries heard loud noises outside the house. Looking out, they saw several hundred Moros dressed for war in festive green or red silk shirts. Every man bristled with weapons—hand grenades, rifles, and sharp, wavy-bladed swords.

Henry thought instinctively, *This is it. We'll all be killed.* Just as quickly, he thought, *If they succeed, at least we'll die quickly.* Henry knew the Moro swings once with deadly accuracy in a slanted cut that severs the head and shoulder of his victim. Such a death offered a more merciful end than the slow torture the Japanese practiced on their captives.

With mounting fear, the defenseless Americans watched the Moros climb the steep ladder and surge into the house. Seizing Gladys and the children, Henry thrust them behind a large tree that formed a supporting column for the house. At least two feet in diameter, the tree offered a degree of protection. Taking his stand in front of the tree, Henry thought in anguish, *At least I'll be the first to go.*

The Moros came yowling and screaming into the house with their swords bared for attack. Henry closed his eyes, expecting imminent death. Clutching each other, Gladys, Gene, and Bud stood motionless as the Moros crowded past, pushing people out of their way, pawing through the bundles on the floor, snatching what they wanted. Meeting no resistance, they used their swords only to slit open the scattered packages.

Henry slipped behind the tree to stand with his family. Trembling with fear, he tried to shield Gladys and the children with his own body. Helpless and distraught, he began to wring his hands in despair. Gene moved quietly away from her mother and stood in front of him. Looking up into her father's face, she placed her slender hands over his shaking fists and reassured him gently, "Don't, Daddy. Don't be afraid. The Lord is watching over us. You know Grandma is praying, Paka and Bepa (Henry's Dutch parents) are praying, our friends are praying. Don't be afraid, Daddy."

Henry stopped shaking. Grateful for his daughter's confidence, he managed to smile and nod his head.

After an agonizingly long interval, the Moros rushed out, satisfied for the time being that they had taken everything they wanted. For a few hours the Americans could count on being left alone.

The welcome interlude proved to be short-lived. Through contacts in the village, the Americans learned that the Japanese, landing in force on Mindanao, had come into Lanao Province and were moving fast around the lake. All hope of evacuation disappeared with the news that General Fort and his staff had surrendered to the Japanese in the town of Dansalan, now called Maramag, across Lake Lanao. Giving in to the inevitable, the general had sent an order through to Salaman that the Americans must come immediately to Dansalan and surrender to the Japanese.

With that report came the terrifying rumor that Moros from all over the district were converging on Salaman. The missionaries knew they had to get away immediately. Before they could cross the lake and surrender to the Japanese, they had to elude the Moros, enraged at the sight of all those Americans slipping out of their clutches.

Hastily, the desperate group bundled together their few belongings and slipped across the road under cover of darkness, heading for the shore of the lake, where outrigger canoes with makeshift coverings offered some protection from the drizzling rain. At the edge of the lake, the men hurriedly lifted the women and children into the canoes. Within minutes they heard Moros in the distance yelling in rage. Sporadic gunfire shattered the still-ness. Here and there the sky lit up briefly with flares shot from rifles. Behind the refugees, a group of Filipino soldiers stood with rifles, hoping to ward off the onrushing Moros.

Exhausted, Henry DeVries fell into the canoe beside his wife and children. Weak and sick, Gene attempted to get comfortable in the cramped space allotted her on top of tin cans and boxes packed tightly in the bottom of the canoe. Gladys rummaged hastily in their knapsacks, trying to find blankets or bathrobes to ward off the chilly night air.

Nightmarishly, the boat motors refused to start. In despera-tion, Henry and the other men seized one end of long bamboo poles as the soldiers on shore grabbed the other end to pull each heavy boat around the lake. A normal crossing with motors took one hour. Working with tortuous slowness in the steady rain, the men worked throughout the night and the next day to pull the canoes around to the other side of the lake.

In the canoe with the DeVries family and a few others was the body of a young soldier who had been stabbed in the Moro attack. An Episcopalian priest assumed custody of the dead man. Kneeling protectively over the corpse, the priest prayed aloud for the safety of the dead man's soul. As the canoe made its creeping journey around the lake, the priest placed his hands on the corpse and prayed for the salvation of each part of the body—the hands, the feet, the torso, the head. The drone of his prayers added a macabre touch to the nightmare of terror in the bone-chilling rain and unrelieved darkness.

As the canoes approached the far shore, Gladys drew out sev-eral white sheets to mount on long poles in a sign of surrender. Word had come that the Japanese promised not to shoot at those who came in bearing white flags.

The canoes landed at the site of an old Moro market, which had been stripped and burned by the Japanese. One by one, the exhausted refugees stepped out of the canoes onto the charred cement. Waiting to receive them were American officers, now prisoners of the Japanese. Three or four Japanese soldiers, their bayonets held ready, impassively watched the group disembark. Stepping forward to take charge, the Japanese commander accepted 46 Americans as prisoners and ordered them to march up the road a half mile to the house designated as a temporary prison.

Henry recognized the house and knew it to be scarcely adequate for a family of five. Now the prison would house 46 people, many of them suffering with dysentery. The house had been stripped of furniture. Through gaping shrapnel holes in the roof, the incessant rain fell to form wide puddles on the filthy floor. The one toilet facility was a hole cut in the middle of the floor in one small room of the house.

It was May 26, 1942. David, if he was alive, was 18 years old, Gene not yet 16, and Bud a boyish 13. Gladys and the children did not yet know of Henry's gnawing fear that David had gone down with the *Corregidor*.

Anxious relatives in Michigan did not get word until July 1, 1943, that the missionary family had been interned by the Japanese. The DeVries family had entered a night of horror that was to last nearly three years.

# Chapter Six

# "God Is Our Refuge and Strength"

Gene lay on a narrow folding cot in the stifling, stench-laden air of the crowded house in Dansalan. When she raised her head high enough to look out the open window, she saw a steady stream of trucks coming in, carrying long rows of American soldiers who filed out dejectedly to stack their guns and surrender to the Japanese. Subsequently, she watched these young Americans prodded into cruelly hard labor and deliberately humiliated by the Japanese.

Military captives met a far worse fate than did civilians. The Japanese took delight in wearing down the physical and emotional strength of the American fighting men. They gave to the American officers servant tasks in front of Filipino officer-prisoners in order to degrade and humiliate the white men. The attempt backfired. The prisoners learned the brotherhood of human suffering.

In spite of all Gladys could do, Gene grew steadily worse. Her mother recognized with horror the symptoms of malaria, added to the severe and persistent dysentery. With proper food and effective medication, Gene had a chance to live. In Dansalan there was no hope she could receive nourishment or medicine.

After several weeks, the prisoners were herded into trucks and moved to Camp Keithley, a rough barracks near Malaybalay. By this time Gene hovered near death from malnutrition, dysentery, and malaria. Her cruelly abused digestive system refused to tolerate the bit of nourishment offered in the daily food ration.

Once each day, 280 prisoners in the barracks shared ten cans of spoiled sardines spread over meager portions of rice. Gene took one look at the ladle of rice spread with a tablespoonful of rancid sardine juice and turned away sicker than before. No self-respecting dog could eat such food.

An American doctor, interned with the DeVries family, examined Gene and told Gladys despairingly, "Gene simply cannot live unless she can get some milk."

Gladys knew they could not get milk, but she continued to pray, trusting God would somehow meet Gene's need. She did not share her anxiety with Henry, who lay seriously ill in the men's barracks.

Before dawn one morning, Henry was awakened by a slight scratching sound near his head. Turning over, he saw in the dim light one of the Bukidnon believers creeping toward him. Reaching his friend, the man whispered, "Sir, we heard that Gene is ill. Perhaps this will help."

He handed Henry a small can of goat's milk, then slipped out of the building as silently as he had come in. Henry roused Bud, who ran over to the women's barracks to take the milk to Gene.

Each morning for two weeks the Bukidnon Christian crept in the darkness to the crude prison, evading the guards at the risk of his own life, to bring a can of goat's milk for Gene. By the time the group moved to another location, Gene's condition had improved. The relieved doctor told her parents to consider her survival a miracle of God's providence.

For 18 months the prisoners were shunted from one place of cramped discomfort to another, through a series of nine makeshift camps. Sometimes their Japanese captors provided adequate food; at other times they let the prisoners approach starvation. At best, the Japanese considered the Americans a necessary nuisance; at worst, they used them as targets for sadistic abuse.

Knowing the atrocities that had been committed by brutal guards, Henry watched his daughter carefully. Gene and Bud chose not to brood over morbid possibilities. When the guards proved friendly, the young prisoners found plenty to do to keep busy. Drawing on natural inventiveness and lively optimism, the camp teenagers contrived games, projects, programs, and even a semblance of school when they found a willing teacher. Henry and Gladys encouraged their children with the attitude that "Whatever our circumstances, we can be sure our Lord makes no mistakes. The only thing for us is to do our best, giving thanks all the time that all of us are alive and can be together."

After several months of captivity, Gladys collapsed under the strain. At that time the family was in a prison near a city with a mission hospital functioning under Japanese control. The guards mercifully allowed Gladys to be taken into the hospital, where she remained long enough to regain her strength.

Gene and Bud noticed that their parents' optimism and acceptance differed from the attitude of many of the other prisoners. Some in the camps preferred to curse the darkness and die. A particularly low point came on Christmas Eve 1943.

After a year and a half of moving from one camp to another on the island of Mindanao, the prisoners were crammed into the hold of a creaky freighter on its way to Manila. Before they learned of the impending transfer, Bud and a friend had scrounged 12 little chickens which they carefully cleaned for Christmas dinner. They brought the chickens with them to the freighter, but the guards seized the clumsily wrapped package, assuring the protesting boys they would be given a chicken dinner on Christmas Day. The chance of one decent meal brightened the darkness of the stinking ship.

At noon on Christmas Day, the prisoners watched avidly as the guards marched into the hold and, with a flourish, set up a table in a small cleared space in the center of the floor. Silently the Americans watched as six soldiers sat down at the table and ate 12 chickens with the trimmings of a traditional Christmas dinner. Wordlessly the prisoners followed the movements of Japanese hands that disdainfully tossed away the chicken bones.

Helpless parents listened to the Japanese laugh at the children who scrambled hungrily for the bones. The prisoners had rotten fish and seaweed for Christmas dinner.

That night, as darkness descended in the airless hold, one of the missionaries, a devout American woman, suggested cheerfully that the pitch blackness of the stinking ship be brightened by the joyous singing of Christmas carols. Her suggestion exasperated some of the other passengers; one man turned on her and cursed her into bitter tears. The other missionaries shared her misery, but there were no Christmas carols.

Later in the darkness, Gene whispered, "Daddy! There's a rat on my neck!"

Henry thought of rat-bite fever and whispered back, "Keep still, Sugar. Don't move."

Seconds later, Henry felt a light touch on his throat, then the drag of a cold tail. With a shriek, he straightened out his cramped legs in a mighty jerk that sent his feet squarely into the stomach of a priest who lay hunched over in the next tiny space. His loud grunt woke up the other prisoners, who began to laugh hysterically. By the time quiet returned, dawn had come and the rats had fled.

Through 11 interminable nights, the wretched prisoners huddled together in thick darkness and stifling heat in the fetid hold as they tried not to breathe the odor of human waste and accumulated filth. Fleas, lice, and huge rats crawled over them. With the approach of daylight the rats disappeared, and the human beings had a chance to take turns in the fresh salt air up on the deck of the freighter.

Early in January, the ship (fittingly dubbed "Hell Ship" by its miserable passengers) docked in Manila. The prisoners were ordered off the ship and loaded into waiting trucks to be transported to Santo Tomas Internment Camp just outside Manila. Before the war, the prison had housed the famed Santo Tomas

University, the oldest university in the Philippines, founded early in the 17th century.

Tropical darkness had fallen when the loaded trucks pulled into Santo Tomas. After a week and a half on the "Hell Ship" and 18 months of near starvation on Mindanao, the prisoners dreaded what might lie ahead. Their first glance at Santo Tomas nearly convinced them they had died and gone to heaven. Piling eagerly out of the trucks, they raced into the dormitories to discover joyfully the almost forgotten bliss of flush toilets and cold-water showers.

Assigned to room 223, the DeVries family found real beds in a room with four walls and a ceiling. After a restful night in relative comfort, each member of the family was issued shoes and clothes to replace the tattered garments they wore. This was the only time they received anything from the Red Cross packages mailed from the United States to the internment camps.

For Gene and Bud, the food ration at Santo Tomas included milk and one egg each day, plus an occasional spoonful of brown sugar. But the family soon found that better treatment by no means indicated a change in the attitude of the Japanese. Santo Tomas was a repatriation center. From there, prisoners were released in exchange for Japanese prisoners in the United States. Therefore, the condition of the exchanged prisoners must be considerably better than that of the battered wrecks found in other internment camps.

The DeVries family did not hope for repatriation. The few prisoners lucky enough to be released were government officials or business executives with powerful connections.

Settling down in comparative comfort, Gene found many of her schoolmates from Bordner High School in Manila. The one face she most hoped to find was not there. For two years the family had heard nothing at all from or about David. Henry alone knew how slim was the chance that David was alive. From the

reports that had come through, he knew hundreds had drowned
in the sinking of the *Corregidor.*

A few days after arriving in Santo Tomas, Henry caught a
glimpse of a young man walking purposefully toward him on the
prison compound. Henry slowed down to wait for him. Looking
carefully in all directions, the young man thrust a small piece of
paper into Henry's hand as they passed. Henry clenched his fist
around the scrap of paper and waited for the young man to dis-
appear. When he opened his hand he saw David's handwriting on
a hastily scribbled note. His hands shaking, Henry read the brief
message. David was alive and only recently had been transferred
out of Santo Tomas to the Los Banos Internment Camp, 50 miles
outside of Manila.

Nearly out of his mind with relief and excitement, Henry
ran to share his news with the family. Later, they found many
young internees who knew David and had played baseball with
him before his transfer. In the camp baseball circuit, David earned
the nickname "Breezy" with his reputation for pitching skills.
With several hundred other men believed to be strong enough
to fight against the Japanese if they escaped, David had been
moved to Los Banos to be held as a "maximum security risk."

Relieved by the news from their brother, Gene and Bud
began to join eagerly in the activities of a lively group of teenagers
at Santo Tomas. They found their place in a makeshift school
taught by willing volunteers: missionaries, teachers, businessmen,
and specialists in a variety of fields. With an occasional battered
textbook, scraps of paper, discarded government forms, and
account books, the instructors held classes and made homework
assignments to be completed without the use of textbooks. The
school-age prisoners eagerly accepted this contrived education.

After three months of increased hope for survival, the
DeVries family heard that Los Banos camp had been enlarged to
accommodate several hundred additional prisoners. They chose
to transfer in order to be reunited with David.

# Chapter Seven

# Execution by Starvation

After a separation of two and a half years, the DeVrieses were reunited in April 1944. For the first months in Los Banos, they considered their transfer not a bad choice. They had less to eat than in Santo Tomas, but conditions in general stayed about the same. Being together far outweighed the added discomforts. They shared the excitement of the other internees when persistent rumors of the end of the war, or of food shipments on the way, flew through the camp.

David had fared much better in Manila than his family had in their long ordeal on Mindanao. But for him, Los Banos proved to be a terrible ordeal. Assigned to the kitchen crew, he went out on work detail to cut green wood for the stoves. Piled on the fires, the green wood produced stinging, raw smoke that painfully irritated his eyes. Often he had to crawl into the cooled down firebox to rake out the ashes in order to start a fresh fire. His eyes smarting, he choked when he tried to breathe without inhaling ashes and cinders.

Anxiety about David's eyes and lungs gave place to worse developments. Though the internees could only guess at the truth, the Japanese, facing defeat under pressure from the Allied invasion of the Philippines, had begun to reevaluate the burden of their captives.

In October 1944, a high-ranking Japanese official, in charge of several large internment camps, came to inspect Los Banos. Before he left, he issued orders for the execution by starvation of the entire camp. Several of the prisoners who understood

Japanese heard the order and passed the word along to other key internees. In secret meetings these men began to lay a plot for the escape of two men who could contact the American forces and inform them of the dire straits of the prisoners.

Responding to the "execution by starvation" order, the Japanese cut the camp's food ration to 100 grams (seven ounces) of wormy rice per prisoner per day. The kitchen crew cooked the wormy mush in huge cans and measured it out carefully to each family or individual.

Henry DeVries ate his portion with his eyes closed and his mind dwelling on an old Dutch proverb: *"Ieder beest het sien vet."* ("Every beastie has its fat.")

In the darkness as they tried to sleep, the family dreamed of the mush they would have the next day or, in tormented nightmares, tasted hot waffles or creamy chocolate fudge. Henry began to draw up long, detailed lists of elaborate menus he planned to order when he went back to a world of restaurants and grocery stores. Gene collected a large file of recipes from prisoners of varied nationalities. On small scraps of paper she carefully wrote out directions for making gourmet dishes. Talking about food slightly appeased their intense hunger.

Lt. Konishi, who demonstrated an undying hatred for any white man, controlled the food supplies. He argued arrogantly, "Why should I give you salt or anything else when the Japanese in my country do without what they need in order to win the war?"

This reasoning failed to explain why the guards turned away loaded wagons of foodstuff driven to the gate of the camp by Filipino farmers who could not get into Manila to sell their vegetables. In the lush gardens all over the rich farming area around the camp, vegetables rotted in the fields while American and British prisoners starved behind the barbed-wire enclosures.

In desperation, a committee of prisoners went to Lt. Konishi to appeal for better treatment. In response to their plea, he smiled complacently, patted his pearl-handled revolver, and said, "Tell the prisoners that if they become violent, I will seize and execute this committee."

His attitude reflected that of many young Japanese, brainwashed into belief in the destiny of their emperor and their nation to rule under divine appointment. These men considered all Americans sadistic, cruel, and inherently weaker than the Japanese. A soldier of such a breed treated his prisoners cruelly; if he detected leniency in another guard, he usually reported it to his officers, who then ordered the execution of the friendly guard.

The hatred of their captors came as a complete shock to the DeVries family. Before the war they had many Japanese friends in the Philippines. Occasionally they saw in the attitude of the guards a trace of the friendly, gracious spirit they had known in their former Japanese acquaintances.

By January 1945, complete starvation became inevitable unless help came soon. Realizing their imminent danger, the kitchen crew began to prepare two prisoners to escape. For several weeks the cooks surreptitiously set aside an extra ladle of mush from each huge can of food and slipped the food to the two volunteers. This small portion of food, scrounged from cans that fed 200 prisoners, kept Jack Connors and Peter Miles noticeably stronger than the other men. Their condition aroused some comment among the other internees, but fortunately did not get the attention of the guards.

The DeVries family shared the emaciated condition of the other internees. Bud, now 15 years old, dropped from 110 pounds to a skeletal 78. Henry lost more than 60 pounds. Gene was a wraith-like 62 pounds. Gladys' health had been undermined to the point that she would never be really well again. They worried most about David, who had marked symptoms of beri-beri and whose eyes had been severely damaged by raw smoke and stinging cinders.

When she could do so unobserved, Gladys slipped part of her own tiny portion of mush onto the plate of one of the children. To appease their hunger by a touch of illusion, she kept back a little of each portion to warm up before bedtime, hoping they would feel they had had something to eat before they went to sleep. When she could, Gene walked to the edge of the camp to search for grass or straggling weeds to add to the dreary mush.

The DeVrieses' room became an impromptu gathering place for missionaries and other friends in camp to come for prayer and mutual encouragement. They prayed for food; they prayed for freedom. As they came closer to starvation, they began to wonder if their prayers were going to be answered.

Fortunately, Jack Connors and Peter Miles successfully escaped from the camp on February 17. To cover up their absence, friends arranged an elaborate scheme to answer for the missing men at roll call.

A day or two later, American planes flew overhead, low enough for some of the prisoners to see photographers standing in the open doors taking pictures.

On February 20, 1945, the Japanese guards set up a row of machine guns facing in the direction of the area where the 2,147 prisoners lined up each morning for roll call. On that same day Lt. Konishi, without explanation, stopped issuing food. The reason was quite simple: the Japanese saw no reason to waste food on prisoners scheduled for execution when they lined up for roll call at 7:00 a.m. on February 23.

On February 22, the missionaries met in their small group for prayer. Too weak to sit up or to kneel down, Henry lay prostrate on the floor and prayed, "Father, if it please Thee, take over this awful situation."

He did not know what else to ask for. All the enchanting rumors about food shipments and rescue attempts had proved groundless. Many prisoners had already died from starvation and disease, and were buried by emaciated fellow internees too weak to do more than scoop out shallow graves into which they rolled the bodies, saving the coffins for repeated use. In the deep lassitude of extreme malnutrition, the internees could scarcely grasp the reality of their plight.

On the night of February 22, the prisoners heard American planes circling Los Banos, bombing and strafing the area. The weakened internees, strengthened by a flicker of hope, hugged the ground outside their barracks, welcoming each thundering crash. "At least they know we're here!" they tried to reassure one another.

"Here," however, was a long way from help. Fifty miles behind Japanese front lines, the Los Banos internees looked for help from American forces who had their hands more than full in the Manila area as they fought to regain the capital and to free prisoners held in camps close to the city. There was no reasonable hope for the rescue of the Los Banos captives. In spite of all the evidence, however, the DeVries family clung to their faith in their faithful God to bring them through. They could not believe He would bring them through all that they had already endured, only to let them die when help was heartbreakingly close.

# Chapter Eight

# Turmoil in the Camp

Two thin, white columns of phosphorus smoke threaded upward behind the sprawling, barbed-wire-enclosed area that was the Los Banos Internment Camp. Five miles away, where the shallow edge of Laguna de Bay touched the wide, white sands of the beach, a matching pair of smoke signals reached above the trees.

Thirty seconds before 7:00 a.m. on Friday, February 23, 1945, responding to the smoke signals, a line of lumbering amphibious tractors veered slightly to the left and headed for a marked spot on the beach at Laguna de Bay. Overhead, nine twin-motored C-47's of the 65th Troop Carrier Squadron roared past in perfect formation. A carefully planned land and air rescue operation moved purposefully toward Los Banos.

Early in February, American headquarters in Manila had learned of the scheduled execution of the internees in Los Banos. An immediate attempt at rescue was out of the question. All fighting units were heavily engaged in other strategic operations. One division had arrived on Tagaytay Ridge, overlooking Manila from the south, but it had little territory, with none it could claim as sanctuary. For the immediate present, the commander had to concentrate attention on Nichols Field and Fort McKinley, U.S. military bases on the outskirts of Manila.

The American forces were paying a high price to regain control of the Philippine Islands. Japanese units bitterly resisted all efforts to seize Manila, Clark Field, and the surrounding area. To liberate Los Banos, the American commander had to have a secure base of operations, skilled fighting units diverted from other engagements, transportation for the prisoners, and a shelter for those who were rescued.

Lt. Col. Butch Mueller, of intelligence, sent scouts to question guerillas. Their report confirmed what he had heard. Fifty miles behind Japanese lines, Los Banos was guarded by 247 Japanese inside the camp and thousands of soldiers deployed in the area. Getting the internees out was only a first step; they had to be transported through 50 miles of strongly protected enemy territory.

On February 18, Jack Connors and Peter Miles met guerilla scouts who led them directly to American headquarters. The exhausted escapees confirmed what was already known and added further details, placing on air photograph maps the exact arrangement of the interior of Los Banos, pinpointing the internees' quarters, the guard houses, the sentry positions, the blockhouses, and the pillboxes armed with machine guns. The two men added one detail that proved crucial. For one brief interval each day, the Japanese guards stacked their guns in a corner and gathered for religious services in formal worship of their emperor. For this quarter of an hour the camp was particularly vulnerable to surprise attack as the Japanese went through their unvarying routine. With their guns out of reach, the guards faced toward Tokyo, stood at salute, then repeated the pledge to their god, Hirohito. In unison they called out a loud prayer, asking blessing and help on the day's mission. After the prayer, the guards saluted crisply, bowed again, rose erect, then gave a bone-chilling yell as they broke from the group and went back to claim their guns.

With this crucial information added, tentative plans began to fall into place. Gen. Oscar Griswold, commander of the XIV Corps, set the target date for February 23, their last chance to find the internees alive.

Specific units came in for assignments. On February 20, Lt.

Johan Ringler of the 511th parachute infantry was given a map and shown a small field just north of Los Banos. He was told, "On February 23, load your company into nine planes waiting at Nichols Field. Exactly at 7:00 a.m., jump the company on the field just north of Los Banos. Proceed at once into the camp, destroy the guards, and organize the internees for evacuation. Within half an hour, expect the remainder of your battalion to arrive on amphibious tractors."

The young lieutenant was warned, "Be sure to tell your men that any bullets fired into the camp might hit internees. For God's sake, be careful!"

"Where will I get parachutes?"

"They will be flown in from Leyte on the 21st. Move the company to Nichols Field on the 22nd."

That evening Lt. Ringler called his company out for briefing. He stated the facts as simply as possible: "2,147 Americans and British are being held 35 miles south of here in Los Banos camp. They are almost dead from starvation, and their execution has been scheduled. We are to attempt a rescue. We'll ask for volunteers, because this is what you're up against: Japs by the thousands are in the area. Our chance to get through is small. To *get out* with the prisoners, the chance is even less, but we're going to try. If you want to be in on this operation, step forward."

The men listened carefully. When the lieutenant paused, the entire company took two steps forward. From the group, Lt. Ringler selected 135 of the more experienced men to make the parachute drop; he then ordered the rest of the men to move in with the amphibious tractors.

After the briefing, Chaplain Alexander knelt to pray with his men. He knew that some in the group never came to the chapel tent, but in the darkness he heard them pray aloud. "You, up there, upstairs, if You're ever going to help us, this is the time!"

The company moved as ordered to Nichols Field. On the night of February 22 the men slept under the wings of their nine planes. Before dawn on the 23rd, they loaded and took off toward Los Banos.

The entire operation depended heavily on the success of 80 Filipino guerillas who had been given three assignments: to infiltrate the camp area and mark the parachute drop zone exactly 30 seconds before 7:00 a.m.; to mark the landing beach at the same instant; to place themselves so that at the same time they could attack and kill the camp sentries, silently if possible.

To allow time for these missions, the Filipinos crossed the choppy Laguna de Bay in native *bancas* (canoes) after nightfall on February 21. Arriving shortly before dawn on the 22nd, exhausted, they had only enough time to reach the woods back of the shore and hide before daybreak. Ahead lay five miles of hazardous terrain dotted with Japanese snipers and complicated by flooded rice paddies through which they must work their way in order to reach Los Banos.

On Thursday night, February 22, each man plodded laboriously for seven hours across the flooded rice paddies. Creeping down from the hills before dawn, they spread out to assigned positions 20 feet from the barbed wire enclosing the camp. They lay there quietly until the signal to move.

There was no moon. Velvet shadows shrouded the battle positions selected for the next day. Men moved under cover of darkness silently and accurately into attack positions. Everything appeared to be in readiness for the rescue operation.

At midnight Gen. Oscar Griswold, division commander, received an urgent message from the Air Corps: "Hundreds of trucks, lights blazing, are reported to be entering Los Banos camp, halting, turning, moving back to the east."

The general faced an agonizing decision. Had the Japanese been alerted? Were they reinforcing the camp? If so, the attack would be suicidal for the American troops and for the prisoners. Or the Americans could force their way through to find a camp deserted of Japanese and littered with the dead bodies of the internees. Similar rescue attempts had resulted in such disasters. Gen. Griswold weighed the possibility of failure against the one chance the internees had to survive, if indeed they were still alive. He also chose not to pass the message on to his troops, who faced enough problems already.

At 1:00 a.m. Gen. Griswold and his staff mounted their jeeps and drove toward Mamatid Beach. On the way, they passed New Bilibid prison at Muntinlupa. It was the only reinforced concrete building between Manila and Los Banos, and it had been chosen as a shelter for the rescued internees. Before the rescue, American forces engaged the Japanese in hand-to-hand fighting for two days before driving them out of the needed facility.

Reassured by the bright lights in the buildings and the orderly preparations being made for the evacuees, Gen. Griswold left New Bilibid to continue his inspection. On his route he passed long lines of trucks waiting behind the American lines for the signal to move forward to the beach to pick up the prisoners when they disembarked from the amphibious tractors.

The general reached Mamatid Beach in time to watch the last of 59 ungainly tractors enter the tepid, dirty, shallow water of Laguna de Bay on the first leg of their seven-mile compass course toward Los Banos. The commander of the 672nd Amphibious Tractor Battalion, Col. Gibbs, led his group with enormous misgivings, which he kept to himself.

Faced with a seven-mile trip on a black night, his craft loaded with paratroopers accustomed to air travel, he had orders to hit the beach *exactly* at 7:00 a.m. He had to maneuver through a right-angled turn in the middle of a blind course and end up at the one spot on the beach where his clumsy floating craft could leave the water. As if that were not enough, Col. Gibbs had been cautioned repeatedly to remember that surprise was the key word for the success of the rescue. Yet here he was, in the noisiest collection of noisemaking machines ever designed, suited for short, direct assault landings across beaches. Clanking his way forward in the darkness, the colonel snorted his disgust. "They expect us to *tiptoe*? 'Surprise'—ha!"

He saw a glimmer of hope in the diversionary action planned north of the San Juan River. The infantry of the 637th Tank Destroyer Battalion waited through the night at fords discovered and prepared by engineers the day before when all the bridges were found to be destroyed. Obviously, the Japanese expected an attack from that direction. Happy to oblige, the Americans planned to give the Japanese what they expected, hoping to hold their attention long enough at San Juan River to give the rescue operation a chance of success. If not, the Japanese would swarm all over the rescue forces, and nobody would live to tell what happened.

The 637th had just completed the bitterest fighting campaign of its career across the open ground of Nichols Field in the face of suicidal resistance and heavy strafing. They had earned a rest break but didn't get it. If the infantry took time out to rest, the prisoners at Los Banos would die.

Thirty seconds after the smoke signals rose behind Los Banos and on the beach at Laguna de Bay, the first artillery round reverberated across the somnolent rice paddies and landed on Lecheria Hill, the Japanese first position at the San Juan River. Machine guns returned fire. The battalion captain fell dead as his troops surged forward. One company turned to the right to block the expected arrival of Japanese reinforcements along the road from Manila. The remainder of the force, in a short and bitter fight, seized Lecheria Hill and moved on toward Los Banos to surround a rock quarry where intelligence reported reserve Japanese troops.

Inside the barracks at Los Banos, Bud DeVries fastened his belt and prepared to take his place in line for roll call. He heard the roar of planes coming in close overhead. Slipping his feet into flimsy *bakyas* (native sandals), he rushed into the cook shack near the doorway. From the north, out of a heavy bank of clouds, nine planes in formation swept in low. One by one they peeled off and circled an open rice field a half mile from the camp.

Even though he knew the planes were too slow for bombing, Bud instinctively ducked when he saw a small load drop from beneath the first plane. Before he could hit the floor, the white bundle opened. In that instant the air was filled with 135 white dots, dropping fast.

"Paratroopers!"

A scream, a prayer, an exploding excitement hit the camp and blew it into turmoil. Beyond the barbed wire, guerillas crept in close enough to attack and kill the sentries before they uttered a sound. Realizing they were not strong enough to take the pill-boxes, the guerillas set up covering fire to hold down the Japanese until the paratroopers could arrive.

Sudden bursts of gunfire exploded south of the camp toward the forest. Men dressed in mottled green uniforms with coal-scuttle helmets and high leather boots raced through the tall, green grass. Crouching low, falling flat to fire grease guns, they darted toward distant ammunition huts which blazed in sudden fury.

Pandemonium broke loose.

Inside the barracks, Henry pulled Gene and Gladys under the protection of a makeshift air raid cover. All around them, prisoners scattered in every direction, sliding under beds to dodge whizzing bullets.

The Japanese panicked. Falling back into the barracks with the prisoners, they lay close to the floor and fired wildly at the swarming invaders. One by one the guards began to run out of the barracks, trying desperately to regroup in the center of the camp. As they ran, they fell, shot down by the attackers.

A prisoner suddenly yelled, "Americans! In our barracks!"

Bud ducked out of his tiny cubicle in time to see the first American pass through the barracks doorway. Others followed in single file and began to set up a machine gun at the rear of the barracks. All over the camp paratroopers surged forward, kicking their way through the barbed wire fences, joining the guerillas already inside, firing on the guards as they ran.

Dazed prisoners looked up to see monstrous machines clanking over the hills, lumbering in and out of the ditches surrounding the camp, snorting, growling, too big to be real, too real to be a dream.

Henry gaped in astonishment. Turning to one of the paratroopers, he pointed with shaking hands to the tractors. "What on earth is that?"

A grin split the boy's deep yellow skin. "Amphibious tractors, amtracs, sir. They'll get you folks out of here!"

The huge tractors headed for the open ballfield in the center of the camp. Paratroopers jumped out and moved quickly among the milling prisoners, urging them to line up as fast as possible.

The dead bodies of Japanese soldiers were sprawled grotesquely about the camp. Guerillas swarmed over the dead, stripping each one of helmet, gun, shoes—everything except trousers. One guerilla looked up regretfully at a priest and said, "I need the pants, Father, but I won't take them. There are Sisters in the camp!"

Col. Gibbs jumped from his tractor and picked his way through to survey the scene. Afraid to believe his good fortune, he stalked through the area, warning sternly, "Look folks, it's not over yet. We've still got to get you out of here. There are about 4,000 Japanese sneaking around out there close by."

Impatiently, he urged the emaciated captives forward. "Come on, come on. Let's get going! If you have anything you want to take with you, grab it fast. We're going to fire these buildings immediately. We want to leave no cover for the Japanese on the way here."

It was 7:30. After a half hour of swift action, 247 Japanese guards lay dead. Not one of the rescue force or the internees had been wounded, though there was a report that one paratrooper sprained his ankle in the jump.

Within seconds, the awestruck missionaries bundled together the few things they had left—Bud's autograph book, Gene's recipes, a Bible, a few tattered articles of clothing. Together, the DeVries family walked over to the line of amtracs.

Jim Harper and his buddies, Joe and Bill, stood beside their tractor waiting for orders to load up. Fascinated, the missionaries watched the three men push their helmets back and light cigarettes. All of the Americans appeared to be afflicted with the same peculiarly deep yellow skin. Later, Henry learned that the skin coloration came from Atabrine, a drug taken to ward off malaria.

Jim caught sight of Gene standing beside her mother. He turned to his friend with a delighted grin. "Hey, buddy, do you see what I see?"

"Yeah, man! What are we waiting for?"

They walked over to Gene and began to gather up the few bundles piled beside the family. Without waiting for the command to board the tractors, the DeVrieses followed Jim and climbed up into the amtrac. The boys picked Gene up, set her on top of the tractor, and put an oversized helmet and goggles on her head. Enjoying their attention, Gene smiled self-consciously.

His eyes smarting with weak tears, Henry watched his daughter respond to the obvious admiration of the young men. Not even her terrible loss of weight could dim that engaging smile.

Inside the tractor, Bud turned immediately to the most important thing on his mind—food. Rummaging eagerly, he found a field rations kit. One of the crew members opened it quickly, took out a can of corned pork hash and gave it to Bud. As he ate, Bud thought that nothing in his entire life could ever again taste so indescribably delicious.

Col. Gibbs barked an order that sent 45 women, children, and invalid men to fill each tractor. Dave DeVries joined the men

considered strong enough to walk out behind the loaded
amtracs. The huge machines began to roll out of Los Banos past
blazing barracks, with the leaping flames forming a surrealistic
tunnel of fire.

Cheering paratroopers lined the roadway, waving and throw-
ing K rations. These sweating, gum-chewing, grinning young men
*were* America—reaching out her hand to take back her own.

Outside the camp, infantry troops formed a protective cor-
don around the walking evacuees as the group started toward
Mamatid Beach.

Hiding in the trees and tall grass along the road were
Japanese who had slipped in from other areas. Fortunately, they
were armed only with 30-caliber guns which could not pierce
the two plates of protective shield on the tractors. Each time the
snipers fired, the long line of tractors halted.

Fascinated, Bud hung close to the tractor opening so that he
could peek out. Scarcely a yard away he saw a Japanese jump
from behind a coconut tree to fire at the amtrac. In that instant
the machine gunner whirled around and in one burst cut the
sniper in two.

Riding inside the tractor with the DeVries family was an old
man who had managed to survive the years in Los Banos.
Hearing claims that the tractor would take them through to the
other side of the bay, he snorted his unbelief. "What're you trying to tell me? This thing goes through water?"

The others laughed. "It's true, dad. You wait and see."

The old man retreated in stubbornness. "I don't believe a
word of it."

At last the long line stopped at the edge of the bay. Each
amtrac then began its slow, splashing descent into the water.
Halfway across the bay one of the men called out teasingly, "Well,
dad, have a look!"

The old man peered over the edge, awestruck. "Well, I'll be
durned!"

On the beach, the commander realized with enormous relief that he could evacuate all of the internees by having the amtracs make two round trips across the bay. This removed one worry: he had thought the walking internees would have to follow ground troops as they fought their way out and that they might encounter strong resistance on the beach.

Rejoicing over their rescue, the evacuees naturally saw the paratroopers as their deliverers. They did not know until later that a higher price for the rescue had been paid by the ground forces in the diversionary action at San Juan, where two men were killed and two wounded. These four were the only casualties of the entire operation.

The infantry unit, still involved in increasingly intense fighting, withdrew slowly to the San Juan River. Their engagement gained 50 miles of enemy territory, which they held until the fighting in Manila ended.

Crossing Laguna de Bay with the prisoners and returning for the combat troops, the tractors became targets for snipers. Twelve P-38's hovered overhead for protection. When a four-inch mortar opened fire from the shore, three planes peeled off, headed for the point from which the shots originated, dropped a bomb, strafed the area, and circled back into formation.

The DeVrieses were in the first group taken across the bay. They waited on the beach for nearly three hours while the tractors made a second trip to pick up the remaining evacuees.

Filipinos living in the area learned of the rescue attempt. They came cautiously to the beach to find out what had happened and to bring food in case it was needed. When they saw the condition of the prisoners, the Filipinos began to weep. The missionaries struggled with their own grief at the sight of Filipinos who showed the drastic effects of their own long years of deprivation. For the Filipinos, every day of the war was a struggle for survival.

When the last load of prisoners and troops landed safely on

the beach, the group quickly transferred into long lines of trucks, waiting since midnight to whisk them all to New Bilibid prison, where hot meals and clean beds had been prepared for them. For the first time in nearly four years, the DeVries family came under American protection.

Within a few hours after the rescue, Henry entered the prison hospital while his family went into their separate barracks. Henry lay on his hospital bed, a board 16 inches wide and two inches thick, with one blanket for a mattress and another for cover. In the women's building, Gene and Gladys had similar accommodations; Bud and Dave bunked together in the men's building, all of them still in "prison," but with quite a difference! Above these protecting walls waved the flag of their own country. Within that security they found clean beds in clean rooms; nourishing, strengthening food; and expert medical attention.

Henry realized his critical physical condition made it entirely possible he would not live, but the miracle he prayed for had happened. After nearly three years of agonizing uncertainty and unbelievable hardship, somehow, by the mercy of God, his family had survived. With careful attention they might be strong again. Tears coursed down his cheeks. They were alive, and all of them were free at last.

For two weeks Henry remained in the hospital with little chance of survival. He still felt as though he were starving to death. On each side of his bed lay paratroopers who were severely jaundiced. When they received their trays of food, they were too nauseated to eat. Henry watched until he could stand it no longer. After three meals he begged frantically, "Don't send your platter away, okay?" He then drank his own soup (all he was permitted to eat), took the platter from one tray, cleaned it up, then turned, as hungry as ever to gobble all of the food from the other platter. Conscience-stricken, he lay down on his cot to pray desperately, "Forgive me, Lord, for being greedy. I know I could rupture my stomach, but I can't help it."

After two weeks, he improved enough to visit his family in their separate buildings. Later, he walked through the hospital, encouraging the other patients as much as he could.

One day he talked to a badly wounded young soldier with his head propped on pillows so he could see what was going on. In mid-sentence, the boy broke off and smiled broadly. "Here come the two angels!" Henry turned to see Gene and her friend Helen, from Australia, who had shared the horrors of Los Banos. To his surprise, he discovered that the girls came often to write letters for young men who had no hands or were too weak to write, and with eager smiles and conversation encouraged them in their battle to survive.

For the first few weeks, the internees remained under careful medical supervision, lining up between meals for a special stew and a vitamin pill. Henry delighted in every scrap of nourishment. Sometimes he and several others got back in line, only to be told gently, "No, no, no more. Please trust us. This is for your own good."

After a month, every member of the family had gained 25 pounds and felt stronger. Constantly they kept in mind their gratitude for their rescue from certain death; over and over they reminded themselves, "We want never to forget what it cost."

All around the area intense fighting continued. Convoys of trucks left the prison loaded with troops. While they were gone, the internees heard guns firing, frequently very close to the prison itself. Less than an hour after the trucks left, they would begin to return, bringing stretchers loaded with men dripping blood, with many men mortally wounded, and others already dead. This ghastly routine reminded them all of the price still being required of these men to win the war.

One day as he walked around the prison, Henry followed four men carrying two sheet-covered stretchers to a section of the prison set aside as a temporary morgue. Before the war it had been a place of execution, and the only place in the room to sit down was the electric chair. Determined to see for himself the price being paid, Henry sat down in the electric chair to watch while the men prepared the bodies for burial or shipment home. When he thought he could stand it, Henry got up out of the chair and looked into the faces of the young men. He wanted to remember for the rest of his life what it took to save his family from certain death. Henry DeVries never forgot.

*Chapter Nine*

# Confidence in God's Good Will

In May 1945, after ten weeks of rest and recuperation in Muntinlupa prison, the DeVries family boarded an army transport truck to the bay north of Manila to board the S.S. *Eberly* for their trip home to the United States. The ship had just completed its maiden voyage across the Pacific, bringing 4,000 troops to the Philippines. The S.S. *Eberly* was the first American ship into Manila Bay after the area had been reclaimed from the Japanese and the bay partially cleared of sunken ships.

The ship filled quickly with a mixture of civilians rescued from internment camps and wounded soldiers heading home for recuperation. The still hungry internees delighted in the food served in the officers' mess. By the order of Gen. Douglas MacArthur himself, they relished ice cream in cereal bowls after lavish steak or chicken dinners. By the end of May, when the ship landed in Los Angeles, Gene had picked up weight and looked more like a normal 18 year old. Dressed in an oversized WAC uniform, however, she still resembled a rescued waif.

Arriving at their assigned hotel, the family luxuriated in carpet soft enough to sleep on. For the first time in years they took baths in warm water. Even in their own home in Malaybalay, they had only a makeshift shower, and for the entire time in internment they had not had warm water to bathe in.

Hotel beds were too good to be true. The morning after their arrival, Henry asked a young man from Los Banos, "How'd you sleep last night?"

He laughed. "I couldn't sleep in that bed. I had to get on the floor!"

The first morning, the family went to eat out with money issued for food. With great delight they sat at the drugstore counter to order whatever they wanted. Henry had dreamed of waffles; now he ate his fill.

On the bus into the city, they gawked with unconcealed awe at the store windows loaded with entrancing treasures. "Look! There's a furniture store! Isn't that bed pretty? Look at the fruit store! Oranges! Apples! Pears!"

The driver probably considered his passengers demented. Each of them was dressed in army issue clothes or garments retrieved from casualties. The men wore army pants and shirts with old tennis shoes. Gene had on her "rescued waif" costume as they headed for Bullocks Department Store to meet a store representative assigned to assist them with their selections. Each man could choose two suits, underwear, two shirts, neckties, socks, and shoes. The women had a comparable allotment.

Gladys suggested to her husband, "Take David and Gene with you and get them what they like. I'll take Bud. He won't know what to get."

Henry had no luck with David and Gene. Neither could decide what to buy. Gladys went along the next day to help. In an elegant section of the store, she sat down at a little mirrored dressing table to buy a hat. Wearing an old white dress she had kept throughout internment especially to wear when she came home, a pair of army shoes a size too long, a pair of pumpkin yellow rayon stockings, and with her thin hair combed back in a prim, old-fashioned knot, she reached for a stylish hat, small and dainty, with a tiny bunch of flowers that drooped over one eye. Gladys began to laugh. She and Gene howled in glee until the tears came. Then Gladys found a larger hat, more appropriate to her "returned missionary" status.

Dressed in a semblance of fashion, the family spent a few days orienting themselves to a "normal" existence that included plenty of wonderful food and restful sleep in an atmosphere of freedom and luxury. They had come home at last.

They eagerly caught a train to Grand Rapids, Michigan, and their much anticipated reunion with beloved relatives. They knew their family and friends in supporting churches would help them make the necessary adjustments to a new way of life for each of them.

David, at age 20, had completed only nine years of normal education, plus the haphazard instruction scrounged in various prison camps.

Gene, at 18, had finished the eighth grade in Manila, and in snatches during internment had been taught by priests, nuns, teachers, missionaries—anyone in the camps who could teach subjects without the help of any kind of equipment, not even textbooks or writing materials.

Bud, at 16, had lost so much weight he appeared to be scarcely older than ten. He, too, had tried to continue the grade school education interrupted by the war.

Henry and Gladys prayed for guidance for their children's education. During the summer, Gene insisted on taking a double load of courses at the local high school in Grand Rapids. Learning rapidly and doing well in each course, she began to realize her education had not been all bad. During the years of internment, she and her brothers had gained from highly motivated instructors a rich mixture of information reflecting many cultures and backgrounds. The emphasis on problem solving, essential for survival in the camps, brought out the learning motivation and intense curiosity that make an excellent student.

Gladys had also prepared her children much more effectively than she realized with her improvised learning experiences and direct applications of all that they learned. This background, added to their natural ability and linguistic skills, gave the three DeVries children a competitive edge over others their age who had received an education in a more traditional but less challenging environment.

In the fall of 1945, Gene enrolled in Wheaton Academy, in Wheaton, Illinois. This Christian preparatory school, associated with Wheaton College, attracted many Christian young people from the same type of conservative background familiar to the DeVries family.

Gene had spent most of her life being "different"—the blonde among people with dark hair and eyes, the Christian in a predominantly pagan culture, the missionary kid in a group of children whose parents never left the United States. Now she needed acceptance and friendship from congenial peers. She also needed normal interests and recreation that would ease built-up tensions and heal tormenting memories.

Since David had enrolled in nearby Wheaton College, Gene had the reassurance of his being close by when they needed each other. Their parents stayed in Grand Rapids, where Bud enrolled in a local high school.

Gene graduated with honors from Wheaton Academy in the spring of 1946, and in the fall she entered Wheaton College with many of her friends from the Academy. There she had found the social and educational milieu she needed. Her fears of not being able to keep up lessened, even though her desire for academic excellence did not diminish.

In the environment of a Christian academy and college, Gene began to wrestle with a decision she did not share with her parents. She had returned from the Philippines with her mind made up: she would never become a missionary. She knew her parents' hearts remained with the Filipino believers and the people who had not yet been reached with the gospel of Jesus Christ. Henry and Gladys looked forward to returning to Bukidnon Province as quickly as possible.

After the war, when news arrived from the area around Bethel Mission in Malaybalay, the missionaries learned, to their great relief, that the believers had held firm in spite of ridicule, starvation, terror, and persecution. As the Bukidnon believers moved from one place to another seeking food and safety, they sang and prayed through long nights of sheer terror. Listening to them, other Filipinos realized these people had something special. Many asked the Christians, "How can you act like this?"

By the end of the war, when Bukidnon Province returned to U. S. control, over half the original believers had died from sickness, starvation, or persecution. Those believers left behind such a powerful witness that returning missionaries found, to their astonishment, that the number of church members had actually increased. Many Filipinos, seeing the courage and strength of the believers facing death, had become convinced of the power of Jesus Christ and had also come to believe in Him. As believers scattered into new areas, fleeing the Japanese, they formed small churches.

Before 1942, 14 churches had been established in Bukidnon Province. After the war, 24 congregations waited for the missionaries to return. Most of the church buildings, built by the believers themselves, had been destroyed by the Japanese. All of the buildings on Bethel Mission compound had been taken over by the Japanese and had been totally destroyed or badly damaged. The missionaries did not depend on buildings, however; their work had been planted in the hearts and lives of the Bukidnon believers.

Upon entering Wheaton College, Gene chose a major in American literature, which she loved. To her surprise, she soon found the courses did not interest her. She almost began to loathe the subject. Not understanding this change, she turned to the Lord to find out what direction He wanted her to take. She then switched to a major in Christian education. Every course proved fascinating; she began to do extremely well in all her classes.

On her college entrance application form, Gene was asked, "What is your attitude toward Jesus Christ?" She answered, "I believe in the Lord Jesus Christ as my own personal Savior, and I endeavor to let Him be my guide in all that I do."

The pattern of her own faith and practice had been set by her parents; now that she was an adult, Gene had to carve out her own course of obedience to the God she believed in. Few people sensed her inner struggle about her future. Henry and Gladys had never pressured their children to follow their own call to be missionaries. They wanted the will of God for their children; they were content to leave the direction up to Him.

As she worked through conflicting feelings of deep love for the Filipinos and a lingering dread of the Japanese, Gene began to meet other young people who had been in the Philippines during the war. Young men who had fought in the Pacific now enrolled in Wheaton College to prepare themselves to return to the Orient as missionaries. Observing their enthusiastic commitment, Gene began to reevaluate her own decision not to consider missionary service.

Gene struggled with her attitude toward the Japanese, even though she knew that their behavior came from the fact they did not know a loving God and, therefore, could not be expected to show love to those they considered enemies. She knew the Americans were despised burdens to the Japanese, who justified their atrocities in the name of national pride.

Gene's disillusionment had not come from her ordeal in the prison camps, nor from any doubt about the power of the gospel of Jesus Christ. Her dilemma stemmed from her loss of faith in some of the missionaries interned with them. Before the war, Gene had been sheltered in a loving environment with parents and missionaries who genuinely loved and served the Filipinos. They had shared in their joy and sadness, success and hardship. Gene naturally expected other missionaries to be like the ones she knew at Bethel Mission.

As the DeVries family was shunted from one place to another, they began to experience human nature under severe stress. Early in their days of hiding, they were thrown together with a group of missionary families out in the forests. The group outlined rules for the protection of each individual and, particularly, for the welfare of the children. To guarantee no one went hungry, they decided to pool all food supplies and distribute them fairly.

Waiting for their regular issue of food one day, Gene and Bud overheard another child say complacently, "Oh, we've got plenty of that!" as his missionary parents reached for their ration of canned milk. Seeing their astonishment, the boy described to Gene and Bud the way his parents had hidden cases of supplies before claiming their share of the community ration.

As the months of hardship continued, Gene saw a few Christians prove that for them, at least, survival came before principles. She also observed some individuals who made no claim to be Christians but who reacted unselfishly, at great cost to their own comfort, to protect or help other people. She began to turn away from God's people in despair at their lack of godliness. She did not turn away from God Himself. She knew Him well enough not to blame Him for the weakness of some of His people.

Gene learned how hard it was to pray or to maintain any type of personal discipline when the constant denial of basic needs crowded out every other thought. When all they could think about was food, all of them found it hard to behave like Christians. Even for believers, hunger sharpened the temper as well as the appetite.

Henry and Gladys deliberately set for themselves a discipline of prayer and cultivation of Christian graces under trial. No matter how bleak their situation, they looked for and found some reason to give thanks to God for His provision for their needs. When they lost everything, even the food they needed to stay alive, they praised God and hung on to life tenaciously. They thanked God they were together as a family to face anything that lay ahead. Above all, they taught their children that their heavenly

Father's divine will could not be wiped out by the evil which men practice. Even if they had to die, they had confidence in God's good and perfect will.

During her first two years in college, Gene satisfactorily resolved her inner conflicts. She accepted the fact that God Himself had proved faithful in every circumstance in her life. She could, therefore, trust Him to continue to prove faithful. She also decided that she could love people and accept them, even though she would not allow herself to place her confidence first in other human beings. In every decision, God would come first; she would depend on Him and not on man.

Gene accepted the fact that what she had been taught about God, as revealed in the Bible, had proved true. What she had been taught of man's weakness and sinful human nature had also proved true. The truth that God could strengthen weak men in trials also had proved to be true. As she thought through her life, Gene could find no instance in which God's Word had not proved valid. Therefore, in confidence, she would believe the Word of God and stake her life on it.

At last Gene reached the point when she could say honestly and freely, "Lord, I'll go anywhere You want me to go—even to Japan, if that's what you want."

Her new understanding wiped her heart free of any lingering bitterness toward those who had treated her cruelly. She began to feel honest compassion for the Japanese people and a growing desire to communicate to them the truth of God's love and mercy. She was ready to go either to the Japanese who had hated her or to the Filipinos who had loved her, but the faithful God whom she served would determine the direction she would take.

# Part Two

# The EBERSOLE Family
## (Russ & Gene)

*"For this God is our God forever and ever;*

*He will be our guide even unto death."*

—PSALM 48:14

# Chapter Ten

# Early Years

Rusty, Russ' oldest child, often kidded about his dad's "war-time" experiences. "While my mom suffered hardships in Japanese prison camps, my dad was in the Navy playing tennis. His only ship was a ferry boat between Seattle and Bremerton, Washington!"

The war years were not the only difference between Russ' and Gene's lives; his background was as different as the geographical distance separating them was wide. Gene's high school years were spent in many Japanese internment camps, while Russ attended four different high schools in New Jersey and Illinois.

The Ebersole family lived in Palisade, New Jersey, a pleasant, middle-class community across the Hudson River from New York City. Russell Sr. commuted daily to the city as he worked with the lamp division of Westinghouse Electric Company. Russ' mother, Sue, was a contented homemaker and devoted mother to Russ and his younger sister, Doris.

Russ' boyhood coincided with the Depression years, which cast economic gloom over most Americans in the 1930s. Russ' parents were no exception, although his father was able to keep his job. As a boy, Russ was never aware those were "hardship" days, and, compared to many, they weren't all that hard. He led a carefree life in elementary school, with many boyhood chums. From an early age, sports were an important part of his life. Whenever he had a free minute, he played sandlot ball in the summer and ice hockey in the winter on one of the small ponds near his home.

Russell Sr. and Sue reflected the solid family values which most Americans held at that time. The family attended church regularly on Sunday mornings, but showed no evidence of a real faith in their lives. Sue's mother was a Roman Catholic, and her father, a good, hard-working man, had little to do with organized religion.

Russ' dad came from a nominal Protestant home. Russell Sr.'s father died when he was a young teen, making it necessary for him to leave school in the ninth grade to support his mother. He was a "self-made man," whose warm personality enabled him to be a successful salesman. During his many years with Westinghouse, he rose to be the general sales manager of the lamp division.

The Ebersoles' next-door neighbors were a Swiss-German couple, Mr. and Mrs. Rudolf Graf. Mrs. Graf, with her quaint Swiss accent, was a thoughtful neighbor. Russ especially loved her homemade bread and strawberry jam, and went often to her kitchen for samples.

Mrs. Graf had a deep personal relationship with the Lord Jesus Christ. She often shared this with Sue, who highly respected this kindly older woman.

One Wednesday night, Mrs. Graf asked Sue Ebersole to attend her small Baptist church. Sue accepted the invitation, and that night, after hearing a simple message on "doubting" Thomas, she received Christ as her Savior. That was the beginning of the working of God's hand in the Ebersole family!

A few years later, Russ' dad was transferred to Chicago as manager of Westinghouse's Midwest division. The family moved to Glencoe, Illinois, on the north shore of Chicago. One of the first things the family did was look for a church. They found the Winnetka Bible Church, whose congregation consisted largely of people from Scandinavian stock.

Russ' mother and father grew in their knowledge of God's Word. After his wife's conversion and obvious change of life,

Russell Sr. revealed something Sue had never known. He had been a fine athlete as a young man, starring in basketball and track. But at the age of 19, he became ill and was hospitalized. There in the hospital, a Baptist pastor visited him and led him to Christ.

However, as a salesman who traveled often, he did not attend church and had no biblical instruction at all. Consequently, he experienced no spiritual growth. His wife's new interest in spiritual things revived his own interest in, and desire for, the same.

As a sophomore, Russ attended the large New Trier High School, in Winnetka. His friends had little interest in the things of the Lord, nor did he. He felt somewhat embarrassed attending Winnetka Bible Church with his parents.

Because Russ expressed an interest in attending West Point, as he prepared for his junior year in high school, his father enrolled him in the Kentucky Military Institute. The pastor's wife at Winnetka Bible Church told Sue, "If Russ goes to Kentucky Military Institute, you might as well forget about his ever coming to the Lord. Why don't you send him to Wheaton Academy?"

At the last minute, that is what happened. In the fall of 1943, Russ, against his will, found himself at Wheaton Academy, on the campus of Wheaton College, 30 miles west of Chicago.

The adjustment of living away from home for the first time, along with his unhappiness at being at Wheaton, made Russ' first few weeks miserable. However, he soon made friends as he went out for the Academy football team. There he met young men who were good ballplayers. There was something else about some of them. They were not just "religious"; their relationship with Jesus Christ was important to them—and very contagious. Russ had never been acquainted with young men like this.

Later that fall, the Academy young people were expected to attend evangelistic services at Wheaton College. One night, Russ was seated in the balcony with his friends. The evangelist, with great sincerity, shared the gospel. Russ' heart was stirred. He knew his friends had something in their lives which he did not possess. As he listened, Russ knew the reality was Jesus Christ. He needed the Savior, for he was a sinner.

As the evangelist ended his message, he gave a simple and brief invitation, asking those to whom God's Spirit was speaking to come forward. Russ was sitting in the middle of the last row in the balcony. His heart was pounding with conviction as he climbed over his seat, walked down the stairs, and went forward where he was led to Christ.

For Russ, many things changed. He was able to enjoy true Christian fellowship with his friends, and his outlook on life was different.

During Russ' junior year at Wheaton Academy, his father was once again transferred, this time to Bloomfield, New Jersey. Russ' parents located a lovely home in Glen Ridge, New Jersey. They decided Russ would not return to Wheaton Academy but would attend Glen Ridge High School for his senior year.

Changing high schools each year is not easy. It involves making new friends quickly, then the process starts all over. During his senior year, Russ concentrated on studies and sports: football, basketball, and tennis.

The Ebersole family found an excellent church—the Brookdale Baptist Church, pastored by Dr. Charles Anderson, an unusually gifted teacher and preacher. There the Ebersoles' knowledge of God's Word increased greatly.

Toward the end of Russ' senior year, the Second World War was "winding down." Russ wanted very much to enter military service; he preferred the United States Navy.

One of his close friends from the Winnetka Bible Church, Earl Roe, also graduated that year. The two young men decided to enlist together. To do that, Russ had to travel to Chicago. In order to synchronize their schedules, Russ needed to leave before his class graduation. He would have to graduate in absentia. Later, he learned that his mother attended the graduation and cried through the whole service.

In Chicago, the two young men were separated during the enlistment processing. Later that day, after Russ had been sworn in, he met Earl. Earl was dejected; he had failed his physical. Later, he was accepted by the United States Army.

Russ spent boot camp at the Great Lakes Naval Training Station, in Illinois. About two months after he entered the Navy, Japan surrendered. Following basic training, Russ and his company were sent to Seattle, Washington, to await orders. After a few weeks, the company was assigned to duty in the Pacific. That is, all but Russ, who was left behind.

Disappointed and discouraged, Russ waited for his orders. Finally, he was sent to the Commissioned Officers' Club in Bremerton, Washington. There he met Lt. McGuigan, the officer in charge. Entering the lieutenant's office, Russ was impressed with the officer's size. He was a huge, burly man who had once played pro football. Lt. McGuigan explained that he had checked the background and records of the men in Russ' company and had chosen Russ as his storekeeper at the officers' club.

Being a common "swabby" and having no experience as a storekeeper, Russ began to object. Lt. McGuigan ordered in a gruff voice, "You are my new storekeeper, and you will also be my new roommate here at the club!"

For almost a year, Russ served in that capacity. While his job provided some interesting and new experiences as well as unusual privileges, it was not what he had dreamed of the day he enlisted in Chicago.

Early in the summer of 1946, Russ' assignment changed. He left the comforts of the Commissioned Officers' Club, moved into one of the barracks, and took charge of the bowling alleys at the Bremerton Naval Base. Again, Russ wondered at his assignment, for he had never even bowled!

He was embarrassed because a few of the petty officers assigned to work under him were veterans who had participated in several battles in the Pacific. It was obvious that they disdained their young "boss" who had never left the shores of America. Russ said, "I sure understand how you feel, fellows. I didn't ask for this job! I'm going to be working right along with you, so let's be friends and make the best of it."

Russ waited impatiently for his discharge. He hoped it would be soon enough to allow him to enroll at Wheaton College in September. He had been accepted in the freshman class.

Russ' discharge came after he had served in the Navy for 14 months. After flying back to New Jersey and a reunion with his family, Russ had just a few days to prepare for Wheaton.

# Chapter Eleven

# "He Will Be Our Guide"

Both Russ Ebersole and Gene DeVries entered Wheaton College in September 1946. Russ was interested in a law career and enrolled as a political science major. Gene, who never again wanted to leave the shores of America, decided to major in American literature. But during that freshman year, God showed each of these young people that He might have different plans for them.

During his freshman year, Russ became involved in athletics, especially soccer and track. Gil Dodds, who at that time held the world record for the indoor mile run, coached the Wheaton track team. Gil was a dedicated Christian whose goals went beyond winning races. He was more concerned with building Christian character into the lives of his runners. Often, as the young men jogged to the track for workouts, Gil stopped them to ask, "What is your Bible verse for today?"

On that track team were outstanding young men who were preparing to serve their Lord overseas as missionaries. Russ became well acquainted with them and teamed up with a few on the mile relay team. As a young Christian, he could not understand why they were planning to "throw their lives away" on the other side of the globe.

Ty Johnson, one of Russ' closest friends, explained to him that God has a perfect plan for each of His children and He wants to reveal it if we are willing to be and to do whatever He desires. Ty questioned, "Russ, have you ever asked the Lord what He wants to do with your life?" Russ had not. It was his desire to be a lawyer, but was that the plan that God had for him?

As Russ read God's Word, a passage from 1 Corinthians spoke deeply to him: *"What? Know ye not that your body is the temple of the Holy Spirit who is in you, whom ye have of God, and ye are not your own? For ye are bought with a price; therefore, glorify God in your body and in your spirit, which are God's"* (1 Corinthians 6:19, 20).

This was a new revelation for Russ. He was not his own; he had been purchased by God with the precious blood of His Son, Jesus Christ. In light of this truth, Russ committed his life to whatever God had in store for him.

Russ and Gene did not meet during their freshman year at Wheaton. They had no classes together and they had more than 350 classmates. However, Russ had noticed Gene from time to time. It was difficult not to notice her, as she was a lovely-looking blonde with a sweet smile. Russ knew Gene was popular with young men on campus, including seniors. He felt that his chances of getting to know her were slim.

At the beginning of their second year, the sophomore class rented a nearby skating rink. The purpose of the event was for everyone to get acquainted. In order to do this, the young men were to skate with a young woman until the bell rang, then they would move up to meet the next one. Russ wished the bell would ring more often, as he saw Gene about ten couples ahead of him.

Finally, he skated up to Gene and introduced himself. Her immediate response was, "Oh, you're the guy who knocked my brother out on the soccer field last week." What a beginning! Russ quickly replied that it was an accident. "I didn't say you intended to do it," Gene countered. "I just wanted to be sure that you were the one." Russ felt sure that he had just experienced his first and last encounter with Gene DeVries. Inwardly, he clung to the hope she would give him another chance.

She did! Russ lived in a private home with five other young men. They were planning a canoe trip and picnic supper. Each was to invite a girl. Russ was timid about phoning Gene, but his helpful roommate dialed Gene's phone number and handed Russ the phone. Gene accepted his invitation—the first of many.

One of the young men on that picnic was Ed McCully, who in 1956, with four companions, was speared to death by Auca Indians along the Curaray River in Ecuador.

Midway through their sophomore year, Russ and Gene dated often and were becoming aware of how much they cared for each other. This presented a problem. By that time, Gene believed God was leading her into foreign missions. Russ, while open to God's will, was not sure. As honestly as he could, he prayed God would show him clearly what to do.

In February 1948, Russ and Gene attended a large missionary conference at the Moody Church, in Chicago, where Gene's father was one of the speakers. After the message, Russ asked to speak to Henry privately. Russ came straight to the point. He explained his love for Gene, and said he believed Gene loved him. He did not want his love for Gene to be the thing that directed him to the mission field. But Russ believed the Lord could use this relationship, along with other ways God had been working in his heart, to help give him guidance. The two men prayed together, each of them asking the Lord to make His guidance clear to Russ and Gene. As the months passed, the Lord placed in Russ' and Gene's hearts a confidence that He was indeed leading them together to foreign missionary service.

Early in 1949, Henry and Gladys DeVries began to make plans to return to the ministry in Malaybalay that they were forced to leave before the Japanese invasion.

During spring vacation, Gene traveled with her parents to Grand Rapids. They spent time at their sending church, Wealthy Street Baptist, before leaving for the Philippines. Russ returned to his home in New Jersey, where he spent most of his time thinking about Gene.

One evening, at the home of his friends Dave and Bette

Scales, he shared his love for Gene and his hope of someday marrying her. Dave said, "Why don't you do something about it? Phone her and propose! I'll even pay for it. Call her and settle this thing." Russ knew Gene would be at a farewell party for her parents at their church, but was encouraged to call anyway.

Over the noise of the party, someone called Gene to the phone. She wondered who was calling at such an inconvenient time and place. To her astonishment, she heard Russ ask her to marry him. There was a pause—not a long one—and she laughingly said, "Yes, I'd love to!" Gladys DeVries asked who had called. As calmly as she could, Gene told her mother, "Russ. He asked me to marry him, and I said, 'Yes.'"

Before returning to Wheaton, Russ purchased a diamond ring and couldn't wait to place it on Gene's finger. On April 19, 1949, he did just that as they stood under a Wheaton streetlight. Gene's parents were visiting Wheaton, and Gene said, "Come on, Russ. I want to show my ring to Mom and Dad."

They ran through the darkened streets toward the house where Henry and Gladys were staying. Gene hurried up the stairs to her parents' room. They sat up astonished as Gene turned on the light and held out her left hand. Her father laughed. "Well, it's about time! We've been fighting this with you two for months. What took you so long?"

As Gene hugged her parents, her father added, "We're glad you settled this before we leave for the Philippines. Now we can see for ourselves how happy both of you are."

On June 15, 1949, Gene traveled with Russ and her two brothers to New York City to see her parents sail on a Filipino freighter for Manila. This difficult separation for Henry and Gladys was eased by their knowledge that Gene and their sons had a second home with the senior Ebersoles.

That summer, Gene worked at the Word of Life camp in Schroon Lake, New York, as a waitress and counselor. Russ drove a truck selling Dugan's bakery products in Lake Mohawk, New

Jersey. Daily letters were the "lifeline" between the lonesome couple.

Their senior year at Wheaton was especially noteworthy for the revival which took place during the winter evangelistic services of 1950. Many lives, touched by God's Spirit then, later took the gospel to the ends of the earth. Russ and Gene's "nifty class of fifty" sent over 130 of their members to foreign fields!

Graduation day was June 12, 1950, but Russ and Gene had little time to savor it. They both took part in the wedding of Gene's brother Dave to Carol Evans, in Washington, D.C., on June 17. Two days later, on June 19, Russ and Gene were married at Russ' home church, Brookdale Baptist Church, in Bloomfield, New Jersey.

To this young couple, joining their lives in service for their Lord, Pastor Charles Anderson gave a reminder that the Lord whom they served is named "El Shaddai, the One Who is enough." Facing the years ahead, Gene and Russ knew that they could trust their faithful God to meet any need that arose.

Engraved in their wedding rings was the scripture text they chose as a life verse: *"This God is our God forever and ever; He will be our guide even unto death"* (Psalm 48:14).

After a brief honeymoon in New Hampshire, the newlyweds served as host and hostess of the adult facilities at Word of Life. The busy summer put them in what turned out to be a "goldfish bowl," living in a ground floor room in the inn with windows from floor to ceiling on three sides.

That summer was highlighted by the presence of Dr. William Pettingill, a speaker who was acknowledged to be among the world's finest Bible teachers. He took a genuine interest in the young couple and invited them to join him and his wife to celebrate his 84th (and last) birthday at a local restaurant. There, Dr. Pettingill shared lessons that proved invaluable to the Ebersoles in later years.

Russ and Gene particularly remember Dr. Pettingill saying,

"I have been in the ministry for over 60 years. I haven't learned all I should have, but there is one lesson I want to share with you. Wherever you serve the Lord, here in America or overseas, remember this: If everything is going well—no difficulties, problems, or opposition—get on your knees and ask God what is wrong. But, if you are serving the Lord with all your heart and everything seems to be going against you—the discouragements are many and the opposition is strong—get on your knees and thank God, for He is working and the enemy is counterattacking."

At the time that seemed like strange counsel, but the coming years proved how right their dear friend was.

In the fall of 1950, Russ and Gene returned to Wheaton, where Russ pursued a master's degree in Biblical literature, majoring in New Testament, at the Graduate School of Theology. Gene served as secretary in the college alumni office for several months and continued writing primary children's materials for Scripture Press publications. Her colleague was one of her former Christian Education professors, Dr. Lois LeBar.

The Ebersoles' first home was an attic apartment at 1005 Santa Rosa Avenue, across the street from the college soccer field. After soccer practice, Russ headed to the cramped quarters for a shower in the bathroom that doubled as a kitchen. This was named the "bath-a-kitch" by one of their dinner guests. Russ' shower frequently disrupted Gene's preparations for dinner since he had to remove the portable oven from the shower stall before he could turn on the water.

During the second year of Russ' two-year program, the Ebersoles learned they would have their first child in August 1952. Russ and Gene spent the final semester at the Ebersole Sr.'s home in Glen Ridge, New Jersey, where Russ wrote his thesis and Gene typed it.

During this time, Russ and Gene investigated several mission boards as they prayerfully considered which team God wanted them to join. As part of their preparation, they planned to attend the 1952 session of the Summer Institute of Linguistics (SIL) at the University of North Dakota, in Grand Forks. There they would immerse themselves in linguistic studies.

However, Gene would be seven months pregnant at the time of their scheduled departure for the 1,400-mile car trip. The DeVrieses had just returned to the States, and both sets of parents and many friends advised them not to go. Gene's doctor was adamant that they could not drive, and only very reluctantly gave permission for Gene to fly.

Russ and Gene celebrated their second wedding anniversary on June 19, 1952, at a small restaurant. Over a lovely candlelit dinner, they discussed the pros and cons of the proposed trip. Russ was especially concerned about all of the negative counsel they were receiving from those who loved them most. He explained to Gene that he hesitated to take her on such a long trip. Gene quickly replied, "We both believe God wants us to take this linguistic training. We can't go wrong following His guidance. He will take care of me and the baby. Let's go!"

Both had peace about their decision, and a week later they flew to Grand Forks. On July 4, they were invited to a picnic with friends from Wheaton, Don and Polly Taber, who were also studying at SIL. As Don drove over some bumpy roads, he jokingly said, "This should bring your baby early, Gene!"

Early the next morning, on July 5, Gene gave premature birth to her first child, Russell E. Ebersole IV. A nurse told Russ of the baby's arrival, and he was elated. The baby was nicknamed "Rusty," to distinguish him from his father and grandfather, whose names were also "Russ." As time passed and the doctors had not appeared, Russ became concerned. Finally, an hour or more after the birth, Rusty's pediatrician approached Russ and said, "You have a beautiful son, but he has a serious, life-threatening problem. The membranous lining covering his lungs makes breathing impossible."

Dr. Silverman led Russ into the room where Rusty lay in a

rectangular glass box which enabled him to breathe artificially. Dr. Silverman was one of the men who had developed this device, called an air lock. Six months earlier, he had encouraged the citizens of Grand Forks to raise money to buy several of them for local hospitals.

As Russ and Dr. Silverman left the room, Russ thanked him and said, "The baby is now in God's hands." Dr. Silverman glowered at the young minister and said brusquely, "I'm in charge here! The baby is in *my* hands!"

As soon as possible, Russ phoned his parents, who were vacationing with friends on Long Island. He told his father of the birth of his first grandchild and namesake. Then he explained the baby's critical condition and asked his parents and friends to pray. He also asked his dad, when he returned home in a day or so, to check if the well-equipped Mountainside Hospital in their hometown had an air lock. Some hours later, Dr. Silverman asked Russ to join him to check Rusty's progress. As they turned from the air lock, Dr. Silverman put his hand on Russ' shoulder and said, "I'm sorry for what I said to you this morning. You were right. The baby is now in God's hands! I have done all I can for him."

By the end of the fourth day, Rusty was able to breathe on his own and was out of danger. God had gone before them and provided, in the small city of Grand Forks, not one, but three of the very machines needed to keep their first child, Rusty, alive. And the man who helped develop the air lock was their personal pediatrician!

Russ phoned his parents to give them the wonderful news. Then he asked, "Dad, did you check at Mountainside Hospital about the air lock?" His dad answered, "Yes, and they don't have a single one!"

Russ soberly told his father, "Dad, if Gene and I had not followed God's leading and come to Grand Forks, you would not have a grandson!"

As they stood on the threshold of their missionary career, God had taught Russ and Gene an important lesson: always follow the will and leading of God as He makes that clear—no matter how many others encourage you to do otherwise. Their confidence in their living and loving God had been immensely strengthened. Russ and Gene saw God's good hand at work to protect Rusty's life.

After Rusty's birth, Gene's mother came to help for several weeks. Then, as the linguistic classes drew to an end in late summer, Russ' mother drove from New Jersey to Grand Forks to see her new grandson and to take the family back home.

One of Russ' former classmates at Glen Ridge High School accepted Christ as Savior while in college. He asked Russ to begin a Bible class for the young men who had been in high school with them. A number of them had returned after finishing college and were now working in the area. Russ contacted many of them by phone and invited them to the first Bible class. One friend responded, "To what? A Bible class? Well, for old time's sake, I'll attend the first one."

The class continued for about six months, with 12 to 30 young men attending. Two of them came to faith in Christ.

Russ and Gene continued to seek God's will regarding the mission He would have them serve with. They believed strongly that "the team you play on is more important than the field you play on." After investigating four or five mission boards, they were directed to ABWE (the Association of Baptists for World Evangelism), the mission Gene's parents had served with in the Philippines.

In April 1953, they attended ABWE's spring candidate classes in Germantown, Pennsylvania, along with 11 other young men and women. For three weeks they were immersed in ABWE's history and policies, and learned about its various ministries around the world.

One incident made Russ and Gene wonder if they would be

appointed. They had asked permission of the hostess, Miss Ruth Woodworth, who served many years in the Philippines, if they could be excused one evening to have dinner with former Wheaton classmates who lived in Philadelphia. The evening was so enjoyable they forgot the time; they arrived at the mission home at midnight. The doors were locked and the lights out! Gene, a bit provoked, asked Russ, "Now what are we going to do? We'll probably never be appointed!"

Russ picked up some pebbles from the driveway and began to throw them at Miss Woodworth's bedroom windows on the second floor. She came to the window to see what was happening. Russ explained their predicament. Finally, the front door opened. It was evident that their hostess was not pleased. Was this the end?

A week or so later, Russ and Gene waited in the ABWE office for their board interview. Miss Woodworth approached them—with a smile—and said, "I hope the board appoints you to a ministry in Iloilo City where I served." The Ebersoles looked at one another and smiled. All seemed to be forgiven!

In their interview, they shared their belief that the Lord was directing them to the Philippines, but they had no preference concerning the six regional areas in which ABWE worked. When asked if they were willing to serve as field evangelists in Iloilo City, on the central island of Panay, they were happy to answer, "Yes." They were officially appointed as ABWE missionaries on April 14, 1953. In their first letter to friends and supporters, the Ebersoles shared information about their assigned area:

"Panay is one of the largest of the more than 7,000 islands in the Philippine archipelago. Its population of over one and a half million is scattered throughout rural areas. We hope to do extensive and intensive evangelism among the people, with the goal of establishing indigenous (self-governed and self-supporting) churches. A number of churches have been established, but at present there is no one to continue this work. The need is great; the call is urgent. What we do we must do quickly!"

Deputation (now called Pre-field Ministry) began in earnest. The Ebersoles visited churches in the East and Midwest to share their enthusiasm for the ministry to which God had called them. Their full support was promised by the end of 1953, and preparations were made for a February 1954 departure from New York City.

Not long before Russ and Gene departed for their first term of service in the Philippines, the Lord gave them an unexpected privilege. ABWE was sponsoring a dinner in the Philadelphia area for friends of the mission and mission personnel. The Ebersoles were surprised and delighted to be seated next to Dr. Raphael C. Thomas, ABWE's first missionary. Dr. Thomas was the catalyst for founding ABEO (Association of Baptists for Evangelism in the Orient), as the mission was first known.

Dr. Thomas, almost 84, was a spry gentleman with a keen sense of humor. He was extremely interested in the young couple seated beside him, and plied them with questions. When he heard that they were assigned to Iloilo City, he almost fell off his chair. "Iloilo City! Iloilo City! That's where I went in the early 1900s. I spent almost my entire missionary career there, directing the mission hospital and preaching the gospel wherever I could. That is where our mission began, young man—in Iloilo City in 1927. Oh, how I wish I were your age again! How I would love to go back to Iloilo with you. But the crazy doctors won't let me."

Dr. Thomas' excitement and obvious love for Iloilo and the Ilonggo people was a great encouragement to Russ and Gene on the eve of their departure. It was another confirmation that Iloilo was God's place of service for them.

During the Ebersoles' first year in Iloilo City, they learned of

Dr. Thomas' death shortly after his 84th birthday. How thankful Russ and Gene were for that special evening God arranged for them.

The Ebersoles were to sail on the *Dona Nati,* a Filipino freighter, from New York City to Manila, on a trip that would last 42 days. On the day of departure, many friends and family joined to wish the couple bon voyage. The ship was to sail at 1:30 p.m., but freighters seldom leave on "passenger time"; the freight is the important thing.

Many hours later, Captain Jose Ferrer told Russ that his parents and friends, who had patiently remained, had to leave. Russ went to his dad, who was holding little Rusty, his only grandchild and namesake. "Dad, you'll have to leave, as the gangplank will soon be pulled." As his father handed the baby to Russ, there were tears in his eyes. "Russ," he said, "this is the hardest thing your mother and I have ever done—saying goodbye to you and Gene, and especially to Rusty." Then he quickly added, "But we wouldn't have it any other way; we know you are doing what God wants you to do, and that gives us great joy!"

Sailing on the Filipino freighter had some wonderful advantages. Captain Ferrer was kind to the young couple and adored Rusty. Many of the crew members were from the area where Russ and Gene would be working and spoke the Ilonggo dialect. They were happy to help the Ebersoles begin learning simple words and phrases in their language.

Gene had grown up speaking the Cebuano dialect, a "first cousin" to Ilonggo, and she also knew some of the Bukidnon dialect from Malaybalay. Her familiarity with these dialects and the Philippine culture proved to be a great asset to them both. The purser, who became a close friend, readily gave Russ permission to conduct "divine services" each Sunday morning for the passengers and crew who desired to attend.

The 12 passengers ate every meal with Captain Ferrer at the captain's table. One day after lunch, Russ and Gene missed Rusty, each assuming the other had him. A frantic search began. Captain Ferrer himself, along with crew members, searched the ship from top to bottom. Finally, the captain said to Russ and Gene, "We've searched everywhere and cannot find him. I'm afraid that somehow he walked out on the deck and fell overboard!" Terrified, Russ and Gene stared at one another. There was nothing they could do except blame themselves for not looking after their precious, tow-headed little boy.

A few moments later, the door of a fellow passenger's cabin opened and out toddled Rusty, his smiling face covered with chocolate. The woman had taken him into her cabin after lunch, where Rusty entertained her as she fed him chocolate candy. She was completely oblivious to the search going on outside. The good hand of our God protected Rusty's life once again.

From that time on, Gene made sure the harness they had brought was securely fastened on Rusty whenever they left the cabin.

One of the Ebersoles' fellow passengers, a university professor, was returning to Manila after graduate studies in the United States. Her husband, who held a high government position, met the ship in Manila. He mentioned to Russ that Ramon Magsaysay, the dynamic president of the Philippines, would visit the *Dona Nati* the next day to officially receive a large shipment of farm implements donated by the Lions Club in San Francisco.

The next day, Russ and Gene accompanied their friends to the pier to get a glimpse of the popular president. As Magsaysay's party approached the ship, Russ stepped out of the crowd with his camera and stood in front of the president.

Magsaysay stopped and asked Russ pleasantly, "What do you want?" Russ explained, "My wife and I arrived yesterday on this ship. We will be living in the Philippines serving as missionaries. Many Americans, including ourselves, admire you greatly. I'd like to take a picture of you."

Smiling, President Magsaysay called an aide and instructed

him to take the picture. Then he stood side by side with Russ as the picture was snapped. After briefly chatting with Russ and waving at Gene, the president boarded the ship.

Russ' new friend exclaimed facetiously, "I've been in government service for years and have never met a president. You arrived yesterday and already you are a personal friend of President Magsaysay!" What a wonderful introduction to the Philippines—welcomed by the president himself!

Early in April, as the Ebersoles left Manila and headed for Iloilo City, in the hot lowlands of Panay Island, Gene suppressed a tiny wish that they could go instead to mountainous Bukidnon Province with its cooler air and familiar friends. Accepting the fact that Panay needed a field evangelist immediately, Gene resolutely put her childhood memories behind her and moved with Russ and Rusty toward their own place of service.

# Chapter Twelve

# The Work of an Evangelist

After years of preparation for their life's work, Gene and Russ were eager to settle down in a home of their own and begin their ministry. Arriving in Iloilo City in early April 1954, they initially stayed with Gordon and Martha Wray.

Gordon was the director of the Doane Evangelistic Institute, one of ABWE's two educational institutions which trained Filipino young people for the ministry. The Wrays' apartment was upstairs in Doane Hall—a large, Spanish-type house that was the centerpiece of the institute's property. The ground floor was part of the training facilities.

Both the Doane Evangelistic Institute and the spacious Spanish home were named for Marguerite Doane, who had been instrumental in helping to start ABWE. She was the daughter of William Howard Doane, a famous hymn writer and an ingenious inventor who had become a wealthy man. His daughter gave generously to ABWE's early ministries.

Soon the Ebersoles found a small but adequate apartment on the ground floor of a two-apartment house in the La Paz section of Iloilo City. This became a comfortable and attractive haven.

About a week after arriving in Iloilo City, Russ was invited to be one of the main speakers at the annual Conference of National Churches. That year the conference was held in the town of Manapla, on the nearby island of Negros.

Russ was thrilled to stay in a Filipino home for the first time. At mealtimes, two teenage daughters served the food. Russ noticed when they looked at him, the girls snickered and repeated something in their dialect. He asked their father, who explained that his girls had given Russ a nickname, "Mr. Blue Eyes." He added that Filipino nicknames were not always that complimentary.

The evening Russ was to preach, he was introduced to his interpreter, a young pastor. The young man explained that Russ didn't have to speak sentence by sentence, but could give paragraphs of thought. Then the pastor would put the thoughts into the dialect. While being introduced, Russ looked out at the crowd of almost 1,000 Filipinos. He was so excited that he completely forgot about the interpreter at his side. As Russ moved along in his message, he noticed two senior missionaries in the front row poking each other and smiling. Russ thought, *Why would they react that way to a new missionary trying to do his best?* Then he observed that many of the Filipinos were doing the same thing. About seven minutes into his message, Russ felt a tap on his shoulder and heard his distraught interpreter whisper, "Sir, I cannot do it!"

As Russ tried to cover his embarrassment, the crowd roared with laughter. Right then, Russ made a silent vow and prayed, "Lord, help me to learn this dialect well so I can preach on my own."

Returning to Iloilo City, Russ and Gene determined to begin language study as soon as possible. There were no language schools at that time, nor even textbooks to help them. They hired a Christian woman from the church to be their tutor. But she had never taught before, and Russ and Gene's time was already full with teaching responsibilities at the institute. So, much to their regret, real language study was limited.

Gene began teaching Christian Education courses soon after they arrived, and Russ taught Introduction to the New Testament. One of the students in Gene's first class was a friend from her childhood days in Bukidnon. Renewing their friendship increased Gene's homesickness for Malaybalay.

The students in Russ' large freshman class understood English, but they had problems comprehending their young instructor's rapid-fire delivery. After a week of classes, Gordon Wray encouraged Russ to slow down and speak distinctly. He said, "Many students have complained that they do not understand anything you say because you talk so fast and your accent is strange to them."

In addition to teaching, Russ was asked to set up the men's physical education activities, including coaching basketball.

Since two of the missionary field evangelists were on furlough, Russ planned extended weekend trips into the provinces of Panay and nearby Guimaras Island in order to spend time with the pastors and people. He lived in their homes and enjoyed their warm hospitality. During those times, he was immersed in the Ilonggo dialect and made good progress in the language.

In addition to her teaching responsibilities, Gene worked on preparing Christian Education curriculum with her missionary colleague, Bonnie Guthrie. She also became involved as teen advisor at the Doane Baptist Church and in home visitation with the church's Bible woman, Mrs. Lopez. In this way, Gene met the women of the church in their own homes and frequently contacted women interested in hearing for the first time about the Lord Jesus. With Mrs. Lopez' help, Gene steadily improved her ability to use the Ilonggo dialect.

In the central islands of Panay and Negros, tent evangelism had proven to be a successful method of penetrating towns with the gospel, many for the first time. ABWE missionary Paul Friederichsen pioneered this method, which was also used by missionaries Bill Hopper and Frank Jenista. Russ had the equipment for tent campaigns but was an inexperienced "rookie."

To help him immeasurably, the Lord provided an outstanding Filipino pastor-evangelist, Rev. Zoilo Anat, to be his co-laborer. Rev. Anat had fought during World War II with the Filipino Scouts and was a true Filipino patriot. More important, he was a devoted "soldier of Christ." He had been trained at the Doane Evangelistic Institute and was an effective pastor and gifted preacher. But his heart was in evangelism, and he readily accepted Russ' invitation to partner in spreading the gospel throughout western Visayas.

The Ebersoles went to Bethel Baptist Hospital in Malaybalay for the birth of their daughter, Cheryl Lynn, on February 18, 1955.

When they returned, Russ and Mr. Anat made final preparations for their first tent campaign in the nearby town of Mandurriao, a stronghold of Roman Catholicism.

The gospel tent was erected in an empty lot near the airport, and the two-month campaign began. At first, many thought a circus was coming to town, and the tent was overflowing for a few nights. Realizing the religious nature of the meetings, a number of them drifted away, but many continued to attend.

Both Mr. Anat and Russ preached nightly from the Roman Catholic edition of the Ilonggo Bible. They used Bible filmstrips, flannelgraph, and chalk drawings to clarify the message of the gospel, which many heard for the first time.

Russ was far from fluent in the dialect but was determined to learn it by continuing to use it. Some of the people complained to Mr. Anat that Russ' preaching "hurt our ears" because of the way he spoke their language. Russ laughed as he replied, "I'm sorry about that, but this is the only way I can improve. They'll have to put up with earaches until I learn it."

Mr. Anat worked patiently with Russ to help correct his mistakes. After each meeting, he reviewed the words and expressions Russ had mispronounced or misused. Russ' knowledge of Filipino culture was also greatly enhanced by his friend's loving counsel.

In spite of strong local opposition and the "Americano's" poor Ilonggo, God's Spirit used His Word, and the lives of many men, women, and young people were transformed by the gospel.

One of the first to trust Christ as his Savior was a local barber, Mr. Sampiano. Fifty years before, in 1905, when he was only five years old, two strangers visited Mandurriao selling black books. A few days after their arrival, the men were killed by residents of the town. The little boy asked his mother why these strangers were killed. She replied, "We were told that the book they were selling was filled with spiritual poison."

The night he was converted to Christ, Mr. Sampiano shared with Russ, "For 50 years I have wondered what was in that book. The first night you began preaching here, I came. Both you and Mr. Anat were preaching from that black book. I came each night to learn what was in it. It wasn't spiritual poison. It had the most wonderful message I had ever heard. It was the Bible, God's book!"

Mr. Sampiano became a charter member of the small church established in Mandurriao and faithfully served the Lord until his death.

That campaign in Mandurriao was the beginning of a fruitful evangelism partnership between Russ and Pastor Anat, a relationship that continued for seven years.

Russ' second campaign was in the town of San Enrique, in the central part of Panay, 60 rough miles from Iloilo City. Russ and Mr. Anat set up housekeeping in an old trailer that Paul Friederichsen used years before. The gospel had never before been preached in San Enrique.

In that campaign, which continued for four months, Pastor Dequito and people from his church, Passi Baptist, five miles away, were a great help. They often provided special music and gave personal testimonies.

The opposition in San Enrique was strong and steady. People attending the meetings were threatened with ex-communication. Disturbances were common. One night a group of drunken men with their *bolos* (sharp-bladed machetes) entered the tent and tried to break up the meeting. Police, who were present each night, removed the drunks, and the meeting continued. Several weeks later, the ringleader of that drunken group, Mr. Pinyol, was San Enrique's first convert. His changed life from brawler and drunkard to sober and enthusiastic believer gave a powerful testimony to the whole community.

The opposition, however, continued. One night before the meeting, Russ stood outside the tent looking up at a gorgeous, starlit sky. He began to pray out loud, "Lord, these people don't want You! They don't want me! They don't want the gospel, Lord. I miss my wife and our two little children. Lord, why did you send me to these hard-hearted people? Maybe I should have been a lawyer back in New York."

As was typical during the tent campaigns, to invite people to come, music was played 30 minutes before the start of each meeting over loudspeakers placed in coconut trees. As Russ was praying, he heard the words to Annie Johnson Flint's song,

> He giveth more grace when the burden grows greater,
> He sendeth more strength when the labors increase;
> To added affliction He addeth His mercy,
> To multiplied trials His multiplied peace.

It seemed as if God were answering directly from heaven. Russ bowed his head and whispered, "Lord, I am sorry. Please forgive me. But Lord, I can't remain here without Your help!"

Although opposition never stopped, the Lord did help, and men and women turned to Jesus Christ for salvation. They were instructed and baptized, a building was erected, and a church started.

Sometimes opposition to the gospel came from established authorities. In a coastal town, 20 miles from Iloilo City, the mayor and police chief would not grant permission for a tent campaign. So the tent was erected a few miles outside the town in the large *barrio* (village) of Kabubugan. Nightly police protection was part of the permission given by the town officials.

One Sunday night in the middle of a meeting, a group of young people threw small, homemade, chemical tear-gas-like "bombs" inside the tent. These caused people's eyes to burn and tear. The tent immediately cleared as people exited. The meeting was over!

Russ was upset because the police, who normally provided protection, were not present, and serious harm could have occurred. After securing their equipment, Russ and Mr. Ronner, a schoolteacher from Iloilo City who helped out on weekends as a chalk artist, drove into town looking for the police chief. They were informed that he was at the town plaza, where the annual fiesta was being held. When Russ and Mr. Ronner arrived at the plaza, the dance was in session with hundreds of people surrounding the cement dance floor. The two evangelists asked a policeman to find the police chief and have him come out to talk with them. In a few moments the policeman returned and said, "The police chief does not want to see you."

Russ and Mr. Ronner then strode across the dance floor, creating quite a stir. Russ said, "Chief, I want to talk to you." The chief, not even looking up, said, "Can't you see that I'm too busy now to talk with you?" as he continued counting the votes for the Princess of the Fiesta. Russ then explained that the meeting was broken up by a rowdy group of young men, and that someone might have been seriously hurt. "Where was the police protection we were promised?" Russ asked. At that, the chief jumped to his feet. As he turned toward Russ, he pointed his cocked pistol at Russ' chest! Mr. Ronner, a bigger man than most Filipinos, was standing at Russ' shoulder shaking with anger and embarrassment. Russ quietly told him not to make a move or someone might be hurt. Looking at the pistol pointed at his chest, Russ was sure that if anyone was going to get hurt, he'd be that man!

The mayor of the town ran over and asked Russ, "What is your problem, sir?"

Russ replied, "Mayor, I think the one with the problem right now is your police chief. Please ask him to put that gun away before someone is hurt." The police chief slowly moved back and reluctantly holstered his gun.

Russ gave the mayor full details about the incident and asked him to be sure police protection was provided at the tent when they resumed meetings in two nights. The mayor said he would try to do that, but did not sound very convincing. Russ then told him, "Mayor, if your policemen are not there on Tuesday evening, I intend to contact the governor of the province and have him send out the Philippine constabulary to protect us."

Russ and Mr. Ronner then left the dance and continued their drive into Iloilo City. On Tuesday evening when the meetings resumed, several policemen appeared at the tent long before the meeting began! For the rest of the campaign, there were no further incidents.

Many years later while visiting Kabubugan, Russ preached in the little chapel that had been erected. After the service, one of the deacons told the Ebersoles that God had called seven young men and women from that little church to prepare to serve the Lord at the Doane Baptist Bible College (formerly the Doane Evangelistic Institute). What an encouragement!

# Chapter Thirteen

# Partners in Ministry

In order to have continuity of personnel, the Ebersoles were asked to take their furlough six months ahead of their scheduled date of August 1957.

This posed a complication—Gene was pregnant with their third child. She was having serious difficulties with eclampsia which threatened her and the baby's lives. The Lord wonderfully provided a young Filipina doctor whose skillful and loving care brought Gene safely through her delivery. With great thanksgiving, the Ebersoles welcomed Beth Alane, born in the Iloilo Mission Hospital on April 29, 1957.

A few months later the five Ebersoles said goodbye to their missionary colleagues and many Filipino friends to begin their first furlough.

Two months before their return to the Philippines, the Ebersoles welcomed a second son, Bruce David, on August 22, 1958. In early November, the family left for their second term of service. They were assigned to Bacolod City, on the island of Negros. Bacolod was the capital of Negros Occidental, one of the largest sugar-producing provinces in the Philippines.

Negros Occidental was also the place in the ABWE world with the greatest number of churches at that time. Here, Russ ministered with many fine pastors, some of whom were old enough to be his father.

The mission owned a house in Bacolod City, and it became the Ebersoles' home. It was a busy hub, as Christian workers and lay people visited constantly. Russ and Gene set up a library of theological books, along with helpful periodicals and flannel-graph stories. As they had done in Iloilo City, they began a bi-monthly meeting where as many as 90 pastors and workers enjoyed fellowship, trained in practical subjects related to their ministries, and ate a delicious dinner.

Russ was always a champion of single women missionaries and their multifaceted ministries. During his first term, as Russ ministered in provincial areas, he was challenged by the work single missionary women had done in ABWE's earlier days.

On one occasion, Russ and Mr. Anat hiked to an isolated *barrio* on the island of Guimaras. The believers there told them, "You are only the second missionary who has ever visited us." Surprised, Russ asked, "Who was the first?" He was amazed to hear that ABWE missionaries Helen Hinkley and Stella Mower had hiked there more than 20 years earlier.

As Russ and Gene settled into their second term, they were impressed with the fine group of Bible women serving throughout that area, many of them in difficult and isolated places. One of those areas was in the mountains of south Negros, where a group of small churches was located. From the time he first arrived in Bacolod City, Russ had a keen desire to visit them.

Finally, he was able to schedule a week when he hiked with the mountain missionary, Mr. Manuel, to 14 churches, visiting and preaching at two churches each day. Most of the hiking that week was rugged and tiring, but still it was a joy to reach each church and be greeted by the smiling Bible women and their members, and to enjoy precious fellowship with them. Each group of believers seemed to thirst for God's Word as Russ shared it with them.

Sometimes their beds were church benches or split-bamboo floors, but after hiking most of the day, sleep was always deep and sweet.

One of the special "treats" during the week was swimming and bathing in the cool rivers and streams. One "bath time" was particularly memorable. Mr. Manuel and Russ had taken off their clothes in what they thought was an isolated spot and "skinny-dipped" in the middle of a cool, refreshing mountain river. Enjoying that welcome respite, they were alarmed to see two women on the bank where they had left their clothes. The women had come to do their washing, which could take an hour or more. The men's brief dip promised to be a long swim.

After a few minutes, the women noticed the men and excitedly shouted, *"Buwaya, buwaya! Andam kamo!" Buwaya* is the word for crocodile. The men shouted back and asked where the crocodile was. The women replied there had been a large croc an hour before at the very spot where the men were swimming! Russ and his companion faced a big decision: streak out of the river to get their clothes, or continue paddling in the river and hope the crocodile had moved on? Modesty ruled the day. No crocodile appeared, and as soon as the women left, the men made a dash for the riverbank and their clothes.

Since churches already existed in most of the towns in Negros Occidental Province, Russ' ministry was different than his first term. Local churches were able to sponsor a number of tent campaigns in Negros Occidental. These helped strengthen the churches and encourage church members to be more active in reaching their own communities with the gospel.

Sometimes, Mr. Anat and Russ held campaigns in large, unreached *barrios* with the help of churches in nearby towns. One of those was in Talaban.

The Talaban campaign was held jointly with the Baptist church in Su-ay, where Pastor Figueroa led the congregation. Religious leaders supplied local ruffians with *tuba,* an intoxicating drink made from the fermented sap of the coconut tree. While under the influence, men pelted the tent with stones on several occasions. Thankfully, no one was injured in any of the stone-throwing incidents.

After several weeks of nightly meetings, Mr. Insular approached Russ while he was putting away his equipment at the end of the service. He asked, "What you preached tonight—was that true?"

Russ replied, "Yes, we preached from God's Word, which is absolutely true. What are you referring to?"

Mr. Insular responded that the preaching emphasized that Jesus Christ could forgive any person of any sin. "Is that really true?" he asked Russ.

Russ assured him that it was, for Jesus Christ came to save sinners, and *"If we confess our sins, He is faithful and just to forgive us our sins, and to cleanse us from all unrighteousness"* (1 John 1:9).

Mr. Insular then asked, "Can Jesus Christ forgive me?" Russ asked him if he was a sinner, and Mr. Insular quickly replied, "Are you kidding? I'm probably the worst sinner in Talaban today!" He opened his shirt to reveal a number of deep scars. "These are the results of drunken knife fights. I'm the worst drunkard in this place. Now, can Jesus Christ really forgive me?"

Russ sat down on the bench with him and opened his Ilonggo New Testament to passage after passage which told of God's love for sinners. As Mr. Insular listened attentively, God's Word convicted him of his sin and revealed to him the Savior. After 30 minutes, the men fell to their knees, and Mr. Insular repented of his sins and asked the Lord for cleansing and forgiveness. He stood up a new man, a glow on his face. Thanking Russ, he left the tent and headed home.

Mr. Anat and Russ always followed up with those who made decisions. Several days later, as they approached Mr. Insular's home, they saw a woman sitting on the small porch at the top of the steps. She got up immediately and stared at the men as she passed them. If looks could kill, Russ and Mr. Anat would have dropped dead on the spot. That woman was a visiting neighbor.

Mrs. Insular welcomed the men into her small *sala* (living room). When she realized her visitors were the men preaching at the tent, her first question was, "What happened to my husband?" Feigning ignorance, Russ and Mr. Anat countered, "What do you mean?"

She was surprised they did not know her husband was known for his drinking and brawling. She told them how he had mistreated her and her children when drunk. "But now," she said, "he isn't drinking and he spends all his free time reading the black book he bought at the tent. What has happened to him?"

Russ asked if she liked her husband better now or before. She smiled and said, "Now, but I can't understand how he can be so different."

The men then explained she had a brand-new husband. Jesus Christ had changed him and given him a new nature. Then Russ quoted 2 Corinthians 5:17: *"Therefore, if any man be in Christ, he is a new creation; old things are passed away, behold, all things are become new."*

On hearing this, Mrs. Insular softly remarked, "If Jesus Christ can change my husband like that, I want Him, too!" Mr. Anat and Russ shared God's Word with her and led her to Christ. Mr. and Mrs. Insular became faithful members of the small church that was established after the campaign. They served the Lord faithfully until their deaths.

And the woman whose looks could kill? A week or two later she came to Russ asking his forgiveness for the way she had treated him. Then she said, "I have been listening to the preaching over the loudspeaker and even have attended a few meetings. God has spoken to my heart, and I have come to ask Jesus Christ to be my Savior."

On November 30, 1959, the family welcomed a third daughter and fifth child, Susan Gay, born, as Cheri had been, at the Bethel Baptist Hospital in Malaybalay. Susie's arrival gave the family an opportunity to spend four weeks in the refreshing coolness of Bukidnon Province. Bruce, not yet one and a half, was already investigating everything and was prone to accidents. Somehow he found a can of kerosene and drank some of it.

Thankfully, Dr. Link Nelson was able to quickly pump his stomach, and Bruce suffered no ill effects.

When Susie was only ten days old, the family returned to their home in Bacolod City. To get there, they had to change planes in two cities. Their first stop was in Cagayan de Oro City on the north coast of Mindanao, only a 20-minute flight from Malaybalay. While waiting for their plane to Cebu City, a friendly Spanish priest, dressed in a long white gown, approached Russ and asked if all the young children were his. "Yes," Russ replied proudly, "including our new baby girl." The priest then inquired if all the children were baptized. Russ responded, "No, none of them are."

On hearing this, the priest was concerned and expressed great surprise since he believed that, apart from baptism, the souls of these children were in jeopardy. Russ quickly explained what he believed the Bible taught about baptism, that the ordinance was only for those who had a personal relationship with God through an intelligent act of faith in Jesus Christ.

During their discussion, five-year-old Cheri stood before the priest and said, "You don't love Jesus, do you?"

Obviously upset, the priest replied, "Little girl, that is not a nice thing to say. Of course I love Jesus."

Cheri was not to be denied. She looked up at the priest and said, "Oh no, you don't love Jesus. I've seen you in your church kneeling down and praying to idols!" By now the priest was very agitated (and Russ very embarrassed). Just then, the loudspeaker announced the departure of his plane, and the priest, with evident relief, hurried off. But the "Cheri adventures" were not over.

Soon the Ebersoles boarded the plane for the second stop of their journey. Arriving in Cebu City, they had a brief layover before taking the plane to Bacolod City—and home. When their flight was called, Russ, Gene, and their children boarded their plane and settled in for the short flight. As they were on the runway, ready for takeoff, Russ checked on his family and shouted,

"We're missing one of our children!" The flight attendant asked Russ, "How many children do you have?"

"Five, including the baby," Russ replied. "But our daughter Cheri isn't here. We must have left her in the terminal."

The flight attendant ran to the cockpit to alert the pilot. He immediately turned the plane around and headed back to the terminal. They opened the cabin door, and Russ ran down the stairs into the building, frantically searching for Cheri.

He finally spotted her but couldn't believe his eyes. There was little Cheri, not quite five years old, standing in the middle of six young American priests dressed in long white robes. Russ rushed into the circle to retrieve his blonde, curly-headed daughter. One of the priests asked, "Sir, is this your little girl?" "Yes," Russ answered, "and we almost took off without her!"

The priests laughed. One said to Russ, "We've been having the most interesting time discussing theology with this bright little girl." As Russ scooped Cheri into his arms, he said, "I'm sure it was *very* interesting, but she has to leave you now." Thanking the men, he ran back to the plane. Gene, the children, and the airline's personnel were all greatly relieved that Cheri was finally on board, ready to fly home to Bacolod with the rest of the family.

Russ' evangelistic campaigns and short-term Bible institutes in local churches often kept him away from home. The responsibility of running a household with five lively children, including a new baby, fell largely on Gene's shoulders.

Besides her full-time ministry with her family, Gene was teaching Rusty using the Calvert Correspondence Course. She was also the advisor of the large young people's group at Fellowship Baptist Church in Bacolod City. She had a great love for Filipino young people, and God used her in the lives of many of them.

One of the young men, Art Inion, visited Gene one day. He seemed quite nervous as he said, "Ma'am, I have a problem."

Gene asked, "What is your problem, Art?"

"The president of our young people's group is going to Manila to study," Art replied.

Gene smiled and said, "Why is that a problem to you?"

He quickly answered, "Did you forget, Ma'am? I'm the vice-president! Our constitution says that whenever the president is gone, the vice-president automatically takes his place. Ma'am, I could never be the president."

Gene realized Art was a shy, retiring young man who would find it difficult to lead the 75 or 80 high school and college age young people. Seeking to encourage him, Gene said, "Art, it is obvious God wants you to be the president. And He has promised to provide us with all we need to do His will."

Art took the challenge and became an excellent president. A year or so later, he again visited Gene. "Ma'am, you'll never believe what is happening." Curious, Gene asked Art to explain.

"I believe the Lord is calling me to preach—but I could never do that." Gene replied, "Art, I've been praying about that very thing. If God is calling you to preach, He will enable you and give you everything you need. Just obey Him and follow His leading."

But Art had a second objection. "Ma'am, I could never afford to go to seminary in Manila." Again, Gene encouraged him with the assurance that God would provide all he needed.

Art obeyed and trusted the Lord. He enrolled in the Baptist Bible Seminary and Institute just outside the city of Manila. During his four years there, he excelled in his studies, music, and Christian service. Gene was able to attend his graduation and rejoiced that he graduated near the top of his class and became a part-time teacher in the school. Some years later, Art, his wife, Phoebe, and their young son left Manila to serve the Lord as missionaries in Thailand with PABWE (the Philippine Association of Baptists for World Evangelism).

*Chapter Fourteen*

# He Makes No Mistakes

On the evening of September 8, 1960, Dr. David Daehler telephoned from Iloilo City. Gene answered and heard him ask the operator for Russ. Gene told the operator, "Russ is not in right now, but he'll be back in a few hours. Could I take the message?"

The doctor replied evasively, "Tell Mrs. Ebersole to have her husband call me back this evening."

About a week earlier, Gene had accompanied a younger missionary to Iloilo City. Her friend was nervous about a scheduled checkup, and Gene offered to go with her to the Iloilo Mission Hospital and introduce her to Dr. Daehler. When the doctor met the women, he recommended that Gene also take advantage of the opportunity for a routine examination. In the course of his exam, Dr. Daehler found a small lump in Gene's right breast. He urged her to have the lump removed the next day.

Gene called home to tell Russ of the delay in her return. After one night in the hospital, she flew back to Bacolod to take up her normal routine, trying not to worry about the pathology exam, which would be done in Manila.

Now Dr. Daehler was asking to speak to Russ. After hanging up the phone, Gene waited for Russ and fought to control her mounting anxiety. After the children went to bed, she wandered aimlessly around the house, picking up scattered toys and books, glancing frequently at the clock. She went into the bedroom, picked out a clean nightgown and robe, and stepped into a cool shower. Relaxing under the stinging spray, she forced back the numerous brooding thoughts that were crowding her mind.

By 9:00 p.m. Gene gave up all attempts at diversion. Turning down the lights, she lay down on the sofa to listen for the sound of Russ' car turning into the driveway. Russ found Gene lying there in the semi-darkness. "Is anything wrong, honey?" he asked. Gene hesitated, "Dr. Daehler called. He left word for you to call him back when you came in."

When Russ did not reply, Gene continued, "I guess we both know what this means."

Turning quickly to the telephone, Russ contacted the doctor, who confirmed the Ebersoles' worst fears: Gene's biopsy revealed a malignancy. Gene had to return to the hospital for radical surgery. The operation was scheduled for the evening of September 15. In the intervening days, Gene and Russ attempted to maintain a normal routine. Rusty's school lessons continued through the last day Gene spent at home before surgery.

When word of Gene's condition spread through Bacolod, friends began to stop by the house to encourage her. She and Russ had made many friends, not only among the Filipinos, but also the English, Chinese, and Swiss business people.

One woman came to visit Gene. As she left the house, she turned to Russ with tears welling up in her eyes. "I can't understand it. How can she face this so calmly?" Gene tried to tell her friends why she was not afraid, but many of them could not understand the peace she found in God.

Preparing to leave home, Gene realistically faced the uncertainties before her. For the children's sake, she held her feelings in check until she and Russ boarded a ship for the two-hour trip from Bacolod to Iloilo. With tears in her eyes, Gene said, "This is the hardest thing I've ever had to do: leave our five children when I'm not sure what is going to happen." But she quickly added, "Russ, the Lord gave me a wonderful promise from His Word this morning." Then she quoted from Psalm 23:4: *"Yea, though I walk through the valley of the shadow of death, I will fear no evil; for Thou art with me; thy rod and thy staff they comfort me."*

Russ had found comfort in the words from Isaiah 26:3: *"Thou wilt keep him in perfect peace, whose mind is stayed on Thee, because he trusteth in thee."*

Within a few hours she wrote to her parents, Henry and Gladys, "How good and wonderful the Lord has been to us during these days! His sustaining is indescribable. Saying goodbye to the kids was, of course, very hard."

Dr. Lincoln Nelson, a close friend and fellow ABWE missionary, flew from Malaybalay to Iloilo to perform Gene's operation. As he had hoped, Dr. Nelson found the lump quite small; he reassured Gene and Russ that the chances of complete recovery were excellent.

Gene wrote again to her parents, "How wonderful to know now that we will be together again. The things the Lord has said to me these days can't be put into words. The Lord has been unspeakably good. His peace is past understanding. We know He makes no mistakes. We trust Him, that's all."

The surgery indicated no spread of cancer into other areas, but the surgical procedures and skin grafting kept Gene in Iloilo for six weeks in the home of ABWE missionary colleagues Carrel and Fern Aagard. Determined to restore full use of the affected muscles in her right shoulder and arm, she began an exercise program, even though the effort brought severe pain.

The physical discomfort proved to be much less difficult than the long separation from her children. Much to her relief, Gene learned that her sister-in-law, Ginny DeVries, had moved from her home on the island of Palawan to Bacolod to spend three weeks with the Ebersole children.

Gene missed them all terribly. Susan, with her wiry body and freckled nose, was less than one year old; Bruce, barely two. Shy little Beth, three and a half, usually clung to her mother for security. Rusty and Cheri, eight and six, were a little more independent, but also needed Gene's supervision and attention.

Gene returned to Bacolod early in November in time to meet the senior Ebersoles, who had arrived for a long vacation with the family. Soon after, Russ took the whole family to Baguio, the one place in the Philippines Gene found even more restful than her own Bukidnon Province mountains. For four welcome weeks, they enjoyed the cool, pine-scented fresh air of the mountains high above Manila.

In the mission guest home, Gene sat by the fireplace, watching the dying embers of the fire and reliving the visits she made to Baguio with her parents in the years before World War II. In this serenity, she felt her vitality begin to return.

After a particularly delightful Christmas back in Bacolod, the grandparents left for home, assured that Gene had regained normal strength. Immersed again in her regular schedule, Gene wrote to a friend, "Ours is a noisy, bustling household, as you can imagine. Sometimes I wonder if I'll live through it! The kids are full of life, and then there's Trixie, the watchdog; Blackie, the pup; Whiskers, the child-hating cat; and Rescued, the kitten we pulled out of the front ditch. I'm glad you can't smell the latter! Also, numerous mice, cockroaches, and lizards, to mention some of the more unwelcome family members."

Gene kept thinking of the uncertain state of her parents' health. In the frequent, detailed letters they exchanged, Gene and her mother kept their promise not to hold back news that might cause concern, though each of them maintained a cheerful optimism. When Gladys developed a heart condition, she mentioned it to Gene casually, but Gene could not shake off the possibility of losing her mother. In her Bible, she found and underlined a promise, *"Casting all your care upon Him; for He careth for you"* (1 Peter 5:7). She quoted the promise in a letter to a friend, adding with a touch of despair, "To *do* this!"

A year after surgery, Gene returned to Iloilo for a minor checkup. A biopsy indicated no sign of further malignancy.

After Christmas in 1961, Gene noticed that the usually lively

Cheri appeared listless and inattentive at her schoolwork. Tests revealed that the seven-year-old girl had developed tubercular-meningitis. For six weeks Cheri lay in bed, so weak Gene feared for her life. Two of the younger children showed alarming borderline reactions to skin tests for tuberculosis, but subsequent tests revealed no further problems.

To reassure herself, as well as her parents, Gene wrote, "If we discount Romans 8:28 and the Lord, this is hard to take. But we have always been very careful with the children and taken good care of them. So we need not feel the blame. This must be how *He* planned it. Things could be much worse."

Cheri responded well to medical treatment; her recovery encouraged the Ebersoles to continue with plans for their second furlough in the spring of 1962.

Brookdale Baptist Church in Bloomfield, New Jersey, offered the Hoffman Memorial Mission Home to the Ebersoles for their year of furlough. The comfortable two-story house was near the children's Ebersole grandparents and many friends. Gene and Russ enrolled the children in school and fell into the pressures of furlough—far-flung speaking engagements, frequent trips out of town, and the active social life involved in renewed contacts with old friends.

As the months flew by, Gene tried not to admit she tired far more easily than she ever had before. Most of the time she fought off total exhaustion. Not yet 36 years old, she tried to laugh off her fatigue as one of the signs of "advancing age," exaggerated by the hectic pace of her life. In addition to normal furlough demands, Gene considered it her special responsibility to watch Cheri carefully to avoid the threat of overexertion.

In January 1963, Gene made arrangements to spend a few days in Florida with her parents. For the first time since her marriage 13 years earlier, Gene was able to visit her dad and mom without the distraction of her children's engrossing needs. She enjoyed the warm sunshine and relaxed conversations with her parents and their friends, and caught up on all the talking she missed in the long years of separation from Gladys and Henry.

Watching Gene with deepening concern, Gladys saw lines of tiredness settle across her daughter's face when she thought herself unobserved. The silky blonde hair was now heavily tinged with gray. Gene began to feel more rested. She needed this extra strength, for immediately after her return to New Jersey, Rusty came down with strep throat, which developed into rheumatic fever. His illness plunged the family into another period of prolonged anxiety. By spring, Rusty improved enough to get up for part of each day and resume restricted activities.

By this time, the Ebersoles had begun preparations for their return to the Philippines. During their furlough, they carefully thought through a major decision concerning their work. For their first two terms, Russ had been a field evangelist working directly with the Filipinos in one geographic area of the country. Now he had been asked to accept the newly created position of missionary-at-large, involving liaison work between the missionaries and the nationals on the field, and between missionaries and ABWE headquarters in Philadelphia. Though Russ hesitated to assume administrative responsibilities, he and Gene believed that God directed them into this new ministry.

While shopping, packing, and planning for the next four-year term, Gene continued to be dragged down by tiredness. Complete medical examinations revealed no specific problems, but her physician cautioned Russ to make sure Gene remained under careful supervision by competent doctors, and that she would have regular X-rays.

When her friends saw Gene's fatigue, they asked anxiously, "Are you sure Gene is strong enough to go back?" Russ could only report what the doctors said and cling to the hope that in their own home in Manila, Gene would regain her strength.

On July 26, 1963, the family arrived in Manila and began the difficult task of house hunting. Because of a dock strike, their shipment of household goods had been sent to Hong Kong, where it remained for several months. During that interval, the Ebersoles set up temporary living arrangements in the ABWE guesthouse. Unfortunately, that was a long distance from Faith Academy, where the children attended school. At 5:30 each morning, Gene pulled her sleepy children out of bed to be ready for their long bus ride to school. When the children got home late in the afternoon, they were tired and fretful.

Three weeks after arriving in Manila, the Ebersoles discovered a lovely house in Quezon City, just outside Manila. They named it "Alta Vista," for the street it was on and for the breathtaking view of the Marikina Valley far below. Chasing around, checking out other possibilities, Gene kept the Alta Vista property in mind even though it appeared to be out of reach financially. How thankful she was when the property became available at an affordable price.

Gene and Russ had returned to the Philippines at a crucial period for ABWE, which faced unprecedented challenges. By September 1963, over 250 self-supporting churches existed within the Association of Baptists for World Evangelism fellowship in the Philippines. The two training centers established by ABWE—Baptist Bible Seminary and Institute in Manila and Doane Evangelistic Institute in Iloilo—were training hundreds of Filipinos for ministry.

Russ worked with 80 missionaries in guiding the ministries of evangelism, church planting and development, and training national leaders. Gene found herself more directly involved in Russ' work than she expected. Both of them often dealt with individuals under great stress.

Added to the Ebersoles' other duties was the pressing need to learn Tagalog, the predominant dialect in the Manila area. This study demanded Russ and Gene's focused attention, but with all their distractions, concentration proved next to impossible.

Early in December, Gene accepted limited teaching responsibilities at the Baptist Bible Seminary and Institute, and began work on writing a new series of Bible study materials. She had learned to drive just one month before leaving New Jersey; now she did not hesitate to drive all over Manila, even though the city is renowned as being one of the world's worst places to drive. Since Russ traveled much of the time, Gene became chauffeur for their children and friends.

During this period of adjustment, Gene struggled not to admit the persistent tiredness that continued to plague her. A medical checkup revealed low blood pressure; Gene assumed her condition resulted from the heat, the uncertainty of her physical condition, and a need for more rest.

# Chapter Fifteen

# The Way He Has Chosen

The 1963 Christmas holidays coincided with Gene's brother Bud and Ginny DeVries' vacation in Manila and Baguio. One of the advantages of the Ebersoles' new location was that the DeVries and Ebersole families could visit each other more often. The family looked forward to being together, especially at Christ-mastime.

A few days before Christmas, Rusty had his tonsils removed. Because of his bout with rheumatic fever, the doctors had to take extra precautions, but he came home from the hospital on Christmas Eve, just in time to participate in the play the children had planned for their parents and guests.

Gene took pains decorating for Christmas, allowing the children to share in the excitement of packages from the United States, trimming the tree, buying gifts for each other, and entertaining guests.

Two weeks after Christmas, at the ABWE board's request, Russ returned to the Philadelphia office to discuss critical field matters. He was relieved that Bud and Ginny would be able to stay with Gene and the children during his absence. For several weeks, Gene had experienced a persistent pain in her chest, and Bud promised to take her for an immediate checkup.

A few days after Russ' departure, Bud drove Gene to Clark Air Force Base, about an hour north of Manila, to be examined by U. S. Air Force doctors. Bud cabled Russ the welcomed diagnosis of a pinched nerve, probably the result of scar tissue. The Air Force surgeons recommended minor surgery, which Gene decided to have in February when Russ went to Malaybalay for field council meetings.

When Russ returned from the U. S. at the end of January 1964, Gene and the children met him at the Manila airport. On the drive home, Russ asked his wife, "What about the examination? Are you sure everything is all right?"

A bit too quickly, Gene answered, "Of course it is! They assured me nothing is wrong."

Russ was not convinced. "Did they do a biopsy?"

Gene reluctantly admitted, "No."

Russ considered the exam superficial. When he left for Malaybalay a few days later, he insisted that Gene accompany him so that Link Nelson could determine exactly what her condition was.

Link saw immediately that Russ' fears were well founded. A preliminary examination revealed another mass had developed at the junction of one rib and its cartilage. Hoping to find nothing serious, Link scheduled minor surgery.

When he had confirmed the malignancy in Gene's initial surgery several years earlier, Link had not wanted to believe the report. Gene was only 33 years old at that time; the type of malignancy she had usually occurred later in life. Before, during, and after surgery, Gene had displayed complete confidence. Link considered all the favorable signs: Gene's youth, excellent overall condition, the small size of the tumor, and, above all, her complete trust in God. He considered her chances for complete recovery to be excellent.

Except for occasional casual contact, Link had seen little of the Ebersoles since Gene's mastectomy, until the Ebersoles came to Bukidnon in February of 1964.

When Gene went into surgery, Link administered a mild sedative of intravenous valium before anesthetizing the surgical area with a subcutaneous injection of Xylocaine. Russ had scrubbed in with Link to observe the process. Link kept the con-

# The DeVRIES Family

Gene as a small child

Henry DeVries, pioneer
missionary to the Philippines

Gladys DeVries at the
medical clinic

In the ditch in Bukidnon

Santo Tomas prison camp

Bud, Gene, and Dave

Gene in tribal dress

Bethel Friendship Dormitory, 1932: Rhoda Little,
Beatrice Keur, Gladys DeVries in front row

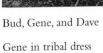

Gene with
her parents
just before
sailing to the
Philippines
in 1954

# The EBERSOLE Family
## (Russ & Gene)

Russ as a young boy

Russ in the Navy

Russ & Gene's wedding

On the deck of the *Doña Nati*
en route to the Philippines
in 1954

The Gospel Tent

The senior Ebersoles
visiting the family
in Baguio

Returning from furlough

Russ with President Magsaysay
the day after Russ arrived in
the Philippines

versation reassuringly cheerful. Believing there was no need for undue concern, he even hummed a little as he made the small initial incision. The tune ceased abruptly when Link caught sight of the ugly cancer protruding in the underlying mass beneath Gene's rib cage. Watching closely, Russ winced at Link's reaction but said nothing.

The surgeon carefully removed a piece of tissue and examined it immediately in his own small laboratory. Sure that his findings indicated cancer, he wanted to remove all doubt by sending the specimen to Manila for thorough analysis.

Probing the incision, Link found that the growth had spread to the lymph nodes under Gene's ribs and sternum. The "lump" was actually the tip of the new growth now extending around the edge of her rib. Removing as much as he could reach, the doctor closed the wound.

Russ had promised Gene that he would tell her the complete truth about her condition. After Gene regained consciousness, Russ told her of Link's strong suspicions. The next day, Russ flew to Manila with the specimen, planning to make arrangements for Gene to receive X-ray treatments.

To prevent acceleration of the growth, Link removed Gene's ovaries the following day. For five days in the hospital, devoted Filipino nurses gave Gene tender nursing care. One of them, Gardenia, was one of the young people Gene had taught in the Bacolod church, and she told her, "I am a nurse in this mission hospital because of your influence."

Early one evening, Gardenia slipped into Gene's room to find Gene's face turned away as she wept softly, believing herself to be alone. As the young nurse began to comfort Gene, the missionary wife turned with a smile, saying, "Gardenia, I'm not afraid to die. I have something bright to look forward to. It's Russ and the children I'm concerned about. Sometimes when I think of the children, I can't help but cry. And yet, I know that God will make provision for them."

That was the only time the hospital staff found Gene in tears. She wrote confidently to her parents, "We just have to leave this all with the Lord. He's ordered it, so it's not bad at all. Let's not make it bad. The Lord will give more grace than we ever dreamed possible, if we allow Him to!"

Russ echoed Gene's confidence in his own letter to the family, adding the promise in Isaiah 41:13: *"For I, the Lord thy God, will hold thy right hand, saying unto thee, Fear not; I will help thee."* He indicated the direction of their plans for the immediate future: "The X-rays will help, but how effective they will be remains to be seen. As you know, these treatments are not at all pleasant; Gene does not look forward to them. Please pray for her concerning this. Also pray for both of us that we can commit this entire matter completely to the Lord Who knows best, and that we can return to Manila with an attitude and spirit that will be a testimony to the children, our friends, and all we meet. I expect we will carry on with our ministries as far as possible. We do not want to create any major change in routine or schedule for the children."

When Gene returned to Manila, she began a 20-day series of X-ray treatments. A complete bone scan did not reveal any evidence of abnormality, although Link Nelson suspected the cancer had spread into several of her ribs.

In spite of the physical discomfort from therapy, Gene continued to supervise her children's activities, including Cheri's ninth birthday party that month. Russ kept on with his work as missionary-at-large, although he curtailed his out-of-town trips as much as possible.

As word of Gene's condition spread to the Ebersoles' friends and prayer supporters, hundreds of Christians began to pray. They prayed that she might be healed of cancer and that the purpose of God would be fulfilled in her life.

Seated by the open windows facing the Marikina Valley, Gene drank in the beauty of the Philippine countryside and thought deeply about the reality of her circumstances. She wrote to a friend, "These days have made me realize so much more clearly that it is the things of eternity that really count."

For the first time in her life, Gene had time to read and study with few interruptions. Meditating on what she read, she turned her attention to the person and work of Jesus Christ, saying, "I may be seeing Him soon. Before I meet Him, I want to find out all I can about His life when He was here on earth."

Once a day, Gene went downstairs for a meal with the family and stayed there to play the piano, read to the children, listen to music, or chat with frequent visitors. She was unaccustomed to such a leisurely life, but she had to yield to her doctor's insistence that she get plenty of rest during the round of treatments.

Gene grieved over the effect of her illness on her parents. Knowing Henry and Gladys DeVries' trusting confidence in God and their practiced serenity in uncertainty, Gene could write to them, "Even though this may not be the path we would choose, it is the way *He* has chosen, so would we want to go any other way? This would never be the way, if it were not best."

Cards, gifts, and other expressions of love poured in from friends around the world, some from people she had not heard from in years. Gene wrote to her parents: "It's quite humbling to see everyone's concern. I realize more than ever that if I have been a little help and blessing to anyone, it is only in the measure that I have allowed the Lord to 'be the only One' (as the Filipinos say). So often I have gotten in His way, instead. Truly, at this point, the immediate future is not known at all, but the *real* future is sure and wonderful beyond our wildest understanding. We must rest in that. I know the Lord is giving you real peace and confidence, and that this fact is evident to others. I do so want the Lord's purpose in this to be accomplished, in us and in others if that is His desire."

On March 21, Russ and Gene flew to Cagayan on their way to Malaybalay and Bethel Baptist Hospital. Because their onward flight to Malaybalay had been canceled, they drove to the hospital in a mission vehicle. Gene delighted in the ride through the familiar route from Cagayan, where she had been born, up the 70 miles of winding roads to her first home in Malaybalay.

Link found Gene in good condition, her wounds healing nicely, radiation burns clearing, and her blood count better than he expected after the doses of radiation she had received. Link encouraged her to get a few more treatments when she returned to Manila.

Encouraged, Gene wrote to her parents: "I live from day to day, trusting Him to make each day count." She added, "I'm getting ready to resume a more normal schedule when I get home, so please pray that I'll have patience with the children. They are such livewires and need so much direction and help. They must not suffer from all of this."

Gene gave thanks for her wonderful household help. Quita, a young Filipina, had stayed with her since Rusty's early childhood. Gene said confidently, "I'm sure the Lord sent Quita to us, even more especially for such a time as this."

As Gene began her next series of treatments, Russ wrote to their parents: "We're taking every medical precaution we know of. With all of this we know the Lord alone knows Gene's true condition, and He alone is able to remove the cancer in her body. We take one day at a time and have experienced a sufficient grace. We know this is due in large measure to the hundreds of friends who faithfully pray for us."

Toward the end of April, the family traveled to Baguio for a brief vacation and a change of climate. They joined the Link Nelson family for several outings. On Mother's Day 1964, Link and Russ took pictures of their families on the grounds of the beautiful Camp John Hay facilities—a rest and recreation facility under the supervision of the U.S. military. Link noted, particularly, the serene radiance in Gene's face, reflecting her complete peace and comfort in the Lord. But he also whispered to Russ,

"Russ, this will be Gene's last Mother's Day."

After several weeks in Baguio, the Ebersole family returned to Manila to continue a schedule far more hectic than Gene could manage without exhaustion. However, she explained to her parents, "It's not as bad as it sounds. I'm up and around and busy."

On June 19, Russ and Gene celebrated their 14th wedding anniversary with dinner in a lovely restaurant. Gene's gifts included three dozen red roses, bargain priced in the Philippines. They reminisced about their years together, thanking God for each experience and reassuring each other of God's continuing faithfulness, even in their present crisis. Their attitude came through in a letter to Russ' parents, when he quoted Psalm 107:29: *"He maketh the storm a calm, so that the waves thereof are still."*

Later that month, Gene and Russ traveled south to Iloilo City for a biennial missions conference. At that time, Link found that Gene's cancer was growing, causing the increasing pain Gene experienced in her chest and back. As gently as possible, he told his friends that they had to decide at once whether or not to return to the United States.

Reappraising their situation, Gene and Russ decided that it would be better to remain in Manila, since it appeared that medical science had nothing more to offer Gene. In Manila they had a comfortable home with capable household help. Their hearts were in the work in the Philippines. And Gene did not need a dramatic reaction to her condition and the emotional trauma of pulling up stakes.

Relieved at their decision for the present, Gene made a valiant attempt to keep up with the sessions at the mission conference. When necessary, she took the pills Link gave her for the burgeoning pain in her chest, back, and abdomen. She managed to look so healthy that her friends exclaimed, "I didn't know Gene was so well. Praise the Lord!"

During the conference, Gene led evening sessions with the ABWE teenage missionary kids (MKs). She wanted to share with these young people what she had learned from her own experience as a missionary kid. Many of them said later that those conferences with "Aunt Gene" taught them a great deal, not only by what she said, but also how they saw her live.

One afternoon, Gene walked through the dormitory lounge to find a friend seated at the piano playing hymns. Gene sat beside her, suggesting, "Let's sing some of these together." They blended their voices, without faltering, through the first and second stanzas of a favorite selection. As they began the third stanza, the young woman glanced at Gene, thinking frantically, *Oh, why didn't I go on to the next song!* Gene, seeing nothing unusual in the words, sang on confidently, "I'll sing when the death dew lies cold on my brow, if ever I loved Thee, my Jesus 'tis now."

Noticing her friend's tears, Gene reassured her, "You know, these songs mean much more to me now than they ever did. I guess it's because it may not be long for me." Her calm acceptance helped Gene's friends to handle their own grief.

Gene grew perceptibly worse after her return to Manila. The growth on her chest protruded just under the skin, three inches wide and pushing more than an inch above the surrounding tissue. She began to take sleeping pills and tried to sleep sitting up in the lounge chair. At times the discomfort grew so intense she said, "When it gets like this, it just can't be over soon enough."

Curious to learn all she could about what was happening to her body, Gene read medical textbooks and picked up information that caused her to be depressed. She began to object when Russ brought her gifts. Turning away from the clothes she once delighted in, she said, "I won't be able to wear it more than once or twice. Why keep on getting pretty things?"

Gene's brother Bud came to her rescue. With a cheerful good sense that sounded a great deal like their mother, Bud reminded Gene, "Look, Sis, you know we have to live for each day as it comes. You can't think about things that might not happen."

Her own practical optimism reasserted itself, and Gene began to consider what to do for her children. "Before long," she confided to her friend, "the children may have to learn to do without me. I believe I should start getting them ready gradually, in little ways, while I'm still here. Then it won't be so hard for them later."

Rusty, a 12-year-old miniature of Russ, had not yet fully recovered from the lingering effects of rheumatic fever, but he was restlessly eager to hurl himself into athletics. Cheri, at nine years old, already indicated a zest for living. Beth's fragile blonde beauty, even at seven years old, resembled that of her grandmother, Gladys. Six-year-old Bruce manfully struggled to adjust to the unaccustomed routine of school. Lively little Susie, nearly five, took great pride in announcing, "I look like my mommy. See? I've got freckles on my nose!"

Each evening, Gene settled the children in bed, talked with each one, told Bible stories, and prayed with them before they went to sleep. One summer evening, Gene went in to kiss Susie goodnight. The little girl threw her arms around her mother's neck and said, "I'm so glad I've got a nice mommy to take care of me." As she left the room, Gene's anguish was written plainly across her face.

For the first eight weeks of the semester, beginning in early June at the Baptist Bible Seminary and Institute, Gene had taught a class in Christian writing. In August, when her doctor told her she must give up that extra duty, she confided to Richard Durham, a friend and fellow ABWE missionary who was the school's president, that she didn't want to give it up. "I love the class; I really want to continue teaching." When Dick took over, the students told him repeatedly how much Gene had meant to them. "She is so beautiful, especially when she is smiling." For as long as possible, Gene had held on to this last contact with the Filipino young people she loved so much.

The Ebersoles' house became a central meeting place for missionary conferences, field council meetings, seminary meetings, and a headquarters for visitors. In late July, Russ received word that an executive from another mission board in Manila wanted to meet the Ebersoles. He called Gene, who replied at once, "Invite them to dinner tonight."

Russ protested. "Do you feel up to it?" he asked.

"Certainly. I want to do it," Gene insisted.

When the visitors arrived, Gene had set a lovely table with candles and her best silver. Both the house and the hostess were so charming that the couple never guessed Gene was ill.

The executive's wife told Russ later, "Our visit with you and Gene was the highlight of our trip around the world. To see Gene, and to realize how ill she was, yet to see how she looked and the way she entertained us, was one of the greatest challenges I've ever had."

In newsletters to friends and relatives, the Ebersoles urged prayer for God's will to be done in the life of each person affected by Gene's terminal illness. Russ told Rusty as much as the young boy could accept and gave basic facts to the younger children, trying not to burden them with a pessimistic outlook. Had not God spared them the worst in many other trials? They hoped for His intervention in this crisis also.

Russ did not spare his and Gene's anxious parents any of the truth, but he assured them, "We would not want to give you the idea that we have given up all hope of the Lord's intervening on Gene's behalf. We know He is able to perform wonderful miracles, and nothing is impossible for Him. We have to do some planning, however, and at the present it does not seem to be the will of the Lord to heal Gene." He added, "Only I know what a wonderful help Gene has been to me in every aspect of the ministry here. Her life has been a blessing and testimony to all our missionaries and the Filipinos. We are thankful the Lord knows our future and that our lives are in His hands."

Gene added a note: "This is a rough letter, but we must face realities, and with His grace we can. We are trying to figure out what to do. May He give us all what we need, that's what He promised. What a wonder—to lean on the knowledge that this has come because of His love. Won't it be wonderful when we see fully the reason? In the meantime, we just 'lean.'"

Gene knew her Lord was real, He was all-powerful, and He loved her wholly. Accepting these truths, she concluded that whatever touched her life had to be a gracious instrument for the accomplishment of God's loving purpose for her, her husband, their children, their families, and for the Filipino people they served. She once said, "I catch my breath with the wonder of it: that God is doing this in love."

In August, Gene planned to give several messages from Philippians to the women at the Baptist Bible Seminary and Institute during their daily period of dormitory devotions. She was able to do that only once because her strength failed, but she kept hoping to go back. Gene's focus was the theme of Philippians: *joy*. Every woman in the room knew of Gene's illness; she shared with her friends a little of her struggle, wanting to be rid of the increasingly arduous burden of living and to be in the presence of Christ, yet wanting also through her life to model Christ. Those who listened to her share Philippians 1:21, *"For to me to live is Christ, and to die is gain,"* never forgot the impact of Gene's testimony.

Late in August 1964, Link Nelson examined Gene and verified the original tumor had returned and was growing rapidly. New X-rays indicated it had spread to her left lung. In answer to Link's cabled inquiry, a cancer specialist in the United States strongly recommended Gene return to the U. S. at once for treatment and possible surgery.

Shortly before Link arrived in Manila, Gene had written to her parents: "I feel quite good part of the time, and I do get around. I enjoy driving! The car is easy to handle and the traffic does not bother me. It feels good to be able to do things. At other times I feel quite weak and short of breath. The inside pain isn't much except when I lie down." To her brother Bud, Gene added, "I like to drive. It makes me feel more like a woman to be able to do things for myself." Though she occasionally mentioned her pain—like "a hot rock" in her back—Gene refused to develop a "poor me" attitude, and urged others to treat her normally. She begged, "Please, I'm trying hard not to be an invalid."

Bud and Ginny DeVries had come to Manila on business and to be on hand to help Gene. The mission committee recommended that Ginny be assigned to a special responsibility in Manila for several months, assisting in implementing a new approach to language study.

Even before these developments, however, Gene and Russ had changed their minds about staying in Manila. Urged on by Link, they decided the family should return to the United States. By leaving immediately, the children could settle in at the beginning of the school term in New Jersey. Bud and Ginny could live in the Ebersoles' home in Manila, which meant Gene and Russ would not have to pack and store their household possessions in order to turn the house back over to the owners.

Another major relief for Gene came with the decision for their helper Quita to accompany the Ebersoles to the States to continue helping with the children and the household.

In the two weeks before the Ebersoles left Manila, they worked with Bud and Ginny to sort clothes, deciding what to take with them and what to leave out for others to use, and what personal items would be packed or left behind.

The atmosphere of the Ebersole household continued to be cheerful. The children rushed about, excited about their trip to the United States.

Sensing Gene's deep desire to revisit Iloilo and Bacolod, Russ arranged for brief trips to these two cities she had called home. There, they visited some of the churches and the Doane

Baptist Bible Institute in Iloilo City. In each city, friends planned a special service. As they joined in worship with their Filipino brethren, Gene and Russ sang a favorite duet:

> Day by day, and with each passing moment,
> Strength I find, to meet my trials here.
> Trusting in my Father's wise bestowment,
> I've no cause for worry or for fear.
> He whose heart is kind beyond all measure
> Gives unto each day what He deems best—
> Lovingly, its part of pain and pleasure,
> Mingling toil with peace and rest.
> —*Carolina Sandell Berg*

Speaking briefly, Gene and Russ witnessed to the faithfulness of their Lord. At times, Gene could not hold back her tears, but she held on to her confidence in God as expressed in a poem she kept in her Bible:

> Our times are in Thy hands;
> Oh God, we wish them there!
> Our lives, our souls, our all we leave
> Entirely to Thy care.
> Our times are in Thy hands;
> Why should we doubt or fear?
> A father's hand will never cause
> His child a needless tear.
> —*W. F. Lloyd*

# Chapter Sixteen

# He Deals with Us Always in Love

On Monday, August 31, 1964, the Ebersole family left Manila. From San Francisco they flew to Chicago, where they were met by a large number of friends from Winnetka Bible Church. One of the women in the group pulled Russ aside to remark in surprise, "I can't believe Gene is as ill as you say. Why, she's radiant! And she handles the two smaller children so capably."

With Quita's help, Gene did indeed manage better than she expected, taking care of the children's needs on the long trip and lengthy stopovers.

On Wednesday, the family arrived in Grand Rapids. That evening, Gene insisted on attending prayer meeting at her home church, Wealthy Street Baptist Church. In response to the pastor's request, she gave her testimony to the group of lifelong friends: "When we left here a little over a year ago, we never dreamed of being back so soon. And yet the Lord knew all about it even then. We are glad to have this opportunity to thank you all for your prayers that upheld us, and that we know are going to continue to uphold us. I've really been blessed in studying Philippians and being reminded again that our joy is from within and doesn't depend on circumstances. I love Philippians 4:13, for I can do anything God asks me to do with the help of Christ, who gives me the strength and power. We are thankful even for this that God has brought into our lives and pray that He will be honored and glorified through it. If the Lord had wished, it would have been easy for Him to have prevented this, yet He knew what He was doing and He hasn't made His first mistake this time." Her voice broke. Pausing to regain control, she concluded, "He deals with us always in love."

On September 4, the family flew into Newark airport. When the doors to the big jet opened, Gene came to the head of the steps, walking confidently, holding several small bags in her hands. Catching sight of the group of waiting friends, she freed one hand and waved a pleased greeting.

In the confusion of welcome, traces of sadness swept away. Waiting in the airport lounge while Russ collected their luggage, Gene helped her friends pass the awkwardness of trying not to ask, "How are you?" When they urged her to sit down, she laughed lightly and replied, "Oh, please don't bother. I can stand."

Russ' parents had moved out of their home into a small apartment so Gene and Russ could have the house for their family. Quita's expert and loving assistance added to the children's sense of security; within days they had settled into school and church activities. Gene maintained the illusion of health by staying out of bed most of the time, busy with small tasks or resting in a chair. The children knew she was ill, but had grown accustomed to it and did not see her condition as frightening. Used to their parents' busy lives, the children accepted matter-of-factly the trips Gene and Russ took into New York City so Gene could begin radiation and chemotherapy treatments.

At first, the doctors tried to spare Gene the full report of their examinations. Finally, convinced she wanted the truth, they confirmed in greater detail what Link Nelson had already said. The cancer was spreading rapidly; surgery would not help. They offered drug therapy to prolong Gene's life and give her a degree of comfort.

Gene called her parents, who waited anxiously for every bit of news. They could not hold back the question, "Why Gene?" Three times in her life, God had spared Gene from imminent death. Surely God in His mercy would not take her away at the height of her usefulness, when her children needed her so much.

Thinking it through, Gladys concluded, "It is God's plan," and buried the sadness deep within herself. As they had done in every acute need, Henry and Gladys continued to pray, "If it please Thee, deliver us. Thy will be done."

One evening several weeks after their return to New Jersey, Gene called her parents. In a strong, eager voice she said, "Hi, Mom and Dad! We're planning on you spending Christmas with us. Come early, at least by the 20th, and help me with packages and decorations."

Suddenly encouraged, Henry exclaimed, "Isn't this wonderful? Maybe the Lord is healing her!" They immediately made plans to spend Christmas in New Jersey.

Early in October, Russ and Gene flew to Florida to spend a few days with her parents. Except for resting frequently, she apparently felt so well that her parents were greatly encouraged. Gene did not conceal from Gladys the ravages of cancer, but they did not dwell on the details of the illness. Instead, they talked of the children and friends in the Philippines. During their visit, the family worked out plans for Christmas. Gene obviously counted on a memorable Christmas.

Returning to North Caldwell, New Jersey, Gene resumed the treatment she now considered futile. Continuing a normal routine, she visited her children's schoolteachers for conferences and, in many other contexts, demonstrated "a sufficiency of the Lord to many others who had rough pathways to walk," as a friend commented.

On November 1, Gene celebrated her 38th birthday. In her fragility, she reminded her friends of a translucent China teacup. Her hair had turned almost completely gray, but her face radiated vitality and youthfulness that spoke of her continuing interest in other people. Pain left its marks on her countenance, but there was no ugly twisting of self-pity or bitterness.

At times, in the middle of the night, Gene whispered against her husband's shoulder, "Why? Why can't I live long enough to watch my children grow up?" With daylight came the strength to say again, "The Lord is not making His first mistake. He has ordered this in love."

On Tuesday, November 17, Gene's doctor and close personal friend, Bob Francis, examined her and ordered her to go immediately into the hospital. At her insistence, he agreed she could go home for the night and enter Overlook Hospital in Summit, New Jersey, the next day.

After the doctor's examination, Russ brought Gene home and put her to bed. That afternoon, propped up on pillows, her face flushed with fever, she welcomed the visitors who dropped by to see her. Clinging to the reality of life that flowed outside her sickroom, she encouraged her friends to talk about their interests and shied away from conversation about herself.

On the following day, early in the afternoon, a close friend, Bette Scales, came by for a brief visit. She found Russ in the bedroom, fruitlessly rummaging in a trunk they had brought from the Philippines, searching for a picture requested by a Filipino friend who had written, "Could we have a picture of Mrs. Ebersole while she is still with us? It would mean so much to us."

Gene knew the particular picture she wanted to send and tried to tell Russ where to find it. He did his best, but found it terribly difficult at that moment to leaf through pictures of Gene as she looked before her illness. Determined to honor their request, Gene would not let Russ give up, even though the effort to help taxed her strength beyond all reason.

Finally, she fell back against the pillows, exhausted. Her cheeks burned with fever. "I'm so tired, so sick," she murmured. "I just can't take care of it now."

Relieved, Russ left the room. Bette moved quietly around the room, gathering things Gene would need in the hospital. Then Russ came back in with a package addressed to Gene. Leaving the package with Bette, he went out again. Bette stripped off the brown paper wrapping and found inside the

Bible Gene had ordered as Russ' Christmas present. Gene waved it away, asking Bette to take it home with her and bring it back later so that Gene could write an inscription inside.

Bette intuitively knew that Gene had to do this immediately. She insisted Gene write in the Bible, but Gene protested weakly, "I can't, Bette. I'm too sick. I'll wait until I feel a little better."

Finally, Bette said firmly, "You must, Gene. You must. If you wait, you won't be able to do it because Russ will be in the hospital room with you and he'll see it. You'll have to do it now."

With shaking hands, Gene took the pen and the Bible from Bette's outstretched hands. Her attempts to write were uneven, and she became impatient with herself. "Look, what a mess! I just can't do it now shaking like this."

Patiently, Bette persisted. "I'll draw in the lines, Gene, and later I'll erase the marks. It will be fine. But you must do it."

Gene looked up to meet the steady, loving gaze of her friend. After a long moment, she dropped her eyes and in silence finished writing the few brief words. She handed the Bible to Bette, who placed it where Russ would not notice it.

Turning back, Bette saw Gene's tears roll down her thin face as she said brokenly, "This will be a very special Christmas for Russ, won't it?"

Her weakened frame shook with wrenching sobs. Gene cried as she had not let herself cry before in the long months of illness. Giving in to the flood of grief that overwhelmed her, she wept for her husband and her children until her face was swollen with her crying.

Both women knew that for Gene the anguish of dying was over. She had faced the fact she was going to die before Christmas. She knew her husband and children would have a life together that she would not share. Yet she refused to back down on what she believed: God would bring to completion His good purpose in her life and in the lives of those she loved, and He would not need her physical presence to do it.

Gene and Russ waited to go to the hospital until the children came home from school. They gathered in their family circle to pray together. After Russ led in prayer, Gene drew her children one by one into her arms and kissed them.

When Gene was admitted into Overlook Hospital late on Wednesday afternoon, November 18, her doctor noted on her chart: "Pale, emaciated, breathing rapid and shallow, temperature fluctuating between 101° and 103°." After thorough examinations he reported to Russ, "I have never seen such extensive liver damage. Get her parents here at once. She can't live more than a few hours."

Sue Ebersole called Henry and Gladys, and Russ told Gene, "Honey, your folks decided to come on now to spend Thanksgiving with us instead of waiting to come for Christmas."

When her parents arrived on Friday evening, Gene talked with them between intermittent spells of unconsciousness. Henry called David, whom Gene had not seen since her furlough in 1963, and he made plans to arrive early Sunday morning. Friends prayed that Gene would recognize her brother David when he came.

Each time Dr. Francis checked Gene's condition, he went to the visitor's lounge, where the family waited through the interminable hours. As gently as possible, he told them, "It can't be much longer, and that's a blessing because the cancer is close to the spine, and we cannot take care of the pain." After each conversation with Gene's family, Dr. Francis prayed with them for the purpose of God to be fulfilled for Gene's life.

When Gene's brother David arrived on Sunday morning, he walked into Gene's room to find her rolled up into a sitting position in the bed, with her eyes bright and clear. She greeted her brother with a smiling, "Hi, Dave!"

For the next half hour, Gene and David talked intermittently of things they remembered from their childhood, particularly in Bukidnon Province.

On Sunday evening, as Russ was leaving the hospital, he turned to tell Gene he was going home to get the children into bed. In response, she puckered her lips for her husband's kiss. That slight gesture was the last sign of recognition Russ saw. From that point on, he knew his Gene had slipped from him, though her body still struggled to stay alive.

On Tuesday night, when it became apparent Gene could not live until morning, her father begged to stay with her, though the strain showed badly in his overwrought nervous system. Dr. Francis pulled him away. "Brother DeVries, you'd better go. You need your rest." Henry protested, but Gladys said firmly, "I think it's best for you."

After Henry left, Russ fell into a chair in the corner of the room to sleep fitfully through the night. At 7:15 a.m., Wednesday, November 25, he went out into the hall to answer the telephone. Hearing Rusty's voice, Russ sent up an agonized plea, "Please Lord, don't let him ask about his mother."

Rusty asked uncertainly, "Dad, should I go to school today?"

Russ tried to answer. "Yes, Rusty, I think you'd better. This is the last day before Thanksgiving holidays; yes, I think you'd all better go to school."

He returned to the room to find his parents had arrived; ten minutes later Gene's battle ended. Russ drew Gladys and David away and went to telephone Henry. "Dad, the Lord took Gene, just three minutes ago."

Blurting from Henry's lips came the cry, "Blessed be the name of the Lord!" Shocked, the grieving father thought wildly, *How could I say a thing like that?* Then he bowed his head and wept. "Thank you, Lord. I know she is with you and her suffering is over."

Later that day, Russ met his children as they came home from school and told them their mother was now with the Lord. Bruce looked up into his father's face to say earnestly, "Then we're glad and sad, too, aren't we, Daddy?"

"What do you mean, Brucie?"

"We're glad because Mommy's with Jesus in heaven, but we're sad because we miss her." A six-year-old child had summed it up for all the rest of the family!

On Friday, Russ took the two older children to see Gene's body; it lay in the small prayer room in Brookdale Baptist Church, the same place where so many had prayed for her.

Gene's memorial service was held in the Brookdale Baptist Church on Saturday, November 28. The church was crowded to capacity with hundreds of friends and relatives. But Russ never felt more alone than when he stood at the rear of the church before the service began.

Just then, Jay and Dorothy Morgan, dear friends who served with ABWE in Hong Kong, ran up the stairs and into the foyer. Russ was amazed to see them. He asked, "Jay and Dorothy, why are you here?" That very morning, across the Hudson River, in New York City, the Morgans' only son, James, was operated on for cancer.

Jay replied, "When the surgery was finished and we talked to the surgeons, we left immediately to be with you."

Russ was overwhelmed with the Morgans' caring, and he thought of Paul's words in 2 Corinthians 7:6: *"Nevertheless God, who comforteth those that are cast down, comforted us by the coming of Titus."*

During the service, Russ sat with Rusty and listened to the comforting words of Scripture. His heart was also moved as he heard the words of hymns Gene loved:

"For I know whate'er befalls me, Jesus doeth all things well."

*and*

"I am not skilled to understand what God hath willed, what God hath planned.
    I only know at His right hand stands One who is my Savior."

Afterward, as he watched the body of his wife moving away from him down the aisle of the church, Russ remembered the way Gene looked as she came toward him down that same aisle on the night they were married over 14 years before. His arm around his son's shoulders, Russ thought, *Where do we go from here, Rusty? Where do we go from here?*

The service ended, and her friends followed Gene's flower-blanketed casket through miles of winding roads lined with the stripped trees of winter. Moving slowly, they stood at last near the stone arches of the Memorial Chapel. The lovely flowers could not blunt the fact it was winter and the day was cold.

Walking slowly away from the grave of his beloved Gene, Russ was numb with grief and pain. He wondered, *Lord, how can I go on without her? What about our children who have lost such a wonderful mother?*

Among the many friends at the graveside service was ABWE board member Dr. Joseph Stowell. He put his arm around Russ' shoulder and said, "Russ, I've never experienced what you are going through. But I want to remind you of one very important thing. Your five children all had a wonderful, godly mother for at least the first five years of their lives. God will use her molding influence on them for the rest of their lives!"

Russ and the children remained in the senior Ebersole home. Russ' parents moved back in to take over the household and to help Russ and Quita with the children. For Russell and Sue Ebersole, this necessitated a complete adjustment in their own lifestyle. Russ' dad was 68 and his mother 64 when Gene died. Both were in excellent health. They loved to travel and looked forward to doing more of it in their retirement years.

Shortly before Gene's death, Russ' parents had shared with him the burden the Lord had placed upon their hearts to help him care for his children. They said, "Our home is open to you and the children, Russ, as long as you need it. We believe this is what God wants us to do, and we want to do it."

# Chapter Seventeen

# The Plans I Have for You

Through all the aching loneliness of the months following the death of his wife, Russ wondered how the Lord would fulfill in his life the promise made to Jeremiah thousands of years earlier:

*"For I know the thoughts that I think toward you, saith the Lord, thoughts of peace, and not of evil, to give you an expected end"* (Jeremiah 29:11).

However, Russ was able to continue serving the Lord with ABWE and maintain his contacts with his adopted land, the Philippines. Russ commuted from his parents' home in North Jersey to the ABWE office on Race Street in Philadelphia, spending several nights each week in the mission home in Germantown, Pennsylvania.

In 1965, the mission administration, under the leadership of Harold T. Commons, president, and Edward C. Bomm, treasurer, asked Russ to be missionary-at-large for the Far East. This position involved regular overseas trips to visit with and minister to ABWE missionaries in Australia, East Pakistan (now Bangladesh), Hong Kong, Japan, Papua New Guinea, and the Philippines.

In this administrative position, Russ was the liaison between ABWE headquarters and 200 missionaries in the Far East. He was also a "trouble shooter," seeking to help resolve problems as quickly as possible. One of the things Russ appreciated about his role was the opportunity he had to preach the Word of God on numerous occasions, both overseas and in North America.

The mission trips often lasted two to three months. The long separations were made a bit easier by regular letters between Russ and his children, and postcards sent from every "port of call." The children had a calendar on which they would cross off each day until Dad returned. They also had a large world map on which they followed Russ' travels from day to day. They prayed specifically for him in each place.

Russ also tried to purchase small items for the children from each country he visited. He either sent the items by mail or presented them to his children when he returned.

Sometimes missionary colleagues or national friends who had known the children would send gifts for them also. But, Russ was not prepared for one "special" gift presented to him by missionary friends in East Pakistan. It was Russ' last morning at Malumghat hospital. He and his traveling companion, Dr. Harold Amstutz, ABWE's candidate secretary and Russ' close friend, were ready to leave by car for the city of Chittagong, en route out of the country.

As the missionaries gathered to say goodbye, Dr. Vic Olsen said, "Russ, you'll have to wait a few minutes. We have a special gift for your children." Russ asked, "What is it, Vic? We have to be on our way."

Smiling, Vic answered, "It's a baby tiger!"

Russ said, "Come on, Vic, you have to be kidding."

Vic replied, "Some men found the cub on one of the trails in the hills last night and brought it down to the hospital."

Just then, there was a knock on the door, and in came a Bengali worker, soaked from the rain, carrying a small woven basket. He reached inside and held a tiny cub in his hands. This would be a *very* "special" gift for Russ' children!

Harold Amstutz said, "Russ, you can't take that animal with us!"

Russ replied, "Harold, this is a wonderful gift for my kids. Of course we'll take it."

A missionary brought out a baby bottle and explained how

Russ could feed the cub. By now Harold was almost beside himself. "Russ, you'll never get that cat through customs, and we have four or five more countries to visit. And, if you think I'm gonna babysit a baby tiger, you're crazy!"

Russ realized, of course, it would be impossible to take the cub with him, as much as he wanted to. He was enjoying "pulling Harold's leg," however. As Russ looked more closely at the cub, he saw it was spotted, not striped, and it looked more like a leopard.

So it was. Russ left the cub with the Olsen family, who kept it for several months, then sent it to the capital city, Dhaka, where it was put in a zoo. This "tiger" turned out to be a rare, clouded leopard. When Rusty heard about it, he said, "Dad, if you had brought that animal back, it probably would have paid for my college education!"

Russ had especially looked forward to their visit to East Pakistan. He wanted to visit the grave of his good friend Harry Goehring, and the home in Hebron where Harry and his family had lived.

During Russ' visit to the lovely hospital compound, he asked to see Harry's grave. Harry was buried behind one of the women missionary residences on a cliff looking over a beautiful tidal inlet of the Bay of Bengal. Russ was accompanied by missionary colleague Jay Walsh and Ancherai Tipperah, the faithful tribal evangelist with whom Harry had trekked the Chittagong Hill Tracts preaching the gospel.

As the three men stood quietly in front of the simple grave, Ancherai said in Bengali, "I loved that man very much. He preached the gospel to my people throughout the hills. And someday I shall be with him again in heaven."

Ancherai's words and demeanor spoke eloquently of his love for Harry. Russ was deeply moved, but he was not prepared for Ancherai's next exclamation. "My heart is burning for my people!"

Jay translated this for Russ. Then, in an even louder voice, filled with pathos, Ancherai almost shouted, "My heart is burning for my people!"

Russ had never heard such an expression of compassion. He thought to himself, "It is no wonder there are scores of 'Jesus Houses' (small churches) throughout the Hill Tracts with a man like this preaching God's Word."

A few days later, Russ and Jay were poled up the Matamahari River in a canoe-like riverboat, headed for the mission station called Hebron. The five-hour trip was pleasant, as the river was bordered by lush foliage.

Russ' excitement grew as they approached Hebron and "beached" the boat. Jay led Russ up the steep embankment and pointed out the house Harry had built for his family. They climbed the stairs leading to the porch, and Russ stared at the largest lock he had ever seen. It spoke to his heart as it meant there was no one to live in the house. No one to take Harry's place to share the good news of Christ with the tribal people in the hills.

Jay opened the door and led Russ into the small house. The rooms were bare, the windows shuttered. Russ spotted a small high chair in one corner—that must have been Faith's, the youngest child. Russ' heart was deeply touched again, and he silently prayed, "Lord, please fill this home again with those who will take Harry and Nancy's place."

Harold and Russ continued their Far East trip, visiting the six countries in which ABWE's personnel then served. In each place they fellowshipped with and ministered to missionary colleagues and national brethren. But in no place was Russ' heart so moved as when he stood by Harry's grave and walked into the house Harry built.

As the months and years passed, Russ was increasingly aware he and his children had needs that could only be met by a wife and mother. Three thoughts, however, made him wonder if these needs would ever be met: He didn't believe he could ever love another woman the way he loved Gene; he didn't believe any woman could ever love him the way Gene had loved him; he didn't believe any woman would be crazy enough to marry a widower with five children!

Was he forgetting the promise of God? *"Call unto me, and I will answer thee, and show thee great and mighty things, which thou knowest not"* (Jeremiah 33:3).

Or was he forgetting the ability of God, which Paul describes? *"Now unto Him who is able to do exceeding abundantly above all that we ask or think, according to the power that worketh in us"* (Ephesians 3:20).

The Lord would soon wonderfully fulfill the truths of these words of God in the lives of Russ and his children.

# Part Three

# The GOEHRING Family

*"Whosoever will come after me, let him deny*

*himself, and take up his cross, and follow me.*

*For whosoever will save his life shall lose it;*

*but whosoever shall lose his life for my sake*

*and the gospel's, the same shall save it."*

—Mark 8:34–35

# Chapter Eighteen

# A Boy from Pennsylvania;
# A Girl from Indiana

## HARRY

A young boy roamed the wooded hills of western Pennsylvania every free moment, often dreaming of the day when he would be a forest ranger. Harry Goehring was the youngest of nine children born to Harry and Ethel Goehring. The doctor warned the Goehrings that their eighth child should be their last because of Ethel's poor health. But God overruled, and Harry Dale Goehring was born on April 16, 1933.

The Goehrings reared their large family during the years of the Great Depression and World War II. Harry's older brother, Harold, served in Germany during the war and was later in the Occupation Forces in Japan. His older sister, Ruby Jean, worked a year in a bombshell factory to earn money for college. Harry's father worked hard at two jobs to support his large family. He was off before dawn on a milk route, then worked during the day as a cabinetmaker. Hard work and frugality were expected from each member of the family. Harry remembered being awakened very early every morning by his father's brusque call, "Harry Dale!" When he heard this wake-up call echoing up the stairs, Harry knew he'd better be down the steps in a hurry to help with morning chores.

Harry attended the small village grammar school in Callery, Pennsylvania, then went to Evans City High School, where he enjoyed sports, especially football. The Goehring family all attended First Baptist Church of Evans City, Pennsylvania, where

Rev. Norman Hershey was the powerful preacher. When Harry was ten years old, Pastor Hershey led Harry to Christ.

During Harry's senior year of high school, his oldest brother, Harold, died through a severe reaction to sulfa. His brother was preparing to become a missionary to Japan, and Harry almost idolized him. Many years later, Harry commented, "It would always seem so easy for Harold to be good, but so hard for me." Harry renewed his dedication to God at his brother's death, yet still felt God wanted him to pursue his lifetime dream of becoming a forest ranger. After graduating from high school, Harry spent one year at Bryan College, before transferring to Michigan State University to major in forestry. He worked in the forestry service in the mountains of Montana after his first year of study at Michigan State. Harry's mother prayed her son would not enjoy his summer in forestry. Her prayer was that God would call him into the ministry. Harry loved every minute of that summer.

Returning to Michigan State University, Harry was filled with enthusiasm for the life's work he had chosen. God did not use a burning bush to arrest Harry's attention, but, rather, it was the demise of his old car that changed the course of his life. Harry told it this way:

" 'Be sure and keep an eye on that oil, prof. This car drinks oil like gas! The speedometer is slow too, so keep it down to 55 m.p.h.' With those words of warning I promptly fell off to sleep. All six of us were dead tired from a fruitless weekend of deer hunting.

"Awaking suddenly sometime later, my eyes fell on the speedometer, 70 miles an hour! In my car that was an actual 85! The oil? Too low! The motor? Knocking like a snare drum! When we came to a shaking stop, it didn't take long for us to realize that I was the object of an unfortunate circumstance. My $350.00 car was useless!"

Since the car was his only means of transportation and he

was working his way through school, it was a great loss. That—
and other circumstances—caused Harry to cry out, "Lord, do You
really want me in forestry?" God's Word spoke to Harry as he
read Ephesians 3:8: *"Unto me, who am less than the least of all saints,
is this grace given, that I should preach among the Gentiles the unsearch-
able riches of Christ."* God intervened. He answered the prayers of
Harry's godly mother. Harry believed God was calling him into
the ministry of Jesus Christ.

Harry returned to Bryan College to finish his college education. During his first year back at Bryan, he attended the
Toccoa missionary conference in Toccoa Falls, Georgia. God continued to melt and mold his heart.

### *WHAT IS LIFE TO ME?*
Mark 8:34–38
*Harry Dale Goehring*


What is life to me, Lord,
If through it day by day
I walk in ways I would, Lord,
Without Thee as my stay;
Without my share of sorrow
Or burden of the cross,
And not to share with Thee, Lord,
The triumph after loss?

What is life to me, Lord,
If through the lonely night
I cannot glimpse my Savior's face
In visions of delight;
If morning does not bring, Lord,
A time to serve Thee new
Instead of fruitless memories
Of things I failed to do?

What is life to me, Lord,
If evening time arrives,
Yet not one word of witness
to guide to Thee the lives
Who with the burden of sin's load
Attempt to find the way,
And here am I, so weak, Lord,
Without Thee as my stay?

What is life to me, Lord,
Unless for Thee to die?
Retain not one small want of mine,
Just on thy Grace rely;
Thy faithfulness to me, Lord,
Is all that I will need
To shed my blood in service
Of planting precious seed.

Oh, this is life to me, Lord,
To daily bear Thy cross,
To daily have Thee search my heart,
To daily burn all dross,
To daily bring to Thee, Lord,
All burdens, griefs, or cares,
To daily walk in childlike trust
Through Satan's tangling snares.

Oh, Christ, The everlasting God,
The Bread of Life to me;
The Living Water from above,
The Rock to which I flee,
In Thee is found all joy of life,
For by Thy Grace and Love,
Life here for me is one great task—
Reflecting God above!

"This poem is written as a result of the Lord's working in my heart at Toccoa Missionary Conference, April 13–15, 1956."

Harry served as class chaplain, sang in the choir and on gospel teams, worked on Christian service assignments, ran cross-country, and served as student coach of the track team. His devotion to Christ was evident. At graduation, he received several honors, but the one that meant most to him was the one given for Christian testimony. Upon receiving that one, Harry took it to his mother and laid it in her lap, saying, "Mother, this honor is yours. It is because of your faithful prayers."

## NANCY

God worked in another life born into the quiet stability of a small farm in Indiana. Nancy Goodman was the third living child of Chauncey and Mildred Goodman. Her father, after graduating with honors from Purdue University, spent only a few years in his field of electrical engineering, in New York City, before deciding he much preferred the fertile fields of his native Indiana. He returned there with his family to spend the rest of his life farming. So Nancy grew up in rural Indiana instead of in New York City.

While Gene DeVries was surviving prison camp in the Philippines, Nancy, then in grammar school, was collecting milkweed pods used to make life rafts for the U.S. Navy, and saving nickels and dimes to buy stamps for war bonds. That, and seeing her cousin in a U.S. Navy uniform going off to war, was the closest Nancy came to the reality of the war taking place halfway around the world.

Nancy spent summer days working hard on the family farm, hoeing the garden and canning its produce, picking wild blackberries to sell and freeze, and helping in the fields. She enjoyed swinging on the high rope swing tied to a limb of the Scotch pine in the front yard, catching lightning bugs, walking in the woods, picking bouquets of wild flowers, and watching rain-storms rush across the field. Like the Walton family of TV fame, at bedtime the Goodman children played word-guessing games, calling from room to room until their mother told them to go to sleep.

It was a great treat when the toot of the horn announced the arrival of the county library truck. The whole Goodman family loved books. Travel books whetted Nancy's appetite to see the world. What Nancy learned from books and watching violent Indiana storms from the safety of their farmhouse's big front porch was the closest she came to excitement. For 12 years Nancy rode the same yellow school bus with the same driver over the same route to the same small school where she studied with most of the same classmates. But when she was a freshman in high school, Nancy faced a dramatic and difficult change. Her father died of kidney failure. Her only brother, then a senior in high school, kept the farm going with his mother's help. Times were lean, but the Goodman children, Roger, Marilyn, Nancy, and Shirley, saw amazing answers to their mother's prayers.

Since Nancy's father did not have a will, the laws of Indiana required that two-thirds of all possessions not owned jointly by the couple must be sold to set up a trust for his underage children. This included crucial items such as farm equipment and a small herd of Angus cattle. Nancy's mother had to buy back two-thirds interest in all the farm machinery the family had already used. Though not a large sum, it was enough to cripple a farming operation as small as theirs. It was harvest time, but it was a very wet fall. The Goodmans couldn't get into the fields to pick the corn. The corncrib stood empty, and there was no corn to feed the cattle or pigs. Nancy's mother and brother tried to pick enough corn by hand to feed the animals but couldn't keep up. Just as the corn ran completely out, a neighbor asked Mildred Goodman if he could borrow a wagon to finish picking. He owned higher, sandy ground, had just filled his corncrib, and still had more in the field. He offered to bring back the wagon filled with corn. Then, when the Goodmans picked their corn, they could repay him by refilling the wagon. Their neighbor's corn kept the Goodman's animals fed until they could get into their own fields. Neighbors then helped them harvest the corn when the ground was dry.

Not long after that experience, Nancy's mother became sick with a bad case of flu. Because she did not have money to pay for a doctor's visit, she did not get treatment. After she had been ill a few days, the Goodman's doctor knocked at their front door. He knew Mrs. Goodman wanted to sell some Angus cattle. When Nancy's mother opened the door, the doctor forgot about the cattle and treated his patient, now ill with pneumonia. Nancy's mother often recounted how God sent her doctor to make a house call when he did not even know his patient was sick, and how God sent a wagon full of corn at a crucial time. Hearing Mrs. Goodman giving thanks to God for those wonderful interventions made a lasting impact on Nancy and her brother and sisters.

The Goodman family attended the Baptist church in the small neighboring town of Mentone. There, Nancy first learned the stories of Jesus Christ and first heard a missionary speaker. She was drawn to missions by men and women who told of their work in distant lands sharing about the love of Jesus, who died for them. Nancy desired that she, too, be able to go to people who didn't know about Jesus. Although Nancy had been convicted about sin during childhood, it wasn't until she was a senior in high school that she made sure of her commitment to Jesus Christ. From that point on, Nancy developed a deep love for Christ and wanted to follow His plan for her life.

After high school, because of financial constraints, Nancy worked for a year to earn money to attend college. During that year, a musical team from William Jennings Bryan College gave a presentation in the Baptist church in Mentone. Those musicians directed Nancy's thoughts toward their school.

The following fall, Nancy enrolled in Bryan College. Nancy enjoyed its location on the top of Bryan Hill, overlooking the small town of Dayton, in the hills of Tennessee. It was not a large college—just the right place for an Indiana farm girl. She majored in Christian Education of children, since she believed God was leading her to prepare for full-time ministry. Every Sunday, Nancy taught a class of poverty-stricken mountain children at the Cove Mission. Riding to the mission was nerve-wracking, but it was worthwhile. She loved her class and looked forward to teaching the children each Sunday.

The first big social event of the year at Bryan College was the freshman reception. Nancy didn't remember much about her date for that night, but she did remember the senior, Harry Goehring, who sang a beautiful baritone solo. A few weeks later, she was pleased to be assigned to the dining table where he was the host. Though Nancy was shy, Harry put her at ease, and she found it easy to carry on a conversation with him. From time to time, he would join Nancy and her friend Linda when they were walking. The more she knew him, the more Nancy admired and respected Harry. Something he said made her think, *He must have a girlfriend back home.* She admired his qualities so much, though, that she prayed, "Lord, when you get ready to give me a husband, please make him someone *like* Harry Goehring." She was amazed when, within a day or so, Harry asked her to be his date for a guest artist program. He added that he might be a bit late, since he would be returning that evening from a cross-country meet.

On the night of the date, Nancy waited until it was almost time for the program to start. Then she decided to go with her roommates since she didn't know if Harry would get back in time. They had been seated only a few minutes when Harry slipped in next to Nancy, just as the program was about to begin.

He commented, "Hmm. I didn't know I was dating the whole room!"

Harry and Nancy were dating steadily by the middle of October. At the college Christmas banquet, favors shaped like gift boxes were set at each place. When the banquet was almost over, Harry wrote something on a small piece of paper and slipped it inside Nancy's favor. When she reached for it, he told her not to open it until they left the banquet. As they exited the dining area, Nancy opened the little box and removed the tiny piece of paper hidden inside. On it were written the words "Will you marry me?" That was the last thing Nancy had expected. Flustered, she replied, "I . . . I think so." And with that, she ran up the stairs to her room. It didn't take Nancy long to make up her mind for sure once she realized Harry really meant it.

When Harry's birthday in April drew near, his classmates Gayle and Charlene Ryle approached Nancy with the idea of holding a surprise birthday dinner in their mobile home. Nancy was excited about this surprise for Harry. What she didn't know was that Harry had set the whole thing up. After dinner, Gayle and Charlene made an excuse to take some ice cream back to the big freezer in the college kitchen. When they left, Harry pulled a box from his pocket and gave her an engagement ring. The surprise was on Nancy!

Nancy was always amazed that God did not just answer her prayer and give her someone *like* Harry Goehring but gave her Harry *himself.* God gave her the man she had so admired and respected, a man of purpose who loved the Lord and His Word and cared about other people.

# Chapter Nineteen

# God's Provision

The wedding date was set for November 21, 1957, during Harry's seminary Thanksgiving break. Around three weeks before the planned date, Harry became ill with a high fever. He assumed it was a virus since the flu was epidemic at that time. Yet the pain in his lower back and stomach didn't fit with the symptoms others had. The doctor decided he should be hospitalized. When exploratory surgery was performed, it showed his appendix had ruptured. Because his appendix was not in the normal position, the doctor had not considered that diagnosis. His body had walled off the infection, and this saved his life. But even so, Harry was still very ill. Nancy sat for her bridal picture for their wedding announcement wondering if she would ever need the picture.

When Harry began to recuperate, he declared he would be married on November 21, even if they had to carry him into the church. As it turned out, he was still hospitalized on that day. Nancy and her mother had to contact all those who had received invitations and let them know the wedding would be delayed by one week.

Harry had not been working long enough for his health insurance to take effect. So Nancy used part of her small inheritance to pay his hospital bill. That way he could be released from the hospital for his wedding. She often teased him about having to pay the hospital a dowry.

Harry lost 30 pounds during his illness and was still pretty weak and pale, but he was determined that the wedding would go on. So on November 30, family and friends gathered at the First Baptist Church, in Mentone, Indiana. Marilyn Rathfon, Nancy's girlhood friend, was her maid of honor, and one of Harry's college friends, William Brew, was his best man. Reverend Irwin Olsen performed the ceremony. Nancy's brother, Roger, walked her down the aisle. The radiant bride stopped partway down the aisle and listened with a heart full of thanksgiving as the groom sang to her in his rich baritone voice, "Thankful God gave me you, Thankful for love so true, I'll always praise my Savior because He gave me you."

Following the ceremony, the couple greeted their guests at the home of the bride's mother. After the reception, they left for an overnight honeymoon in Plymouth, Indiana. The next day, they returned to the little rented farmhouse that became their first home. Thanksgiving break had come and gone, and Harry's busy school and work schedule began once again.

In their early years of marriage, the couple was forced to trust God to supply their needs. Harry was firmly convinced he did not want his wife working to pay his way through school. God provided Harry with a job at the Litchfield Creamery, in Winona Lake, which gave him short winter hours and long summer hours. By the time Harry finished seminary, the Goehrings had not only kept ahead of their seminary expenses, but also managed to pay off money Harry owed his parents for college.

Harry and Nancy saw God provide their needs in answer to prayer, and they learned how to make a little stretch a long way. Nancy had a $5 weekly budget for groceries. They only used powdered milk (good training for the mission field) and bought hamburger, chicken, or pork only when they were on sale for 29¢ a pound. Fresh salads were a luxury they ate only on Sundays when they had dinner with Nancy's mom.

One day Nancy got word that Harry's sister, Lola, her husband, Lowell Hoyt, and their seven children would be in town for dinner. Nancy had potatoes and vegetables she had canned, but no meat. Their week's money was gone, and Harry's paycheck was not due for a couple of days. Nancy prayed God would show her what to do. No one but God knew of her pressing need. Later that morning, her mother arrived at her door with a ham. Usually Nancy scrimped and saved for several weeks to have extra money to buy food for guests, but this time God provided for the unexpected.

The Lord blessed Harry and Nancy with two children during their four years at Grace Seminary. Harold Allen, named for Harry's older brother, was born August 14, 1958. Joyanne, born on May 22, 1960, was as contented and joyful as her name suggested. With Harold's birth it became impossible to make the trip out to the Goodman farm to wash diapers and baby clothes, so the young couple prayed for a washing machine. At a farm auction, their bid of $5 was accepted for an old Maytag wringer-washer, and the auctioneer even threw in the rinse tubs. Nancy had grown up using a Maytag washer, so she had no difficulty using equipment that would prove frustrating to someone who was used to an automatic machine.

During that time, Nancy's mother worked in the yard goods department of a store in Warsaw and was able to get cloth remnants. But Nancy didn't own a sewing machine. The Goehrings prayed again, and Nancy went to a sewing machine dealer in Warsaw to see about buying a used one. Although the dealer offered many new and expensive electric machines and some used ones, none of them was within Nancy's price range. Back in the corner sat an old Wheeler-Wilson treadle machine. When Nancy asked about it, the salesman told her she could have it for $5. Nancy tried the machine. It worked like a charm and made beautiful, even stitches. She bought it on the spot. Nancy spent many happy hours at that machine creating little garments from remnants while Harry worked nights at the creamery. Harry and Nancy saw how God provides every need for those who are committed to Him.

During seminary years, the Goehrings served in First Baptist Church of Mentone, where Nancy had grown up. Harry was a gifted teacher, able to motivate his college students to discover the truths of God's Word. Nancy, who loved small children, was the superintendent in the pre-school department and delighted in teaching little ones about Jesus. They both worked with Vacation Bible School, sang in the choir, and helped wherever they could.

While attending seminary, Harry considered being a teacher, a pastor, or doing home mission work. At the beginning of each chapel, he prayed, "Lord, if it be Thy will, show me today what you want me to do." On March 8, the Holy Spirit, through Dr. Keul of the mission agency TEAM, caused Harry to face the fact that he had never honestly considered foreign missions. How could he, as a pastor, challenge young people to a ministry which he had never faced squarely himself? That afternoon when he arrived home, Harry went to an upstairs room and spent time reading God's Word and considering this all-important issue. The Lord let him understand John 3:16 in a new way: "God so loved the WORLD!" God's purpose was to reach the world with the gospel. With real joy Harry surrendered his will to that purpose. Having made this commitment, Harry felt responsible to do all in his power to make himself available for the job. He was ready to enter the world of foreign missions.

God worked quickly in response to Harry's obedience. Within a few days, Dr. Viggo Olsen visited the Mentone church and helped crystallize Harry's ideas toward a specific mission board and field of service. Dr. Olsen explained his vision to help open a hospital in East Pakistan, a country surrounded by India, with overwhelming needs, both physical and spiritual. During Vic Olsen's presentation, he included a couple of pictures of the tribal people in the country. He mentioned the need for evangelism among those tribal people and for the Bible to be translated into their own language. Amazingly, those few slides and comments, which were not Dr. Olsen's main emphasis, arrested Harry and Nancy's attention. They both felt East Pakistan was God's place for them.

The Goehrings applied to ABWE, praying that God would direct them to work among tribal people in East Pakistan. Even though serving God was Nancy's deep desire, she admitted to honest doubts.

"After applying to the mission, Satan tested me by reminding me of my incapabilities—and doubt stole in. But God is so good! One evening as I was reading my Bible, the Lord spoke to my heart through 1 Thessalonians 2:4, *"But even as we have been approved of God to be entrusted with the Gospel, so we speak . . . "* With my mind upon the people of East Pakistan, I went into the kitchen and my eyes fell upon a calendar verse. *"This people have I formed for myself; they shall show forth my praise"* (Isaiah 43:21). I knew then that God had led us, and that Satan could no longer cause me to doubt."

Harry and Nancy were members of the 1961 ABWE candidate class. Many in that class were headed to East Pakistan, including Dr. Donn and Pauline (Kitty) Ketcham, Drs. Ralph and Lucy Ankenman, nurses Becky Davey, Jeannie Lockerbie, and Jean Weld, and church planters Mel and Marjorie Beals. Dr. Vic and Joan Olsen had challenged many of them to be part of opening the work of medical/surgical evangelism in East Pakistan.

During a devotional time at candidate class, Harry blended his voice with Jeannie and Jean to sing Avis Christiansen's song:

Only one life to offer—Take it, dear Lord, I pray;
Nothing from Thee withholding, Thy will I now obey.
Thou who hast freely given Thine all in all for me,
Claim this life for Thine own to be used, my Savior,
Every moment for Thee.

On October 15, 1961, at the Haddon Heights Baptist Church, in Haddon Heights, New Jersey, Harry and Nancy Goehring

were appointed by ABWE to serve in East Pakistan. In address-
ing the appointees, Dr. Harold T. Commons said, "Missionary is
not a biblical word. It simply means 'one with a mission.' Our
mission is to sound out the message until we see Him face to
face."

# Chapter Twenty

# Gathering a Support Team

Harry and Nancy were filled with joy knowing that they were now missionary appointees preparing to go to East Pakistan for evangelism and Bible translation among the many hill peoples there.

They returned to Nancy's mother's home to prepare visual aids and charts about translation to use on deputation and to set up a schedule of meetings. Both Harry and Nancy looked forward to sharing their burden for the ministry God had guided them toward. The only thing they dreaded was asking others to back them financially. Both came from independent backgrounds and had earned their own way through school. This made it even harder to think of asking others to support them. Pastor Irwin Olsen encouraged and helped them, and both Nancy's home church in Indiana and Harry's in Pennsylvania began helping with their support. Every Sunday in December 1961 and January 1962 was filled with meetings in Indiana and Michigan. They then moved to the missionary home at the Evans City Baptist Church, in Pennsylvania, for meetings in February and March.

The family enjoyed the travel. After years of long hours apart as Harry went to school and worked nights, it was a treat to be together. The children were secure in their parents' love wherever they were. Harold was a bit shy about going into new situations, but Joyanne loved the attention. As they pulled up to a church one Sunday morning, she asked, "Is this another one church?" When her parents answered in the affirmative, she replied with great confidence, "They will love me!"

Joyanne gave Nancy one of life's embarrassing moments. After a Sunday morning service, a talkative lady cornered Nancy. Joyanne, eager to be moving about, kept tugging on Nancy's hand. After some time passed and the woman showed no sign of stopping, Nancy noticed Harry was standing by the door greeting people. She decided she could let Joyanne go since she knew she would not run in the church. The woman kept right on talking. When she finally took a breath, she said, "Well, you've trained her well, haven't you?" Looking behind, Nancy saw two-year-old Joyanne walking around with the offering plate which had been placed by the door for the love offering for the Goehrings.

In April 1962, Harry told supporters of their plans to spend the summer in linguistic training and mentioned they planned to travel by ship to East Pakistan in November.

During July, as they studied at the Summer Institute of Linguistics, in Grand Forks, North Dakota, two-thirds of their support was promised through churches. Then an individual promised to provide any support still needed in November. It seemed as though a November sailing would be a reality.

That summer at Grand Forks, Nancy realized God was giving the Goehrings an unplanned blessing; she was pregnant with their third child. The Goehrings wrote to the team in East Pakistan about their good news, but were disappointed when word came back that they should remain in the States until after the birth of the baby. The mission hospital was not yet built, and medical facilities in the country were far from ideal. This meant a delay of several months, when the Goehrings were anxious to reach East Pakistan as soon as possible.

Near the time of the baby's birth, Indiana experienced a few weeks of intensely cold weather, with sub-zero temperatures and many snowstorms. The Goehrings' car often would not start because of the intense cold. They lived ten miles from the hospital, and Harry had meetings scheduled on most Sundays. Nancy was plagued by the "what ifs." She found her faith dwindling.

"What if I go into labor and we can't start the car? What if Harry is away? How will I get to the hospital on snowy roads, and who will stay with the children?" Around that time, Nancy read a poem containing the following words: "Faith is sweet repose and quiet love that knows each step is ordered from above . . . " That quieted her fearful "what if" questions.

Harry was home when Nancy went into labor, and the car started. Grandma Goodman stayed with the children while Harry took Nancy to the hospital. On February 9, 1963, the Lord gave them a little girl; they named her Faith Ellen.

Since Faith's arrival had delayed their departure, Harry felt it would be wise to have more churches behind them than to have a large amount from one individual. He continued holding meetings after their summer of linguistic study. A year and a half after God had provided their first support, the final amount needed was promised. The Goehrings had 27 churches and one individual on their support team

# Chapter Twenty-one

# The Long Journey

At last, word came that the *Hellenic Spirit*, the Greek freighter on which the Goehring family had booked passage, would sail May 24, 1963, from New York harbor. The last crate was nailed shut and the last barrel packed. The quarter of beef, lovingly canned by people in Nancy's home church, was carefully stashed in the mid-section of several barrels to provide food at the Hebron mission station, where meat was scarce.

The Goehrings were scheduled to sail with Dr. Donn and Kitty Ketcham and their three children. Donn and Harry each set out from their homes driving rental trucks with their freight. They met at the home of Harry's sister, Betty, and her husband, Gordon Fletcher, in Zelienople, Pennsylvania, and continued on together. Arriving at the 57th Street pier in New York City, Harry and Donn made arrangements to have their freight loaded onto the ship.

In the meantime, Nancy's mother and the mother of her dearest friend, Annabel Rathfon, drove Nancy, Harold, Joyanne, and Faith to Zelienople, Pennsylvania. There, Nancy said goodbye to her mom, who preferred not to witness the actual sailing of the ship. Mildred Goodman said that seeing them off on a ship would feel too permanent. After meeting up with Harry, the family rode to his sister Ruby's home in Stratford, New Jersey.

On Friday, 11 people (the five Goehrings and Ruby's family) crowded into a station wagon around footlockers, suitcases, boxes, and bags. In these cases were the things the family would use en route to East Pakistan.

About 1:10 p.m., the group was able to get on the enclosed dock next to the freighter. Stevedores raced around, loading everything from spearmint chewing gum to new cars. Harry managed to get their things up the step-ladder-like gangplank and onto the ship, then up the narrow stairs to their stateroom at the top of the freighter.

Several men from the ABWE office in Philadelphia conducted a short service before the missionaries sailed. Candidate and deputation secretary Harold Amstutz read from Psalm 40. Vice-president Joseph Stowell prayed for blessing upon the missionaries and the loved ones they were leaving. Then Edward Bomm, treasurer, assured the missionaries they were prayed for by name at the ABWE office and thought of continually, even though at times they might feel alone and forgotten. Ed Bomm said they would be no further away than a cablegram or telephone conversation, if it was necessary. He told the missionaries' families the mission office was always ready to inform and serve them concerning their loved ones and invited them to feel free to call on mission personnel if needed.

After the service, everyone went to investigate the staterooms. The beds, small table, and closets were all built into the walls. Each room had a tiny adjoining bath. Faith's crib had to be fastened to the floor so it would not roll. Passengers could walk freely on the deck, but the parents had to constantly watch the children as there wasn't much protection to keep them from falling off. Nancy and Harry decided they had better get a harness for helter-skelter Joyanne, who turned three a few days before they sailed.

The *Hellenic Spirit* did not get loaded in time to leave on Friday, as planned. In fact, the ship developed engine problems which caused a four-day wait. This was only the beginning of many delays. The passengers were starting breakfast on Tuesday, May 28, when Donn Ketcham said, "There's our tugboat!" Everyone jumped up and went out to take pictures. The bay was full of ships, and the *Queen Mary* had just docked. The *Hellenic Spirit* passed under the Verazano bridge, then being constructed between Staten Island and Brooklyn. In an hour, the Goehrings and Ketchams were out to sea. They felt the rolling swells, even though the ocean looked calm. Nancy was seasick at first but became accustomed to the motion by evening.

In addition to the Goehring and Ketcham families, a history professor going to teach in India, his wife, and a novelist going to Greece were on board. They all ate at the captain's table. Since this was a Greek ship, everything was saturated in olive oil. The kids were intrigued by the whole fish with its eyes looking at them.

The boat had no laundry facilities for the passengers, so the two couples set up a daily laundry regimen. The men scrubbed the clothes on a scrub board in a baby tub. The women rinsed, the men wrung out the clothes, and together they hung them to dry on lines on the deck.

The children soon became accustomed to their new home and playmates Tom, Becky, and Marty Ketcham. Looking out the porthole one morning, Harold was excited to see schools of dolphins. The fifth day out, the Ketcham kids excitedly dragged everyone outside because a whale was spotted. Donn and the first officer saw a huge whale arc out of the water, and Harry sighted it blowing and saw its back and tail before it went down. After seeing some flying fish, Harry remarked, "We're not alone in this vast ocean after all."

On the sixth day, they saw land—the Azores—which was a welcome sight. Harry thought about how Christopher Columbus must have rejoiced to see land after months at sea.

Donn and Harry spent the first few days listing and pricing every item in their barrels and crates in preparation for customs inspection. When that was finished, they began listening to Bengali language tapes.

On the ninth day, faintly on the skyline, the passengers saw the mountains of Africa on their right, and Spain's lower hills on their left. At lunchtime, they sighted the magnificent rock of Gibraltar. Later, off the coast of Morocco, they saw the Pillars of Hercules. Then at sunset, they passed the mountains of Granada, the highest in Spain, magnificent and snow-covered at 11,700 feet. The Mediterranean Sea was clear and smooth under a beautiful full moon. The passengers were grateful for calm seas, as once again the ship was plagued with engine trouble; they sat idled for two hours as the crew tried to do repairs.

A day short of two weeks out, the *Hellenic Spirit* arrived in the harbor of Piraeus and Athens, Greece. The crew was jubilant as their wives and relatives came by small boats to board the ship. Some had not seen their families for more than a year.

On June 11, Donn and Harry, with Faith, went to shore to see about getting Faith's yellow fever shot, since the ship would not be able to enter Karachi if she had not had it. Harry and Donn were shuffled from office to office, thankful for the Greek officer from the ship who was with them. He could at least understand what was being said. When they at last got to the right building and room, father and doctor tried to have the shot given in her buttocks. But they jabbed the needle into her tiny arm, then said, "Tomorrow, cholera shot."

The day had a better ending than beginning, as both families went on a three-hour bus tour of the Acropolis. Even in its decay, the Parthenon was beautiful, its majestic Doric pillars outlining what had been a lovely temple, now open to the sky created by our all-powerful God. They saw Mars hill, where Paul preached and told the Athenians about the "unknown god." In Athens, while waiting for engine repairs, the two families learned of the cyclone that had just passed through East Pakistan, devastating the land and killing many. They could only thank God their freighter was not yet in the Bay of Bengal when that storm swept in, and pray for those who had suffered.

The next port of call was Alexandria, Egypt, and a harrowing trip down the Nile River road to Cairo. At the national museum they saw amazing treasures taken from the pyramids: jewels, golden mummy caskets, and more gold than they dreamed possible in the whole world. Even monkeys, the gods of life, were mummified with the king. From the museum, the tour group went to the mosque of Mohammed Ali, with its walls of alabaster. After a lunch stop, they were taken to the tomb of the Pharaoh Cheops, which took 100,000 men 20 years to build. Granite stones, weighing two and a half tons each, were brought 700 miles from the quarry. The pharaoh's tomb was in the very center of the 486-foot-high pyramid. After visiting the tomb, the Goehrings rode camels. The children were most impressed with that experience, but it was a blistering hot day—110°F in the shade—and their ride back to Alexandria was through the desert.

After six days, the *Hellenic Spirit* pulled up anchor and headed toward the Suez Canal. About two-thirds of the way down the 90-mile-long canal, it opened up into Bitter Root Lake. Here their southbound convoy passed a northbound convoy of ships. Passengers couldn't see much, since they were passing in the darkness. By morning, they were anchored in Bitter Root Lake, allowing the northbound convoy to pass, a process which took six hours. As the *Hellenic Spirit* entered the canal once again, the passengers saw a narrow strip of palm trees and farms on the west side in Egypt, but saw nothing but desert on the Sinai side.

Soon they saw barren mountains to the west, the barrier which kept Israel from fleeing when they arrived at the Red Sea. Harry could understand now why the Israelites murmured and how the lack of water would test the flesh to the uttermost.

The ship reached Suez City by 5:30 p.m., then entered the Red Sea, which is 1,400 miles long. Jeddah, the first port, is the city where Muslims arrive on their *haj* (pilgrimage) to Mecca. It took seven days to unload the cargo. Passengers were not allowed off the ship in the daytime, lest they contaminate the pilgrims. But the missionaries docked within 15–20 feet of a small freighter from Yemen jammed with pilgrims. The children were fascinated as that ship unloaded cattle, goats, and camels, the latter being unloaded with a rope sling around their middle. The goats were unloaded in metal boxes about five-foot square and four-foot deep. They watched as 38 goats untangled themselves and escaped from those boxes.

An Indian family joined the passengers in Jeddah. The following Sunday, Harold kept reminding his father to invite the new passengers to join them for their worship service held in the dining room. Harry was surprised when they came. The Indian man was amazed that Harold paid close attention to the service. That opened the door to further discussion about the Lord.

After leaving the Red Sea and entering the Gulf of Aden, the temperature dropped 20°, much to the passengers' relief. Passing from the Gulf of Aden to the Arabian Sea, the seas became rougher. Nancy was once again seasick and spent most of one day in bed. Faith, now a little over four months old, enjoyed her mother's predicament—she got more attention that way.

During a short stop in Karachi, West Pakistan, Harry got a cinder lodged in his cornea, directly over the pupil. He was grateful for the skill and steady hand of Dr. Donn, who anesthetized the eye and removed the cinder. Harry looked like "Patch the Pirate" for several days.

The ship was again delayed in Bombay (now Mumbai), India, waiting for pier space. Harry commented that they were beginning to see some of the reasons for their delays. Three storms had moved up the Bay of Bengal from Burma to East Pakistan's port city, Chittagong. The last occurred only four days earlier. Had they been on their planned schedule, the *Hellenic Spirit* would have been caught in that storm. The missionaries also received word in Bombay that the Matamahari River had overflowed its banks, and the house at Hebron where the Goehrings planned to live was flooded.

After seven and a half days, the ship finally left Bombay. As they neared Rangoon, they learned the radar had gone out on their ship, and visibility was down to half a mile. The captain stayed on the bridge, keeping a careful vigil over his ship. At last, the harbor pilot boarded to guide them into Rangoon. With only one day in port, the Goehrings and Ketchams were eager to see the famous Shwe De Gong Pagoda. After filling out various forms, they were allowed to go onshore in a drenching downpour. They boarded three-wheeled baby taxis and rode past the open bazaar through the crowded downtown area, then up a wide boulevard where they glimpsed the golden spire of the pagoda. At last they came to the main entrance, a 100-yard-long series of steps covered with an ornate roof and wall. On each side of the stairs were little shops where worshipers could buy objects to offer Buddha: flowers, trinkets, candles, and incense. The Goehrings and Ketchams decided to ride the elevator rather than walk the steps. They exited on the white stone pavement surrounding the pagoda. Visitors could not enter the pagoda itself, as it was sealed over 2,500 years before. Inside the pagoda were four relics of Buddha, one of which was a water filter. Surrounding the pagoda were many small stupas and shrines containing intricately carved images of Buddha. There, the people placed their gifts before the statues, then sat and prayed. Harry thought, *All of this to honor a dead man.* How these people needed to know about the living Savior.

The families hurried back to the *Hellenic Spirit* for the last leg of their journey, but it was two days before they pulled up anchor and departed from Rangoon. The next port of call would be Chittagong, East Pakistan, their destination. They passed the southernmost extension of East Pakistan, where it joins Burma. Traveling north, they sailed past Cox's Bazar. Both couples went up on the bridge expecting quickly to see the port. Instead, they saw the twinkling lights of many ships waiting in the harbor outside the mouth of the Karnaphuli River. Because of the cyclones, 24 ships loaded with relief goods were waiting their turn to go the final 10 miles upriver to the docks in Chittagong.

After four days sitting at anchor, a pilot boat approached their ship. On board, they saw a very tall man, their colleague, Dr. Vic Olsen. He had arranged a trip to the ship to bring mail that had been awaiting their arrival. Vic told the Goehrings the house at Hebron was under three to four feet of water, and that they might need to build a new home on higher ground. Previously, Harry had expressed how glad he was there was a place to live at Hebron, because he had never even built a doghouse. Now it appeared he would need to learn how to build a house.

Harry's daily diary entry read "Still waiting" for more than a week. Finally, the ship received word they would be allowed to go in the following day. They got ready, but were disappointed no pilot ship came.

The ship was getting extremely low on diesel fuel. Within two or three days it would be without power, lights, or cooking possibilities. At last, on August 12, at 3:00 p.m., the pilot boat came to the *Hellenic Spirit,* and at about 5:00 p.m. they came in view of the dock. Waiting for them was Vic Olsen along with ABWE nurses Becky Davey, Jeannie Lockerbie, and Juanita Canfield. A torrential rain suddenly poured down, and the welcoming committee jumped agilely into a nearby boxcar to wait it out. A monsoon welcome! It was too late to pass customs and immigration that night, but before they left the ship the next day, the captain said to the Goehrings, "This place is the end of the world. You will not want to stay here. I will be leaving again in three days. If you want to go with me, I have space for you."

After breakfast on August 13, 1963, Vic Olsen took the families and their luggage to the homes where they would live at first. The Goehrings stayed at 32A Housing Society in the apartment of Becky Davey, Jeannie Lockerbie, and Juanita Canfield. Becky gave the Goehrings her room.

Donn and Harry remained at the docks to see their things cleared through customs. Miraculously, by 5:00 p.m. everything had cleared customs without hassle and without charge.

# Chapter Twenty-two

# Introduction to Hebron

The day after their arrival, Harold celebrated his fifth birthday. Joyanne was three years old, and Faith almost six months old. Half of Faith's life had been spent in a cozy cabin on board ship. The first day off the ship, Faith screamed continually. She would look around the big room, then scream. Evidently the high ceilings and the ceiling fan made her insecure.

Harold and Joyanne joined the nursery school Jeannie Lockerbie conducted on the veranda and had a wonderful time playing with the Walsh children, who lived downstairs. Nancy looked up to Eleanor Walsh, who so lovingly cared for her family of six, including two-year-old twins.

Jay Walsh was to introduce Harry to the tribal work, Hebron station, and life in East Pakistan before the Walshes left on furlough. Jay first explained how the Hebron mission station came into being. On a 1957 survey trip to the southern end of the Chittagong Hill Tracts District, ABWE's first missionaries to East Pakistan, Victor and Winnifred Barnard, and Paul Miller arrived at a government outpost called Lama, located on the banks of the Matamahari River. Lama, which might be compared to a county seat town, had a police station, a post office, and a bi-weekly bazaar. Merchants from up and down the river arrived by country boat with merchandise to barter, trade, or sell to the tribal people who trekked in from the surrounding hills. Moghs, Tipperahs, and Murungs, distinctively dressed in their native garb, carried their products to sell: rice, cotton, tobacco, brooms, wild honey, *choan* (elephant grass), and chickens.

Observing such a mixture of colorful tribes gathering in one place, the missionaries were quick to recognize Lama as a key spot for tribal evangelism. Since the government prohibited purchasing property in the Hill Tracts District, the missionaries decided to select a site as near as possible to Lama, in the adjoining Chittagong District. Studying a crude map of the area, they discovered that only a mile from Lama, along the same Matamahari River, a promontory of land lay within Chittagong District, where there were no restrictions on land purchase. Satisfied that this was an ideal location for a mission station, they purchased the land and named it Hebron.

The nearby village of Bilchari is made up of Bengali-speaking people. Although the Hebron missionaries felt specially called to work among the tribal groups, they could not neglect the Bengali people who make up 96 percent of the population.

Within ten days, Jay and Harry went to Hebron to take kerosene and other supplies to missionaries Donna Ahlgrim and Lynn Silvernale and to look over the house where the Goehrings had expected to live. The men borrowed a 16-foot boat from Major Zaman, who lived on the bank of the Matamahari River and, using Jay's 25 hp Evinrude engine, headed up the river. The boat leaked badly, so Harry used the top of a thermos jug and bailed for the entire 22 miles. The trip took four and a half hours through steep, jungle-covered hills. Scattered here and there on the slopes, patches of hill-rice were growing. Muslim and Hindu villages dotted the riverbanks. At 4:30 p.m., Harry saw Hebron for the first time. It was a precious moment. He wished Nancy could have shared it, but the trip was too hot and difficult for the baby.

After a short rest, Jay and Harry looked at what would be the Goehrings' home—the bamboo house with the corrugated tin roof, plaster walls, and cement floors. The water line where it had flooded was at the three-foot mark on the inside of the house. Workers had done a good job of scraping out six inches of mud, but the house was still very dirty, with goat dung everywhere. Harry felt that when it was cleaned and painted the house would be livable. He was glad Nancy hadn't seen the house as it was now.

The next morning, Jay and Harry were awakened at 5:30 a.m. by someone earnestly praying. Ancherai, the Tipperah evangelist, had arrived and was praying with Benu Pundit, the Bengali language teacher. He brought along Tawa, a new convert, from a nearby village. Ancherai poured out his heart for his people and for the missionaries, calling them all by name.

Ancherai prevailed upon them to go to Tawa's village for a service. Jay and Harry left Hebron at 5:30 p.m. and arrived at 6:45—a fast six-mile trek through the rivers and up the hills. Jay and Harry stayed in a one-room woven bamboo tribal house built on five-foot stilts and covered with a grass roof. They were refreshed by a bath on the back porch as they poured water from clay pots over their heads. They had a great time of fellowship with Ancherai and the Christians. Harry learned this had been entirely a Satan village until a few months before. Then four households professed Christianity.

The men hiked back to Hebron the next morning. Before returning to Chittagong, they discussed with Ancherai and Benu plans for the short-term tribal Bible school to begin in November at Hebron.

Within two weeks, Harry and Jay went back to Hebron to clean the house and to take painters to whitewash the inside walls. After long hot days of scrubbing out the house, Jay and Harry cooled off in the river before going to sleep.

When Jay and Harry returned to Chittagong this time, the Goehrings' Hebron home was ready for occupancy. But it had been decided that Harry should build another bamboo home on higher ground before the next monsoon season.

In October 1963, Harry's next phase of introduction to the tribal work began. Jay and Harry trekked deep into the Shangu hills to enlist students for the upcoming Bible school. Jay, Harry, Khoka Sen, a Bengali Hindu convert, and Ancherai, the Tipperah evangelist, left early Wednesday morning for the Shangu River, 30 miles south of Chittagong. It took two hours to travel that far on an old bus. They then contracted for a boat and two *majis* (boatmen) to pole them 90 miles upriver.

Having started on Wednesday afternoon, the group arrived at their jumping-off place into the hill country on Saturday afternoon. During those long, hot days on the boat, Jay reviewed colorful Bible flashcard stories in Bengali with Ancherai, who would in turn teach them to his people in the Tipperah language. Trinity Baptist Church, in Pasadena, California, had made multiple sets of the pictures, which accompanied the Bible stories in the "wordless book."

Friday, Harry came down with a high fever and pounding headache, so severe he began thinking of turning back. Ancherai took Jay aside and they prayed for Harry for a long time. God gave Harry the verse, "I will go in the strength of the Lord," and he determined to continue.

The four men started for the first village, supposedly only 20 minutes away. A bad thunderstorm hit just at that time, making the muddy mountain trails as slick as grease. In some places, the path was nothing but footholds cut out of the side of the slope. After falling and sliding up and down the hills, they reached the village utterly exhausted. The village, called Ramdu, consisted of 16 woven bamboo houses perched on stilts with thatched roofs. The floors of split bamboo were smooth and clean. In the corner of each house stood a clay stove with an open fire. Eight of the 16 households professed to be believers. Villagers had erected a little bamboo church, or "Jesus House," with a bamboo pulpit, platform, and benches. They had no pastor or Bible but met faithfully four times a week: Wednesday and Saturday for prayer and twice on Sunday for worship. Each person entered the church and quietly bowed his head in prayer. Then the drummer started, and the singing began. Someone would tell one of the few Bible stories they knew. Harry saw firsthand how the Spirit of God was working among these simple and uneducated people who loved the Lord, yet had so little. His deep desire to translate the Bible into their own language was intensified as he spent time with these believers. The plan was to translate the New Testament into Tipperah using the Bengali script. Until that time, other tribal translations had used letters from the English alphabet. Choosing to use the Bengali script meant a Tipperah person would learn to read the national language as well as his native tongue. But Harry knew learning the language, reducing it to writing, and translating Scripture required many years.

The great need for trained leadership among the tribal people was also evident. Harry and Jay hoped the people of this village—and others—would send young men to the short-term Bible school. The Christians in each village were to choose a man who could speak Bengali to attend. He would be taught to read and write Bengali, taught Bible stories using the flashcard visuals, and taught simple doctrines. Then he would return to his village to teach his people.

Monday morning the men left for the second village. Steady rain continued to fall, and their path led them up and down steep slopes, through gorges, and over large, slippery rocks. Six and a half hours later, they dragged themselves up to the top of the ridge, and there, across the gorge, was Duni Rum village. Men ran to meet them, and as they climbed the last slope, singing children lined the paths. They were taken to the headman's house, which soon was filled with people. This village also had 16 houses and a church.

Since the rains continued, it was decided Jay and Harry would stay where they were, and representatives from other villages would come to them. Tipperahs were far more able to navigate the slippery trails. Their days in Duni Rum were filled with teaching and answering questions. Services were held each night.

When the group left that village on Friday, the people were in tears. The trip out was another six and a half hours of hard trekking through beautiful bamboo forests and jungles. Harry was so glad God had given him strength to press on when he was so ill. He truly did go "in the strength of the Lord."

While Harry was away on his first trek, the Lord tested Nancy's faith. One day when Juanita, Becky, and Jeannie were away, Joyanne became quite sick, the refrigerator broke, and the washing machine wouldn't work. That very afternoon Nancy received six letters stressing that folks at home were praying for the Goehrings. The news encouraged Nancy's faith, and both she and Harry recognized more than ever the importance of the prayers of God's people.

Jay and Harry had one more trek into the Tipperah villages in the Matamahari River area before the Goehrings moved to Hebron. Harry and Nancy used the time between Harry's treks and work trips to Hebron to get ready for their move. They ordered handmade beds, dressers, tables, and chairs from a local furniture maker. They would need kitchen help in order to live in a place as remote as Hebron. The nearest market, Lama, was over a mile from Hebron, and everything had to be carried from there. A man would be needed to do the marketing in this Muslim country. Nancy was told no literate, trained cook would ever go where they were going, but she and Harry felt led to ask God for one. God provided a faithful cook named Barua (because of his Buddhist faith), who was willing to accompany them. The day before the move, he and Harry shopped for supplies not available at the small Lama Bazar market.

On November 4, at 7:00 a.m., their crates and drums and supplies were loaded on a truck. Then Harry took another truck to the place where their furniture had been built, only to find the shop owner had not arrived, and the workers refused to release the furniture. Two hours later, the furniture was finally loaded. At 11:00 a.m., their caravan of two ancient trucks, which Harry called "mechanical mishaps," and the open-sided jeep started south out of Chittagong. ABWE missionary Gene Gurganus was driving Nancy and the children as far south as the Matamahari River. Harold, now five years old, and three-year-old Joyanne were in the back seat with Lynn Silvernale and Shupria, a young woman from the village near Hebron who had come to Chittagong for medical attention. Nancy sat in the front seat holding Faith, a wiggling nine-month-old, as they bounced on and off the bumpy one-lane road. The ancient truck carrying the barrels broke down just two miles out of town. Gene and his passengers drove back to Chittagong to arrange for another truck. By the time the missionaries returned with a different truck, the first dilapidated machine had coughed back to life, and after much persuading and a wad of gum on the fuel pump, they were on their way again.

The caravan reached the Matamahari River at 3:30 p.m., after four hours navigating the first 60 miles of the move. Here, men transferred the two truckloads onto riverboats. These were about 25 feet long and four feet wide in the center and were pushed upriver by *majis* (boatmen) wielding long poles. Lynn, Shupria, and the Goehring family started the 22-mile trip upriver about 5:30 p.m. They traveled in a small canoe-like boat which sat low in the water, propelled by a Johnson motor. Because of the floods, the river had become a mass of shallow sandbars. Harry and Lynn soon lost track of the times they jumped into the river to push the boat into deeper water. After only 45 minutes, darkness fell suddenly, as it does in the tropics. The group found themselves stuck on yet another sandbar. Since Harry did not know the river, to go on would be impossible, so they looked over the "bedroom" possibilities. Lynn and Shupria squeezed side by side in the canoe. Harry found a semi-dry spot where he laid the tarp from the boat's hood. Blankets covering the furniture on the truck kept them warm during the cool night, but no one slept. *Majis,* singing their songs, poled boats past them within a few feet. Sounds from along the riverbank carried out across the water. A radio with Pakistani music, so strange to their ears, played most of the night. From far in the distance, the drums and pipes of Riang tribal music could be heard.

At the break of dawn, they left their sandbar and pushed on for Hebron, arriving around 9:00 a.m. Donna Ahlgrim had a wonderful breakfast awaiting the hungry travelers. For the next week, the Goehrings enjoyed the hospitality of Lynn Silvernale and Donna while they tried to make a home from the mixed-up contents of 21 drums and 12 crates. Lynn and Donna were very helpful, and everyone had fun.

One week after arriving in Hebron, Harry, Nancy, and the kids slept in their own home for the first time in two and a half years. The home had a bathroom; however, there was no running water. Bathwater was carried from the river and stored in the 55-gallon drums they had unpacked. Drinking water was carried from a community tube well, in a village about a mile away. That water was then boiled for 20 minutes before drinking it. There was no electricity at Hebron, so they used kerosene lights, stove, and refrigerator, and a gasoline washing machine. People from the nearby Bengali village and the tribal people were fascinated by the gasoline washing machine—an audience gathered every time Nancy did the laundry. After obtaining a kerosene fan before the next hot season, the Goehrings found living without electricity and running water was not that difficult, especially with a cook who knew how to use the kerosene stove and a helper to go for the running water on foot and to light the lamps at night.

The Goehrings settled down to a busy schedule. Harry oversaw and helped construct their new home. He helped with the Tipperah Bible School and began full-time language study. Jay Walsh supervised the Bible school and taught Harry about building the house. But Jay was soon to leave on furlough. Harry felt somewhat like Solomon must have felt as he cried out to the Lord for wisdom.

Nancy spent mornings teaching Harold and Joyanne in a combined kindergarten/nursery class, and studied in a two-hour Bengali class with Harry. Faith kept busy trying to interrupt everyone, even though a neighboring village girl tried to keep up with Faith during her parents' language class. Village children also came to play with the Goehring children on their veranda. They were especially intrigued by the children's tricycle and Joyanne's doll.

Harold and Joyanne usually played together inside the house or on their veranda during Bengali language class, knowing not to interrupt except if there was an emergency. The cook was available in the kitchen for their normal needs. One day during their two-hour language class, Harry and Nancy overheard Harold and Joyanne talking on the veranda. Harold was talking about how Jesus came to earth to die for our sins; he went into quite an explanation. Then he told about Noah, with Joyanne adding comments now and then. Harry and Nancy assumed they were playing church. When they looked out a little later, they were amazed to see a Muslim man wearing a prayer cap squatting beside the children. They had never seen the man before. Harold told them later that the man wanted to know about Jesus and he understood English, so the children told him. Benu, the language teacher, then explained the gospel in Bengali and gave the visitor a Gospel of John. How matter-of-fact a child can be, and what an example to us.

Harry wrote to his sister:

> We really enjoy this beautiful place. Each morning at 6:00 a.m., I walk up past the bamboo house where the Tipperahs live and study up on a little hill, where we are building our new house. The heavy mist clings to the large, vine-covered trees as the sun attempts to penetrate the wet blanket. After getting the men working on the house, we eat breakfast at 7:00 a.m. Then my duties are quite varied, running between the house construction, the Bible school, and my study.

At 10:00 a.m., Nancy and I have a two-hour language class with Benu and then have dinner. At 1:45, I round up the Tipperahs and we all work on the house until dark, 5:30 p.m. After supper and time with the children, I visit the Tipperahs. Even though I can't understand their language, they enjoy the interest. I can talk a little Bengali, enough to encourage them in their work.

Nancy has had perhaps the harder adjustments. I am busy with the people and the work. Nancy stays home with the children. When she tries to study and do her other tasks, she is often interrupted. Life is different for a housewife here. Things that were so much a part of her life at home no longer are here, and in their place are often things that bring frustration. It's difficult for Nancy not to have other young mothers to talk to. The three children demand a lot of time at this stage, as you are well aware.

Building has never been one of my talents, but being out here makes you do a lot of things you never did before (I even went along once to help deliver a baby). The house is coming along and should be finished in another three months. It is 54 feet by 36 feet, having a six-foot veranda on two sides. It is on brick pillars, 35 of them. Right now I am laying the rooms on top of the sub-flooring with two by fours. After this is finished, I'll start framing the thing and pour a two-inch concrete floor. Men are preparing bamboo for the walls. The bamboo is split, flattened out, and then woven in a nice pattern. After the walls go up, the windows and doors will be cut out.

Language is coming along even though we don't have proper time for study. The workers can understand the things I want done most of the time. Many times it's amazing to me that they do. I can get the gist of most things they say when they speak to me, but sometimes I miss a lot.

Faith is in good health. Harold and Joyanne really love their baby sister. Today, Faith took three steps by herself. Our home is a wonderful and comfortable retreat.

Then he signed off by sending his love to his sister and her family.

Jay Walsh had already gone on furlough when the first Short-Term Tribal Bible School ended. Gene Gurganus came up for the closing ceremonies. He spoke in Bengali, exhorting the students from Scripture. Each student gave a short testimony. Certificates, stating they had finished the first term of Bible school, were handed out, and the students also received a book of parables, a pencil, and a plastic case in which to carry the Bible story flash-cards. At noon, students, teachers, and missionaries sat down to-gether on the mats laid on the schoolhouse floor and enjoyed a feast of rice and curry. The students were sent off with a prayer that they would use all they had learned to teach their own people.

The Goehrings left the next morning for Chittagong to spend Christmas with the missionaries there and to pick up supplies. The Goehring family stayed in the home of Mel and Marjorie Beals, who were with the Goehrings in the ABWE missionary candidate class of 1961. Doctors Ralph and Lucy Ankenman arrived during that time, and the Goehrings were able to meet the ship bringing yet another couple from their candidate class. During the trip back upriver, the family shared happy memories of a delightful Christmas including the children taking part in a Christmas program with other MKs (missionary kids).

# Chapter Twenty-three

# Second Year at Hebron

A Bible conference for the new Tipperah believers throughout the hills was top priority. Since they were still few in number, meeting together with other believers would encourage
them in their newfound faith. A service was also planned for
those who desired to follow Christ in baptism. The invitation for
the conference was sent with the Bible school students to the villages scattered throughout the Chittagong Hill Tracts. When the
Hebron missionaries returned after Christmas, they learned
rumors had circulated throughout the hills that the missionaries
planned to give away food and clothing. All day long on
December 31, groups of Tipperah men, women, and children
poured into the compound. The Goehrings never dreamed such
a crowd would come. Harry scrambled all day trying to organize
sleeping mats, cooking pans, and food.

Benu Pundit and Khoka Sen had not yet returned, so Harry
was the only man there. By evening, over 360 people had arrived.
Most were from the Tipperah tribe, although about 70 were Mru
tribal people. Every available sleeping space was taken—under
the house being constructed, in a tent, on the Goehrings' veranda, and in the Bible school building.

That first night, Ancherai and other Tipperahs preached.
Though many had come for a handout, God brought them to
hear the gospel of Jesus Christ. The missionaries felt as Peter did:
we don't have silver and gold, but what we do have is of far more
worth, and we will share that with you.

Harry was relieved on January 1 when Gene Gurganus arrived with a group of missionaries from Chittagong. Khoka Sen
and Benu Pundit also returned from their Christmas vacation.
When the tribals learned this wasn't a big giveaway program,
some left, but many stayed and heard the gospel.

On January 3, 1964, Ancherai, Gene, and Harry interviewed
50 people, of whom 41 were baptized in the river that afternoon.
Khoka Sen baptized Ancherai, who then baptized his wife and 39
others. He shook with cold but kept going. What a great and
blessed day—the baptism of the first Tipperah converts!

The first Bible conference for tribals was over. The tribal
people returned to their villages throughout the hills, and the
missionaries from Chittagong traveled downriver, heading home.
Life settled back into the normal routine at Hebron. Harry continued constructing the house, overseeing the tribal Bible school,
and learning Bengali, as well as interacting as often as possible
with the villagers. Nancy taught the children, continued studying
Bengali, and accompanied Lynn Silvernale when she visited the
nearby villages or had classes in her home.

One night, Harry surprised Nancy by asking, "How would
you like to go to a Tipperah village tomorrow?" The Goehrings
had been invited to the wedding of Rundaha's son in Goli Rum,
the first Christian wedding in the village. Goli Rum was one of
the nearer Tipperah villages, and the path was not as difficult as
most.

The Goehring family, along with Lynn and several Bible
school students, left the next morning after the fog lifted and the
sun came out. It was a clear, warm, winter day. Bible school students carried Faith and Joyanne; Harold was determined to walk.
He started off at a slow trot to keep up with the adults and managed to continue the pace the entire two-and-a-half-hour trek as
the paths crossed and recrossed the same shallow stream.

When Rundaha saw the hikers, he formed a singing welcoming committee on both sides of the trail entering the village.

The villagers were delighted to see the entire Goehring family had come to the wedding. The *Karbari* (headman) invited them into his house. The group climbed the notched log steps up to the veranda of his bamboo home, which was on stilts. After resting a bit, they were honored with a feast of chicken and hawk curry. Any kind of meat was a real delicacy in that village.

At about 1:00 p.m., Tipperahs began congregating in the bamboo chapel for the Tipperah version of a Christian wedding. There were to have been two marriages, but one of the brides was so shy she ran off into the jungle to hide. One couple was married that day. Mats forming a "T" were placed before the pulpit, and the bride and groom knelt before the assembled guests. The groom had a fresh haircut, skin greased with coconut oil, and was wearing a new loincloth and white jacket. The bride wore a new skirt and blouse. Khoka Sen had instructed Ancherai concerning "proper" Christian wedding procedures the night before. During the ceremony, Khoka read from Ephesians 5, 1 Peter 3:1–7, and 1 John 4. Ancherai directed his comments on these passages toward the bride and groom. Finishing his remarks, he forced the groom to place a set of rings into the bride's hand. Both the bride and groom looked extremely shy. The bride knelt with eyes downcast and tears running down her cheeks. Harry and Nancy wondered if the bride was forced into this marriage, since she literally had been dragged into the church by two older ladies and now was in tears. When they asked about this, Khoka Sen explained this was all according to custom. It would be improper in their culture for the bride and groom to seem happy about getting married, for then it would appear they were eager to leave their childhood homes.

After the service, Harry took pictures of the bride and groom and gave gifts. Then the trekkers had to start back to Hebron to make it home before nightfall. Harold's legs gave out after hiking nine miles, and he had to be carried the last mile home. It certainly had been a wonderful excursion, and what a joy it had been to witness the first Christian wedding.

Every two or three months, the Hebron missionaries made a trip down to Chittagong for supplies unavailable at their remote station. Building supplies had to be purchased in Chittagong and sent up to Hebron by country boat. Food supplies were also purchased in the city. For example, they would buy over 100 eggs to store in the kerosene refrigerator, because eggs at Hebron could only be bought one or two at a time by walking through the nearby village and asking at each house if anyone had eggs to sell. Nancy canned vegetables and fruits not available at Hebron.

While in Chittagong, the Hebron missionaries attended field council meetings with the other ABWE missionaries. During the dry season, getting to and from Chittagong was a long trip, because sandbars made it impossible to use the boat's engine on the Matamahari River. The group was confined in the small canoe for up to six hours, then rode in a bus on the bumpy single lane road for three more hours.

Most trips were uneventful, but on one, Joyanne leaned over to splash some water on her face and fell into the river. Harry was poling the canoe from the rear of the boat, and his back was toward her. When he heard the splash, he dove into the river after her. Though the river was shallow in most spots, she had fallen into a deep place where the water was over her head. Harry managed to rescue her before Nancy, who was in the covered part of the boat with the baby, realized what had happened. From that time on, the children always had to wear life jackets, even when the river was low.

During the six months of basically dry weather, when it was impossible to run the boat's engine, poling up or down the river was exceedingly slow and tedious. There was also the underlying question, "What would we do if a missionary or local resident had a medical emergency and had to be evacuated?"

With designated gifts, the Goehrings purchased a flat-bottom boat powered by a Lycoming aircraft engine and propeller.

The boat was called an AirCat®, and the advertisement for this vessel read:

"Over land, sea, muck, or mire
It goes like a cat with its tail on fire."

The AirCat® was a seven-day wonder to people living along the banks of the Matamahari River. They had never seen—or heard—a car, motorcycle, or airplane. At first, as Captain Harry steered from his chair perched high above the water, people, cows, and goats scurried to safety. Eventually, curiosity got the best of them, and villagers ran to wave and greet the missionaries and their visitors en route to Hebron at what, to the villagers, was lightning speed.

Harry left from Chittagong on his second trek into the Shangu hills in March 1964. Gene Gurganus and Dr. Ralph Ankenman went with him. They trekked through virgin forests and huge bamboo clumps and over challenging mountain trails. This time Harry was well, and, as an outdoorsman, enjoyed every minute of it. They had gone once again to enlist tribals from each village to come as students for the new term of Bible school. On this visit, they witnessed the baptism of 21 believers who had trusted Christ through the witness of the headman in another village. The infant church among the Tipperahs was growing.

After returning to Hebron, Harry, with village helpers, kept making good progress on the house. Monsoon season was coming, and they needed to move before it arrived. In early April, a storm hit. Harry and Nancy found water was gushing in under their kitchen door. Both of them started mopping as fast as they could, but it was coming in faster than they could mop. When the storm stopped half an hour later, there was about an inch of water in all of the rooms of the house but one. One house in the nearby village was destroyed, and others lost part of their grass roofing. The Goehrings thanked the Lord for safety, but realized the urgency to move to higher ground.

Moving day, April 22, was picturesque. Nine Tipperahs, in their loincloths and tucked-in *longis* (skirts), carried everything piece by piece, box by box, and drawer by drawer, up the quarter-mile footpath between the houses. By late suppertime everything was moved, and not one thing had been broken. Lynn Silvernale kept the children throughout the day, so that both Harry and Nancy could concentrate on getting settled into their house. Nancy wrote home, "We're now settled in and glad to be up where we get the breezes. The trimmings still have to be put on, but the house is livable, and we are already enjoying the lovely patter of rain on the tin roof. So the monsoons cannot be far off."

Every market day, many tribal people passed by on the footpath in front of the Goehrings' new home. They were welcome to drink water from the new tube well and rest a bit. Often they would stop to rest. As they rested, Harold played Gospel Recordings records on a hand-cranked phonograph. While the tribal people drank from their well, the Goehrings prayed that, as they listened to the Word, the tribal people would drink of the water that would never run dry. Many people said, "Please come to our village and tell us about Jesus. We heard it's the way of peace and joy."

In his diary entry for June 14, Harry wrote, "The Lord has been dealing with our hearts here individually and has laid upon our hearts to pray each morning. Lynn came from her home at 6:15 a.m., and we prayed for 15 minutes. We read Philippians 4:5–7." This was the beginning of early morning prayer meetings when Lynn, Harry, and Nancy poured out their hearts to God. They often sang a favorite hymn, "Unto the hills around do I lift up my longing eyes."

A week or so later, Harry wrote, "Reading Isobel Kuhn's books has made us wonder what it will take of us to break through the hearts of the Bengalis here. What *kind* of sacrifice?" The Hebron missionaries were heavily burdened for Bengalis in the neighboring villages around them—Hindus, Buddhists, Muslims—all seemed so closed to the gospel of Jesus Christ. Although the village people did not want their message, they would tell the missionaries when they returned from their Chittagong trips, "We are glad you are back. It's very dark when you are gone." As of this time, no one in these villages had openly believed in Christ.

Language study consumed much of their time as their first-year Bengali exam approached. They both hoped to take their exam in August, along with the class studying in Chittagong. Trips to Chittagong for supplies and meetings, building and moving into the house, and treks into the tribal villages had all interrupted their language study. Yet Nancy would begin teaching Harold first grade in September and wanted to have passed that language hurdle before his school year began. So they were spending long hours in concentrated study that rainy season. Lynn taught the children for a couple of hours each day during the last month before the exam, so she could spend more hours in reviewing. Harry and Nancy were thrilled to pass their first-year exam one year to the day after their arrival in Chittagong. That night, they also celebrated their first-year anniversary of arriving in Chittagong with Donn and Kitty Ketcham.

The Goehrings went back to Hebron with lighter hearts. Now both of them began their second year of Bengali language study. Harry had slowed his pace so Nancy could finish the first year of study with him. Now he forged ahead at his own pace. Nancy taught the children and continued studying Bengali. Every day she enjoyed being at Hebron even more. She and Harry talked together often of the wonderful privilege God had given them to serve at Hebron and work with the tribal people. They would not have traded places with anyone in the world.

Harry oversaw the second year of tribal Bible school that year. Each evening after the formal classes were over, he sat on the woven mats with the students and Ancherai. The students would ask questions. Sitting by the lamplight, Harry would try to answer, and Ancherai would translate from Bengali to Tipperah. One evening someone asked what kind of bodies we would have in heaven. When Harry opened the Scriptures and explained to them, Ancherai exclaimed, "What you just shared with us is worth more than thousands and thousands of *rupees* (the monetary unit of Pakistan)!"

As often as possible, Harry traveled to tribal villages with Ancherai to share the good news of salvation. They looked forward to the day when Ancherai, whom the missionaries called "the apostle Paul of the Hill Tracts," returned from his preaching tours in the tribal villages high in the Chittagong Hill Tracts. He would arrive with a big smile that lit up his whole face and greet Harry with an enthusiastic handshake. Ancherai said, "*Namascar, bhai* (Hello, brother). I'm empty. Teach me more, so I can go back and teach my people." The two men would sit together for hours as Harry taught Ancherai from the Word of God. Then Ancherai left for another preaching circuit, anticipating what God was going to do among his people.

Sometimes the tribal people came to Hebron, as Harry tells in a *Message* article, "An Amazing Interview With Murungs":

> How often I had heard of these primitive people living far back in the inaccessible jungle hills of East Pakistan. Four sullen-faced men, their reddish-brown bodies clothed only in loincloths, watched curiously as Jay Walsh and I drifted slowly past in our country boat.
>
> Their curiosity was no greater than ours was. How interesting they were with their long black hair tied in a knot on one side of their head. Beautiful jungle orchids decorated the lobes of their ears and red paint was smeared on their cheeks. These were primitive Murungs.
>
> For several months they had serious sickness in their village. These men had come a full-day's trek to the banks of the Shangu River, there to make intercession to one of their gods.

On the altar of woven bamboo lay the skull of a goat. Blood splattered the ground, their attempt to appease the anger of the god.

With this experience as a background, how much more amazing becomes this recent encounter when ten men in loincloths strode briskly into our yard. All had the typical knot of hair on the side of the head and on their backs were carrying woven baskets, suspended from their foreheads by pieces of vine.

With the help of our cook I was able to communicate with these Murungs. They claimed to be Christians who were without rice. They had heard that we were giving out rice to those in need. I explained that we had received a supply of relief goods from the government, but this had been distributed. They seemed content and left the house.

Through the remainder of the afternoon we noticed that they were still on the property. They heard that Ancherai, the Tipperah evangelist, was coming, and hoped to communicate their need more satisfactorily through him.

When Ancherai came, he said that he had met these men in the bazaar. They had told him that they were Christians and had no rice. Ancherai had shared our suspicion that these Murungs were merely saying they were Christians in order to get rice. Therefore, he had asked them, "You say you are Christians, but where are your *Jesus Houses* in your villages?"

Pointing to his heart, one quickly answered, "This is my Jesus House. You Tipperahs all have *Jesus Houses* in your villages. Does that mean you will all go to heaven? You could have three Jesus Houses in your village but if your heart is not a Jesus House you would not go to heaven."

A surprised Ancherai hung his head. Later he asked, "If you are Christians, where is your offering to the Lord?"

They replied, "You have never taught us about an offering to the Lord. If you will teach us, next year we will bring our offerings."

Amazed by this report, I determined that in the evening

I would meet with these men and quiz them further concerning their faith. As I approached the house that evening, what a sight greeted my eyes. There was Ancherai seated in one corner of the veranda with two other Tipperah Christians by him. Before him were the ten Murungs. He was reading from Romans and said he wanted to preach. Before he began, I suggested we ask them a few questions.

Turning to the Murung who seemed to be the leader, I started talking to him in Bengali. He couldn't understand. I asked Ancherai to interpret my questions. (Although Ancherai has never had a day of schooling, he speaks five languages, one of these being a dialect of Burmese which the hill people understand.) I questioned in Bengali; Ancherai interpreted in Burmese. The men discussed in Murung, and back came the answer.

The first question was, "These men say they are Christians and they believe in Jesus. Ask them who this Jesus is." One of the Murungs said something back to Ancherai, who burst out in a smile and exchanged astonished remarks in Tipperah with his friends. The Murung had simply said, "Jesus and God are one. Jesus is God's Son."

Question: "You say you believe in Jesus. Just what do you believe concerning Jesus?" The answer was longer, and again Ancherai responded with a laugh of joy. They had said, "Jesus is in heaven. But when we believe in Jesus, He comes from heaven down to earth and lives in our hearts."

Question: "What did Jesus do for you?" One answered, "I was a sinner. When I believed on Jesus, He gave me new life."

Question: "What did Jesus do for your sin?" Reply: "Jesus died on the cross for my sin."

Question: "Do you now have a new life?" Reply: "I was a sinner and Jesus took the old man away from me and gave me new life. I used to offer sacrifices to idols, drink liquor, and do other sinful things. Now I no longer do these things. I used to have a *dead life,* but now I have a *living life* and have joy in my heart."

I was shocked by the insight of these primitive men who had received no teaching from missionaries. Question: "Do you have friends who do not believe in Jesus? What will happen to them?" With real emphasis, the spokesman stated, "Many times I have preached to my friends, but if they do not believe, what can I do? I am not Jesus. I cannot give to them salvation myself. If they will not believe, then there will be a *separation* between us and them!"

How amazingly accurate were his words in describing what would happen in the Day of Judgment! I could hardly believe my ears, and I asked Ancherai how these people had learned these things. He said that from time to time while he was touring from village to village, he would stop overnight in this village and preach. He then went on to say, "Certainly God lives in their hearts, and God Himself has been teaching them these things." How amazing is the work of the Holy Spirit of God amongst a people who have little opportunity to learn, but have simple faith to *believe*!"

By June 1965, Harry was scheduled to take his final Bengali exam before starting to learn Tipperah, then he hoped to translate the Bible for the Tipperah people. At that point, there were no other missionaries on the horizon to translate Scriptures for any of the main tribal language groups of the Chittagong Hill Tracts. Undaunted, Harry told Nancy that if the Lord didn't send others to help in the translation work, perhaps he, like William Carey, would need to translate the Scriptures into several tribal languages.

Nancy felt at home now in East Pakistan, and enjoyed her relationship with the village women. As they came to fill their water pots at the well near their house, the women often stopped to visit. She looked forward to designing primers to help teach tribal people to read. Everything seemed to point forward to a wonderful and fruitful ministry working with tribal people in East Pakistan.

# Chapter Twenty-four

# God Knows What Is Best

In the Goehrings' June 1965 prayer letter, Harry told the following account:

"Sahib, a Mogh chief wants you to tell him of Jesus." I had noticed this man with others of his village who were in the Tipperah village I was visiting. Finding he could speak some Bengali, we squatted in a circle and I illustrated the gospel using a stick and the soft earth. Oh, that language barrier! Having never heard of Jesus before, this chief could not understand even the simplest of gospel terms in Bengali.

Thank God for Ancherai. A few days later, he and I made the 30-mile trip to that Mogh village by AirCat®. For nearly five hours, broken only by a chicken curry supper, Ancherai told the gospel story using the Mogh language. The interest was intense even among women smoking their home-rolled cigars.

The chief was definitely interested but was counting the cost of turning from Buddhism. He voiced the often-asked, soul-chilling question, "If I become a Christian, will the mission help me (meaning financial help)?" We emphasized we will gladly give him the news of eternal life, but nothing more.

Later that week we were amazed to find this Mogh chief and several Tipperah Christians sitting on our porch. The chief spoke, "I have come to hear more of Jesus. I don't want anything else. Just help me to become a Christian."

Sensing his earnestness, I sat with him in the shade of a tree and slowly and simply retold the gospel. This time, with the background of Ancherai's preaching in his own language, he began to understand. I met with this group of men again in the evening. After more teaching and questioning, right there in front of his Tipperah companions, he bowed his head and said his first simple prayer to the true and living God, "I am a sinner. Please save me from my sin and give me a new life. I want Jesus Christ to be my Savior. Amen."

Until that day, the door to the 50,000 Moghs had seemed closed. Now that door has begun to crack. Here are babes in Christ. Someone must raise them to manhood in the faith. Pray fervently that young men will meet the challenge of these tribes.

Harry and Nancy were also concerned about Bilchuri, the Buddhist village closest to the Hebron compound. Harry read the verse in Colossians 1:24, paraphrasing Paul's words, "But part of my work is to suffer for you; and I am glad because I am helping to finish the remainder of Christ's suffering for His body, the church." As Harry and Nancy discussed this verse, relating it to the people in the nearby village whose eyes were so blind to the gospel, Harry said, "Dear, I wonder just how much the Lord would have us suffer in order that these people may become part of Christ's body?"

On June 9, 1965, Harry began running a fever. At first no one was alarmed; sudden fevers were not unusual. The children had contracted a variety of illnesses as they adjusted to East Pakistan. By late that night, however, Harry's fever spiked and wouldn't go down. Jean Weld, the nurse who now ran the clinic at Hebron, did not know what else to do to help him. There was no means of communication from Hebron. Ham radios were not allowed in the country; the only telephone, over a mile away at the Lama market, was out of order when Jean attempted to use it. Neither Nancy nor Jean had learned to operate the AirCat®. The only way to get word to the mission doctors was to send a messenger. Abra, a young man from the local village, was chosen to carry a letter to the ABWE doctors in Chittagong (the hospital was not yet built, and the medical staff were studying language in Chittagong). Abra walked several hours until he reached the road, where he caught a bus that arrived in Chittagong late that night.

Through the day, as Abra was making his trip, Harry's condition worsened as those at Hebron anxiously awaited help. Nancy bathed her husband with cool water and tried to find ways to comfort him. He loved music and expressed a desire to hear some. Nancy found a tape of his friend Jim Reese singing in his rich baritone voice. She put it on the Wollensack® battery-powered, reel-to-reel tape recorder. As the tape began to play, Nancy wished she had checked the songs first. They were all about heaven, about laying burdens down. Nancy inwardly cringed and cried out to God, "No, Lord, not this." She wanted comfort that Harry would get well. As Nancy looked back later, she realized God was gently trying to prepare her for what was ahead.

Harry had another difficult night. He begged to be put in a tub of cold water, but that didn't seem to help. At the break of dawn, Drs. Donn Ketcham and Ralph Ankenman walked up the path from Lama Bazar. As soon as the messenger had arrived in Chittagong the night before, the pair began the difficult trip to Hebron. When Donn saw Harry's condition, he said he would have to be evacuated to Chittagong. Donn supervised getting Harry to the AirCat®, and Nancy got the family packed and locked up the house. She thought as she left how different this was than the time they left before, when they so carefully put everything under lock and key. She remembered thinking, *I don't care if the whole place walks off, if only Harry gets better.*

For three days, four doctors and four nurses worked feverishly to help Harry, who lay in the medical clinic in Jeannie Lockerbie's house. The medical team determined his kidneys had shut down and were talking of evacuating him to the U. S., since the equipment needed was not available in East Pakistan.

Nancy and the children stayed across a lane at the Olsens' apartment, and often walked over to be with Harry. On one visit,

Nancy read Ephesians chapter one at Harry's request. The children were restless after a while. Nancy decided to take them back to Vic and Joan Olsen's home for lunch and a nap. After lunch, Nancy had settled the children for rest time when Vic told Nancy, "Harry is failing rapidly." Nancy felt as though someone had plunged a sword deep in her heart. She cried out to God in utter helplessness, "Lord, I am not ready for this. Please prepare my heart." She turned to the paraphrase of Philippians and picked up where she left off. As she read, it was as though the Lord's presence permeated the room. "For to me, living means opportunities for Christ and dying, well, that is better yet" (Philippians 1:21). It was as though the Lord encircled her in His arms and whispered, "Nancy, I am taking Harry now." God's peace and comfort swept over her as she whispered, "It's okay, Lord, he's yours."

Nancy read on, and what she read sounded the way Harry would have instructed her had he had the opportunity, knowing that he was leaving her behind. "But whatever happens to me, remember always to live as Christians should, so, whether I ever see you again or not, I will keep on hearing good reports that you are standing side by side with one strong purpose, to tell the Good News fearlessly, no matter what your enemies may do. They will see this as a sign of their downfall, but for you it will be a clear sign from God that He is with you and that He has given you eternal life with Him. For to you has been given the privilege not only of trusting Him, but also of suffering for Him."

This excerpt from *Daktar/Diplomat in Bangladesh* details the situation:

> Harry was gravely ill. After examining him, findings indicated that Harry's kidneys were so terribly damaged (presumably by infection), they had shut down completely. Overnight, in response to treatment, Harry's temperature dropped dramatically from 104° to 100° and he felt somewhat better. His

kidneys, however, remained steadfastly shut down throughout the day. During the night, however, small quantities of urine began to flow and tenderness over the kidneys decreased.

Early the following morning, Dr. Ralph Ankenman flew to Dhaka to obtain chemical tests on Harry's blood and bring back materials for peritoneal dialysis, which we would use, if necessary, to help remove waste products from Harry's blood until his kidneys could do the job again. At midmorning, Harry took a turn for the worse. Over several hours his condition continued to deteriorate. His strong heart was failing. The medical team applied every conceivable treatment but Harry died.

As the medical staff and missionaries prayed in the living room next to the clinic, Ralph returned from Dhaka with the equipment in hand. Just then, at 3:30 p.m., Vic stepped out of the room where Harry lay and said, "Harry is gone." Vic then walked across to his house and told Nancy that Harry was with the Lord.

Though the pain was intense, God gave comfort. Now Nancy needed to tell her children their daddy had gone to heaven. Faith, only two, wanted Daddy to come back. He often went away to the hills, but he always came back. When Nancy explained he couldn't, Faith responded, "Then let's go there!" Harold responded with brave realism. He wanted to go and see his daddy's body one more time. Joyanne, then five and a real Daddy's girl, in tears said, "I don't want to see Daddy's body. I want to remember my daddy just the way he was." It was hard for Nancy to think of her precious children being without their wonderful daddy. Their daddy, who romped and played with them, their daddy who, with great fascination could take a leaf from a tree and show them all its parts, who would pick up things along the beach at Cox's Bazar and tell them all about them. Now, they would miss all his fun, instruction, and wonderful love.

Nancy realized Hebron would have to close because, as a mother with three small children, she would be more of a liability than an asset to the cause of Christ in East Pakistan. She realized she would have to say goodbye to the ministry among the tribal people that was going so well. The key to that ministry was gone; the translator was missing.

That night she read the children a story that quoted a verse: "You must go to your own country now, but do not be afraid for I will go with you." She quoted that verse, inserting each child's name. She said, "Harold, you must go to your own country now, but do not be afraid. God will go with you." Then she inserted Joyanne's name and finally Faith's. She felt God led her to that Bible story that night.

At the first opportunity Nancy had to be alone, she had a deep desire to read Ephesians 1, the chapter Harry had requested the morning of his death. Nancy read that, even before He made the world, God chose us to be His very own. She thought, *I no longer have Harry's love down here, but I am still covered with the love of God. How wonderful!* She read in Ephesians 1:5 that God's unchanging plan has always been to adopt us into His own family by sending Jesus Christ to die for us, and He did this because He wanted to. Nancy thought, *I never wanted to give up the one I love most. But God willingly gave up His beloved one for me that I might have life. What amazing love this God has for me that He would give up His beloved one.* Verse 8 caught her attention, as she considered that God showered down upon us the richness of His grace, and He understands us and knows what is best for us at all times. *How well He understands me,* she thought, *and knows what is best for me all of the time.*

Nancy talked to the Lord, "This surely isn't what I thought was best, but You understand me more than I understand myself. You know what is best for me. Help me to believe You in this." From verse 11 she realized that all things happen just as God decided long ago. Nancy thought, *Lord, this didn't take You by surprise the way it did me. When You called us to East Pakistan, it seems*

*this is what You planned. All things—including this very hard thing—
happened just as You decided long ago.* Had God not given Nancy
this verse, she knew she would have felt Satan had won a victory
by causing a mission station to close and setting back the Bible
translation by many years. Instead, Nancy was convinced God
was still in control and would somehow be glorified through taking Harry home to heaven at the age of 32. Although the tribal
people would have to wait for the Scriptures in their language,
God would continue to work among them.

She also read verses 19–21: "I pray that you will begin to
understand how incredibly great His power is to help those who
believe Him. It is the same mighty power that raised Christ from
the dead and seated Him at the place of honor at God's right
hand in heaven, far, far above any other king or ruler or dictator
or leader. Yes, His honor is far more glorious than that of anyone
else, either in this world or the world to come."

Nancy responded to God, "Lord, your power has been
incredibly great today. You gave me peace—the peace that passes
all understanding. Lord, I just knew that if anything like this
every happened to me, I would completely fall apart. I would
never be able to be a testimony for You in a time like this. And
yet, Lord, I have your peace. You have given your grace. You have
given your strength. Lord, truly your power is incredibly great to
help those who believe You. Lord, it is the same power that raised
Christ from the dead and seated Him at your right hand. Lord,
help me to believe You in the days ahead. Help me to draw on
this power you have promised me."

Plans were soon under way for Harry's memorial service, as
in that climate he had to be buried within 24 hours. ABWE and
other missionaries, friends from many countries, and local believers made floral arrangements and traveled the 65 miles to
Malumghat. At Nancy's request, Harry's body was laid to rest
under the beautiful gurjun trees on the hospital property. The
service was simple and beautiful.

The gravestone reads:

### HARRY DALE GOEHRING
16 April, 1933–16 June, 1965
"WITH CHRIST"
Mark 8:34,35

Dr. Olsen continued the account,

> Several days later the microscope slides taken from specimens and cultures confirmed that Harry's kidneys had been shattered, not by infection, but by some toxic substance. But where had it come from? A minute, careful, extensive, prolonged investigation of every factor surrounding his illness and death failed to answer that mysterious question.
>
> (Olsen, Viggo B. with Lockerbie, Jeanette, *Daktar/Diplomat in Bangladesh*, Moody Press, Chicago 1973, pgs. 170–171.)

The missionary team rallied around Nancy and helped her in the ensuing days. The Goehrings' equipment and belongings had to be sorted through. Instructions were given for the disposal of items left behind. Nancy packed a few bags to carry with her, and co-workers packed the few possessions that would be shipped to the United States. As Nancy sorted through everything in their home, many villagers came to express their sorrow. The Lord gave Nancy numerous opportunities to share with her Buddhist neighbors the wonderful assurance she had that Harry was in heaven. The village carpenter, who helped build their home, said, "I have much sorrow in my heart for Goehring Sahib. He built this home and now he can't live in it." Nancy was able to share with him the fact that Harry is in a much better, more beautiful home than this one. "That is the home where Jesus is. Jesus had made a beautiful home for him up in heaven. But I have much sorrow in my heart for you, because you still do not have a home in heaven. You need to trust Jesus' death alone to save you from your sin, so that you too can have a home in heaven."

Years later, a young man in Hebron came to Nancy and quoted her very words back to her, and then he stated, "I am a believer and have a home in heaven."

Donna Ahlgrim flew back to the U.S. with Nancy and the children. They were met in Chicago by Dr. Paul Jackson, who represented the ABWE mission board, and Nancy's family. Once more Nancy returned to the farmhouse where she had grown up. Her mother opened her home to Nancy and her children. This was where she would spend the next few years. God's promises and His faithfulness would become more precious to her in the days ahead.

### A Tribute To Harry Goehring
### From His Fellow Missionaries
(Reported in the *Message*, September 1965)
*"These all died in faith . . . "* Hebrews 11:13.

Harry Goehring came to East Pakistan in August 1963 with the confidence that this missionary service was God's way, with the consecration to do God's will, and with a commitment to follow the principles of God's Word. It was our privilege as a group of missionaries to work with him as he "ran with patience the race that was set before" him. Certain things of Harry's life commend themselves to us now as we think of the brief 22 months of service God allotted to him here.

Harry made it his primary concern "to be about His Father's business."

It is easy to become side-tracked in this land and to major on minors. But during the "minor" task of building a home for his family at Hebron, Harry concentrated on the major task of learning the Bengali language. We often credited his amazing success in grasping Bengali to his natural language ability, but the truth was he disciplined himself to spend hours in language study.

Harry met the scriptural qualifications of being one of God's ministers. The standards of 1 Timothy 3 were exemplified in his life. He ruled well both himself and his own house. His discipline was firm, but guided by love.

He went about his work with an earnestness that produced results. Usually a missionary is not able to accomplish much in his first term. By the time language study is finished, it is nearly time for furlough. But Harry, though here less than two years, left behind a legacy in this land. He built a dwelling at Hebron, guided the Tipperah Short-Term Bible School for two years, and wrote a simple Bible doctrine course for use in the school. By these things, *"He being dead, yet speaketh."*

Harry was a man of varied qualities and he used each of them in the Lord's service. His clear baritone voice often lifted our hearts in worship to the Lord. The years spent in athletic competition had given him a strong body that could trek tirelessly in the jungle. His leadership ability was exercised in taking over the direction of the Hebron station after only three months in the country. From the beginning, his godly wisdom and genuine concern won the hearts of the people.

Our work will suffer because of the loss of Harry's abilities, but we will feel even more deeply the loss of Harry as our close friend. He approached difficult tasks and misfortunes with humor. He could romp with his children in the evenings, or get heatedly involved while playing games. We can see his broad smile of welcome and remember the hospitality he showed to visitors in the jungle.

Harry was a vital part of our team. His loss affects every one of us. But we rest all this with our God. For when a life is committed to Him, not only the steps, but also the stops are ordered by the Lord. Harry has ceased from his labors on this earth, but the sweet aroma of his life lingers on. We wait now for the day when we shall be reunited and be forever with the Lord.

East Pakistan Field Council

# Chapter Twenty-five

# God Is Always Good

Nancy was back in Indiana, but her heart was in East Pakistan. She grieved not only for her husband, but for the ministry with the tribal people they had barely begun. Yet she realized she must let God be God. A missionary friend wrote her, "A sovereign God does not owe us an explanation. You must rest in the fact that God knows best and He is in control even in those circumstances we would not choose."

At that time, Nancy read a story about a young woman who was elated over something delightful that had happened. She exclaimed, "Isn't God good!" A gentleman who had walked with the Lord many years replied, "In good or in ill, God is always good."

By September, Nancy felt she should report to their supporting churches. Although she preferred a less visible role, she found herself sharing God's amazing faithfulness with her supporters. She asked them to pray for the tribal Christians and that the Lord of the harvest would send laborers into His harvest. God protected her as she drove her little red Volkswagen. Sometimes the children went with her; other times they remained at home with Grandma. Once, while driving to a church in Endicott, New York, Nancy was unsure of its location. As she drove down the main highway, she asked the Lord to guide her. She thought she should stop at the next service station and phone the church. When she did, she discovered she was within a few blocks of her destination. That answer to prayer increased her faith that God would continue to direct her path. Nancy was able to report to all her supporting churches during her first year back. God not only gave her strength, but also gave her joy in her speaking ministry. But it was time to think about the future.

Nancy had greatly enjoyed teaching her children, using the Calvert correspondence course. She felt awed at having taught Harold to read, opening up the world of education to him. Since Nancy hadn't finished college before her marriage, she decided it would be wise to complete her degree. She prayed for clear direction from God. She believed God had called her to serve Him in missions and had not removed this call. Teaching at a missionary kids' school would give her the same schedule as her children. It would allow her to serve the cause of Christ in missions and still be a good mother. Nancy was accepted at Grace College, only 20 miles from home. She could commute, and the children could continue to attend Mentone school. Nancy found her place in McClain Chapel that first morning with feelings of sadness and misgiving. This was the same chapel where she had watched her husband graduate from seminary only a few years earlier. A lump came to her throat, and she fought back tears. Wasn't there some way she could serve in missions without three long years of study? A young man began to sing a special number written by Mrs. R. R. Forman, called "Submission." God brought peace to Nancy's heart through the words,

> Not what I wish to be, nor where I wish to go,
> For who am I that I should choose my way?
> The Lord shall choose for me. 'Tis better far, I know,
> So let Him bid me go, or stay.

Nancy wished to be in East Pakistan, but the Lord had chosen for her to finish her education. To her amazement, most of her churches determined to stand with her in financial support and prayer.

Those years at Grace College were a time of learning and growing for Nancy, who had led a sheltered life. From her moth-

# The GOEHRING Family

Harry as a young boy

On their wedding day

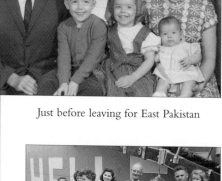

Just before leaving for East Pakistan

Harry's graduation day, with Harry's
mother and Nancy's mother

Russ (holding Joyanne)
prior to his friend Harry's
departure

Nancy's class of
mountain children

Tribal visitors to Hebron

The Goehrings in Hebron

Harry heading upriver with
Khoka Sen and evangelist
Ancherai

Harry's grave site

Nancy with the
children in Indiana

# The EBERSOLE Family
## (Russ & Nancy)

Russ with his five children,
just before visiting Nancy
in Indiana in 1968

Hijacked to China

Entire family
in Loyola
Heights in
1973

Wedding day, June 1969

Nancy visiting a village home in
Bangladesh in 1972

Russ preaching in Thailand with
Roberto Geguillana, first PABWE
missionaries

Part of the Second
Baptist Church in
Oradea, Romania

Visit to China

Russ and Nancy, December 1976

*Gospel Launch* taking
campers to "Treasure
Island"

Russ and his mother,
Sue Ebersole

er's care, she came under her husband's protection. Harry, with his German background, did not want an independent wife, and Nancy, who had never lived on her own, could adjust easily to Harry's wishes. Yet, he was loving in his protectiveness and never made decisions without considering Nancy's desires. The shock of suddenly being on her own, depending on the Lord alone, was a great learning experience for Nancy. Now she must make plans for her family and carry them out. She must schedule her time wisely. She had to keep track of family finances. She alone had the final say in guiding and disciplining the children. She was so thankful for Harry's loving firmness and consistent discipline, because it had borne fruit in respectful and obedient children. But as any parent knows, that loving firmness must continue. Nancy had depended heavily on Harry in this area. Now he was gone, and she could never say, "Honey, I am at my wits' end. You take over."

Nancy learned what it meant to depend on God for help with the children. After disciplining one of the children, she saw the child frequently was not repentant for wrong-doing. Nancy would go to her bedroom and fall on her knees and pray, "Lord, you promised to be a Father to the fatherless. You had better keep Your promise to my little girl right now. Please work in her heart. I don't know what else to say or do." On several occasions, just minutes after praying, that child came to Nancy and repentantly said, "I am sorry, Mommy, for being bad."

By the time Nancy graduated from college, she was a far more independent woman than the one who had entered three years before. In a sense, however, she was not independent at all. These were years of total dependence on God.

Though our sovereign God owes us no explanations, He does at times, in His mercy, pull the curtain aside and give us a peek at some of His purposes.

God showed some of His purposes soon after Harry's home-going; other ways in which God used Harry's death were not revealed at this time—they would be revealed many years later.

God used the last hours of Harry's life to draw Promilla, a Hindu woman, to Himself. As Harry's medical colleagues feverishly labored over him, Debindra Das, a new believer from Hinduism, was ironing in the hallway outside the medical clinic where Harry was struggling for his last breaths. Debindra was amazed at the peace Harry manifested and at his lack of fear. He had never seen a Christian die. Later that day, Debindra said to his wife, Promilla, "I was ironing clothes in that hallway. I could see Goehring Sahib through the open door. I watched his face. I watched him die. Goehring Sahib died peacefully. That is what it's like for a Christian to die. Not like when Hindus die. You know how our people die." Fearing death, Promilla asked the Lord to save her because of the simple testimony of a Christian's peaceful homegoing. Promilla was the first fruits of a death that seemed so untimely.

Debindra and Promilla served the Lord faithfully and reared their children in a godly way. Today, their older son, Bidhu, directs the Bible Correspondence School in Dhaka, Bangladesh. Their younger son, Nidhu, opened a Bible Correspondence School in Grand Rapids, Michigan, as an outreach to the thousands of Bengali-speakers in North America.

Within a year or so of Harry's death, many young couples, who had known him, soberly evaluated their lives, asking if they were really counting for Christ. One was Harry's cousin Jim Sutton, and his wife, Nancy. Jim left his secular job and began working for Moody Press, a leading Christian publisher.

Others were challenged to yield their lives for missionary service in East Pakistan, which was a specific answer to Nancy's prayers. One of these was a widower, Willard Benedict. He married Donna Alhgrim, the young woman who accompanied Nancy and her children back to the States. Another was George Weber, who met his wife, Shirley, at ABWE's candidate classes. Both of these couples later served at Hebron.

Many years after Harry had died, Nancy returned to Bangladesh for a ministry of encouragement to ABWE's missionaries serving in that land. While there, a Bengali man named Daniel asked to talk to Nancy. After a few minutes of small talk, he told this story: Daniel had come to faith in Christ many years before. He had actually "borrowed" without permission a Bible which had been given to Menindro, a man serving as a cook at Malumghat. Daniel had seen the black book and was curious about what it said. When the cook was working, Daniel would slip into the bamboo house where Menindro kept his Bible and borrow it. He did this for several days. As Daniel read the Bible, he became convicted of his sins, and one day fell on his knees before the Bible, crying, "Lord Jesus, Lord Jesus, save me! Save me!"

When Daniel obtained his own Bible, he began to be persecuted, harassed, and heckled. After his baptism, he was severely beaten and exiled to Kutubeia, an island in the Bay of Bengal. After three months of exile, he was able to escape and came back to the hospital. But that did not end the persecution. He suffered numerous beatings. His life was threatened time and again. At one time he was rescued just as a vicious man was about to cut his tongue out. In all these persecutions, he remained true to his faith in Christ.

He then told Nancy a part of his story she had never known. When his persecution was most intense, he noticed the cross and memorial stone on Harry Goehring's grave. He asked Dr. Olsen what that cross and stone meant. Dr. Olsen explained that it marked the burial place of a young man who had given his life to bring the Good News of the message of Christ's love to the people of East Pakistan.

From that point on, whenever Daniel was enduring great persecution, he would go to Harry's grave and say to himself, *"This young man died that the people of my country could come to Christ. I have not yet suffered to the point of death."* God used that marker to give him courage to go on in the faith. Nancy had not known until then what part Harry's death had played in strengthening that young believer's courage during his years of greatest testing.

Daniel endured many years of testing, and still stands firm. Several of his children are committed followers of Jesus Christ. His son, Theophil, is a professor at the Baptist Bible College of Bangladesh and a church leader. Donna, his daughter, is a young woman with a great heart for evangelism. She helped translate the "Jesus" film into the Chittagonian dialect. She also has been a language teacher and helper for new missionaries. Philip, another son, is a medic in the hospital, with a great heart for God. Baby, the youngest, has been a wonderful help as a language instructor.

Nancy thanked God that He used Harry's memorial stone and the testimony of his purpose in life to help a persecuted Christian stay true through great adversity.

# Chapter Twenty-six

# God's Amazing Ways

God's hand was working in another matter during those years of furlough ministry and college. Even to this day, Nancy says, "It was the Lord's doing, and it is marvelous in our eyes." Not long after Harry's homegoing, during a time of reading and meditating on God's Word, a strong, almost tangible thought came to Nancy. The thought troubled her greatly. She pondered this and wondered if it was from God. The thought was this: *Russ needs you now.* This brought no emotional response, except to reflect that either this is from God, or I am the most horrible person in the world. How could I ever have such a thought at this time?

Russ Ebersole and Harry Goerhing became friends as soon as they met in a missionary conference at Brunswick Baptist Church in Gary, Indiana. They were kindred spirits who felt as though they had always known one another. When the Goerhings sailed for East Pakistan, Russ came to New York to say goodbye. Harry and Russ corresponded between the Philippines and East Pakistan. When Gene's cancer recurred, the Goehrings prayed earnestly for the Ebersoles.

Nancy never met Gene, but became concerned for her. So much so that one day, as she and Harry were studying Bengali, Nancy began to cry. Harry asked, "What's wrong, honey?"

Nancy answered, "I was thinking about Gene Ebersole; if God does not heal her, she will leave her children behind before they are grown. I don't think God could ask anything more difficult of a mother."

Harry replied, "Let's pray for her right now." So the couple left their Bengali books on the table and knelt beside their bed. They prayed God would heal her if it was His will. But if it wasn't, that God would especially give Gene grace to face leaving her five children behind. The Goehrings prayed even more earnestly for Russ and his children when word came that Gene's cancer had claimed her life. Harry said, "I don't know what I would ever do if I were in Russ' shoes." He identified with his friend's great loss and prayed often for him. He wrote Russ a beautiful letter of comfort, telling him he was beloved of God, and they would pray for him and his children. Only six months after writing that letter, Harry, too, entered his heavenly home.

After Harry's death, Nancy continued to pray for Russ and his family. Now she understood firsthand the pain of loneliness her husband's friend faced. Was it because she could identify with his pain that she was dealing with this disturbing thought? She prayed, "Lord, if this is from You, bring it to pass in Your time. If it is not from You, please take it from me; I want nothing to do with it." Nancy did not know Russ well; she only knew Harry thought highly of him, and she knew Harry to have keen perception into human character. So at times she thought, *If God is in this, it could be wonderful.* At other times she would think, *Eight kids! I don't think I am that nuts. I don't think I could handle that, Lord.*

After Nancy returned to her mother's home, the Mentone church held a memorial service on Sunday, July 18, 1965. Unbeknownst to Nancy, the pastor contacted Russ Ebersole to be the speaker. When she found out, this disturbed Nancy, as she was already wrestling with her troubling thoughts. She was blessed by Russ' message but relieved when he left without her having much contact with him.

A few weeks later, Nancy was the missionary speaker at Beachwood Lake Camp in southern Indiana. She and the children stayed with Jess and Joyce Eaton, who directed the camp that summer and were going to East Pakistan as missionaries. Nancy had not yet thanked Russ Ebersole for his ministry at her husband's memorial service. She thought she should do that, but felt awkward about writing. This was so much on her mind that she decided she had to talk to the Eatons. She explained the situation and asked, "Does God ever lead like that? He has never dealt with me in that way before. Do you think this idea is from God, or is it something psychological because we prayed so much for Russ and his children? Should I even write him a letter of thanks?"

Joyce's immediate response was, "I believe that thought was from God." Joyce related a couple of experiences when God had directed her in the same way. Jess was not so sure. But both Eatons felt it was proper for Nancy to thank Russ for his part in the memorial service. Nancy typed her letter and asked Jess and Joyce to read it. She wanted to be sure it was a letter he could read if Gene had been sitting beside him. Nancy felt if this thought was God's plan, He would need to work in Russ' heart in His time, and Russ should never know it from her. At times, Nancy almost succeeded in pushing the thought from her mind, but when she did, God ordained a circumstance to bring it back forcefully.

Once she was speaking to a women's group in Greensburg, Pennsylvania. Nancy shared with the women some verses God had used to strengthen and comfort her. As she finished speaking and sat down, the woman beside her leaned over and asked, "Do you know Russ Ebersole?"

Nancy was startled. She gulped, and tried to calmly and truthfully reply, "I don't know him well; my husband knew him better than I do." Nancy learned later that this woman, after reading in the *Message* magazine about Gene and Harry's homegoings, had prayed that God would lead Russ and Nancy together.

ABWE asked Russ Ebersole to become the missionary-at-large for the Far East. Nancy prayed that if God was leading them together, Russ would accept that position. That way she would remain part of the Bangladesh team of which Russ would be the administrator. By this time, more than two years had passed since Harry's death. She continued to pray about Russ, yet it was Harry she missed. One day Nancy shared with one of her married girlfriends at school how much she missed Harry's love and companionship, how much she missed the one who always believed in her on her good days or not-so-good ones, how much she missed his firm, loving hand with the children. She was driving home after that conversation and talking to the Lord. She said, "Lord, if you really do have Russ up ahead for me, could you please give me some sort of sign?"

The first thing Nancy did when she arrived home was pick up her mail from the rural mailbox. That day, the first letter she opened was from an elderly woman in Philadelphia. She had written on every bit of space on the paper, then added a post-script on a scrap of paper that looked as if it had been torn from the edge of a newspaper. When Nancy opened the letter, that scrap of paper fell out. Nancy read the words, "Where is Russ Ebersole now?" She was amazed. The next letter was from Harry's older sister, Lola, stating, "Nancy, we are praying God will give you a new life partner." Nancy bowed her head and said, "Thank you, Lord."

Nancy's only contact with Russ was the quarterly reports she sent him as her administrator. He acknowledged the reports and always took time to share something helpful from the Word of God. This, Nancy believed, was one thing God used to begin to put love in her heart for Russ. Another year passed, and still there was no indication that God was moving Russ in Nancy's direction, or in any other direction for that matter. Nancy read the book of Ruth and asked the Lord to uncover Russ's feet because she couldn't. Years later she realized this was the wrong prayer; he was such a sound sleeper, it took much more than uncovered feet to wake him up!

Toward the end of her junior year, on her way home from school one day, Nancy stopped to pick up Faith. Her friend Phyllis Kantenwein cared for Faith while Nancy attended class. Phyllis' husband, Lee, a seminary student, asked Nancy that day, "If one of the seminary guys asked you to the spring banquet, would you go?" Nancy thought a minute and said, "No, I couldn't." She realized at that moment that she felt as bound to Russ as if she wore his ring on her finger. She felt that until God provided a wife for Russ, she could not encourage any other man.

On the drive home that day, she again talked to God. "Lord, I sure am lonely. It would be so special to have a corsage and a gentleman to open a car door for me. Just to feel like a lady again for a little while instead of mother, father, and student all bound up together. Lord, could you again reassure me that Russ is somewhere up ahead?" There was a letter in the mailbox. This time it was from Russ. Only Nancy realized the importance of what the letter said. Russ hadn't a clue at that point. As he was going through his files, getting ready for a trip to the Far East, Russ came across the letter Harry had written to him when Gene went to be with the Lord. He sent Nancy a copy of that letter, realizing it would be precious to her now. The concluding sentence read, "Russ, we are praying that God will provide for *every need* for both you and your children." *"Need?"* Need, that troubling, ever pursuing thought: *Russ needs you now.* God again gave reassurance.

As the end of her junior year approached, Nancy felt responsible to let her supporting churches know the next step as soon as she could. Was God going to lead Russ into her life upon graduation, or would she go to some mission field as a teacher for missionary kids? Nancy decided to write the Eatons, who were now in East Pakistan. They were the only ones who knew of Nancy's conviction that God was going to bring Russ into her life. She knew Russ would be in East Pakistan on his Far East trip. She wrote to Jess and Joyce and requested that they ask Russ two questions. First, had God led anyone into his life whom he planned to marry? If this was the case, Nancy would assume this whole thing was some psychological trick, and she would be released to pursue teaching missionary kids. Second, was Russ willing to let God lead anyone into his life?

When Russ arrived in Bangladesh, Jess immediately asked to see him. Russ thought he must be having a terrible problem and gave him a high priority. When they sat down together on the Eatons' flat rooftop to talk, Jess asked Russ, "Do you know Nancy Goehring?" Jess felt led by God to be far more direct than Nancy had planned. He let Russ know that somehow Nancy felt someday God might lead them together. When they finished talking, Jess asked Russ what he thought about what he'd just heard. Russ was floored, and said, "Jess, I don't have any pipeline to heaven on this, and I sure don't believe in crystal balls!" To that, Jess replied, "I was afraid you'd react that way. Well, I've handed you the ball, and you can either fumble it or make a touchdown. Joyce and I will be praying every day for you, that God will guide you in this." Russ replied, "Well, I sure do need your prayers!"

During Russ' Far Eastern trip, Nancy visited her sister in Toledo, Ohio. One evening they had dinner with Joan Olson's parents, the Baurs. During the meal, someone mentioned Russ Ebersole would be borrowing their pastor's travel trailer to take his children to Camp Gitche Gumee, in the northern peninsula of Michigan. Since Nancy had not sought this information, she felt God had given it to her for some purpose. It was time for her to send a quarterly report to her administrator. So she added a P.S. She mentioned that if he was in her area, he would be welcome to stop by, like many of the folks from East Pakistan did.

When Russ returned home, he read Nancy's quarterly report, but this time he did so with greater interest. When he read her invitation, he thought, *I'm going to plant myself right in front of her, and God will have to hit me over the head if there's anything in this.*

Then, late one Saturday in early September, Russ arrived at

Nancy's mother's farm with the travel trailer and five children. The children had a great time together. This was something Nancy had prayed would happen if God was going to bring them all together some day.

After dinner, when the children were settled in the trailer and the house, Russ and Nancy sat in the living room. They talked about Gene, about Harry, about the adjustments to living without them. Russ asked many questions. But he gave no clue as to what Jess had shared with him.

Next morning, they drove to Nancy's church in Mentone. She did not want to sit with Russ and his children because she felt it would make people read more into the situation than there was. After teaching her junior-aged Sunday school class, Nancy determined she would wait, then enter the auditorium at the last possible moment. She knew her children would be waiting for her in the back. When Nancy reached the rear of the auditorium where her children were standing, she was stunned to see Russ' children waiting with them. But there was no sign of Russ. His kids asked, "Where's Dad?" The only thing Nancy could think of was that the deacon-in-charge must have asked him to sit on the platform and lead in prayer that morning.

Nancy asked Harold to go to the balcony to see if there was room for all nine of them. He returned, reporting there was not that much space up there. The only available space in all of the auditorium was in the second row! Nancy felt like a mother hen, parading in with all eight children just as the service was about to begin. Yes, Russ did appear and take a seat on the platform. When the deacon introduced Russ to pray, he said, "By the way, Russ is here visiting Nancy Goehring for the weekend!" Nancy wanted the floor to open and let her fall through. Russ wanted to throw a hymnbook at that deacon! Neither was having very spiritual thoughts. *Well*, thought Nancy, *if these folks hadn't jumped to conclusions before, they sure will now!* She was embarrassed, and wondered what Russ was thinking.

After the service and a delicious dinner at the farm, Nancy got the pony out so the children could ride. The two families spent a great afternoon together, until it was time for the Ebersoles to go. Well past time actually, because Toledo, Ohio, was in a different time zone, and Russ was to speak at Emmanuel Baptist Church, in Toledo, that evening.

When Russ arrived at the church, the pastor was finishing the message. He remarked from the platform, "Well, here's our speaker, just in time for the benediction!" He closed the service, then came to meet Russ. "Did you have a good time?" he asked. "Isn't she a great girl?" Nancy's sister was his secretary, and he knew where Russ had been.

Russ returned home, and Nancy began her senior year at Grace. They started to correspond without secretarial help or typewriters. Russ wasn't sure how he felt, but his interest was enough to pursue getting to know Nancy.

On election night that November, the only telephone in the farmhouse rang at about midnight. Nancy's mother, sleeping in the downstairs bedroom, was awakened and went to answer the phone. It was Russ asking to speak to Nancy. Her mother came upstairs, passing through the rooms where the children slept, to the last room, where Nancy had just fallen into a deep sleep after an evening of study. Nancy's first thought was, *There is another crisis in East Pakistan.* She ran down the stairs, trying to clear her head. As she talked to Russ, her mother stood within three feet, certain that something terrible had happened. Why else would anyone phone at midnight? But nothing had happened except that Russ, staying up alone watching election returns at the mission house in Germantown, was lonely and took a notion to call. After trying to chat a few minutes with Nancy in a half-awake state, they said goodbye. Nancy's mother asked, "What did he want? What is wrong?"

Nancy replied, "He didn't want anything," and went back upstairs to bed, thinking, *He called me! And he didn't want anything at all! He called me!* She was so excited that she couldn't go back to sleep. That was the first of many phone calls.

By January 1969, Russ decided he needed to visit Nancy to get to know her better. His interest seemed to be growing, and he wanted to spend some time with her. Before leaving, he told his parents he had become interested in a young widow. His mother's comment was that she'd about given up on anything like that ever happening. He also talked to his children, asking them how they would feel about God giving them a new mommy. Their first question, of course, was, "Who?" When he told them, they asked, "Oh, you mean the nice lady in Indiana with the pony?" Their reactions seemed favorable.

On that next visit, Russ told Nancy he knew she believed God would lead them together some day. He then asked what made her think that. Nancy tried to avoid the question. After dodging the issue three times, only to have Russ bring it back up again, she gave up and told him about her recurring thought. Before the weekend was over, Russ asked Nancy if she thought she could love a man like him. She simply replied, "I already do." After that reassurance, Russ asked if she would marry him. Before he left, they had pledged to marry one another.

Russ came back to visit later that winter, bringing Nancy her engagement ring. It wasn't until then that they removed the rings Harry and Gene had given them and made the announcement of their engagement.

It was a unique courtship. Precious moments alone together were rare. As soon as they thought they were alone, and Russ would take Nancy in his arms, pixie-like Faith, in pigtails, would peek around the corner and say, "I see you!" The children, ever interested, would lay on the upstairs floor at the open-grate register to watch and listen to everything happening below. When Russ made telephone calls to Nancy from his home in New Jersey, more often than not, his children would try to listen in on the other phone.

During Easter break, Nancy went to New Jersey to get to know Russ' family. Russ' mom gave a beautiful open house to introduce her to their friends and family. The couple set June 28 as their wedding date. On April 21, Russ left on his Far Eastern trip to visit the missionaries for whom he was responsible.

Of course, one of the countries Russ visited was East Pakistan. For years, missionaries there had struggled with the difficult question of multiple marriages, divorce, and remarriage. In a country where polygamy and child marriage are common, new believers from non-Christian backgrounds bring many problems when they accept Christ as Savior. The theologians on a research committee to study this issue looked forward to discussing the matter with Russ, who usually had biblically sound answers to perplexing questions. This time, however, Russ seemed unusually distracted. Finally, he commented, "Well, I'm really more interested in marriage than I am in divorce right now." That was how the East Pakistan missionaries learned that God was beginning a new chapter in the life of their much-loved Nancy.

When Russ left on his trip, he and Nancy did not know where they would live after their marriage. While Russ was overseas, the Lord provided a large apartment at the Houses of Fellowship, in Ventnor, New Jersey. He returned to the U.S. just a couple of weeks before the wedding and brought the youngest three children to the farm a few days before the wedding.

June 28, 1969, was a beautiful day in Indiana. Both Russ and Nancy planned to drive to the wedding, held at Community Baptist Church, in South Bend, Indiana. Nancy would take Bruce and Harold in her Volkswagen, and Russ would drive Beth, Sue, Joyanne, and Faith in his station wagon. The older two, Russ and Cheri, would be coming with Russ' parents from Fort Wayne, Indiana, where they had stayed the night before.

Nancy started the drive with joyful anticipation. But they had not gone far when 11-year-old Bruce suddenly burst out, "I hope we have an accident before we get there so you can't marry my daddy!" Nancy had no idea Bruce was opposed to their marriage. She later learned that he had told his big brother, Rusty, who had threatened him within an inch of his life if he dared say anything to his dad. Now Rusty wasn't around, and Bruce felt safe in voicing his feelings. Nancy tried to reach out to calm him. He jerked away. As both cars stopped at a restaurant for lunch, Bruce's parting shot was, "Well, I hope the Lord comes back before two o'clock so you can't marry my dad!" Nancy's first words to Russ when they met to go into the restaurant were, "Russ, if I weren't absolutely sure God was in this, I'd call the wedding off right now." Shocked, Russ asked, "Why?" She then explained the situation.

Russ talked to Bruce before lunch, and afterward they continued on to the church. As Bruce entered into the occasion, carrying gifts into the reception hall, no one would have ever dreamed he was an unhappy boy. Rusty was his father's best man, and Kitty Ketcham, on furlough from East Pakistan, was matron of honor.

It was time for the wedding ceremony to begin, but the best man had not yet arrived. The organist played on and on. Russ' flustered parents at last arrived with Rusty and Cheri. They had not realized there was a time zone change between Fort Wayne and South Bend, Indiana. Rusty quickly changed into his suit, forgetting to change his shoes. From that point on, the ceremony went beautifully.

When the wedding and reception were over, the newlyweds were ready to leave for their honeymoon at Singing River Ranch in Colorado. As they were saying goodbye to their eight children, Bruce practically crawled in the car window on the driver's side. "Dad," he stated, "I don't know why you're not taking me with you. I like horses a lot more than Aunt Nancy does!" It was impossible to explain to an 11-year-old boy why he was not coming on the honeymoon. His grandpa had to practically pull him away.

Colorado was beautiful, and Russ and Nancy reveled in the joy of being together. The realization God had worked in such an amazing way to bring them together gave them great faith for the days ahead. The honeymoon trip came to a close, but it was just the beginning of many wonderful years together.

Part Four

# The EBERSOLE Family
## (Russ & Nancy)

*"Oh, magnify the Lord with me, and let us*

*exalt His name together."*

—PSALM 34:3

# Chapter Twenty-seven

# Major Adjustments

Ventnor, New Jersey, was the place Russ and Nancy and their children worked at becoming one family. Russ and Nancy had the children put a penny in the piggy bank each time they slipped and called either parent "Aunt" or "Uncle," as they had before the marriage. The game worked! They quickly learned to call their new parents "Mom" and "Dad." Rusty opted to live with his grandparents, since he was a senior in high school and sang in a group at his church, Brookdale Baptist.

The girls seemed to have few problems adjusting. Cheri (15) and Faith (six), the oldest and youngest, shared a room; Cheri was Faith's protector. The three middle girls, Beth (11), and Sue and Joy (both nine), shared another room.

Harold and Bruce, only seven days apart in age but light years apart in personality, shared another room. Their adjustment was another story. They simply could not get along. Bruce was gregarious and outgoing, and he knew everything there was to know—almost—about sports. Harold was shy, and had spent much of his playtime roaming the woods alone, BB gun in hand.

How different could two boys be? Many times, the girls would tell Nancy that Bruce was not nice to Harold when they were out playing. On numerous occasions, other mothers voiced their concern to Nancy over how Bruce treated Harold. They said, "Bruce was trying to humiliate Harold in front of the other children." Bruce never behaved that way in front of Nancy, placing her in an awkward position, since she made it a practice not to act on matters she had not observed herself. She felt responding to hearsay might hinder her ability to form a good relationship with Bruce. When she casually asked Harold how he and Bruce were doing, Harold answered, "Fine." Nancy determined this was a matter she would have to ask God to work out. She prayed that the boys would learn to love each other as brothers. The answer to that prayer did not come immediately.

Two years later, when the boys were at Faith Academy in Manila, they competed for the same position on the wrestling team. Of course, one lost and the other won. At the end of the match, they both cried. Each wanted to win, yet each wanted his brother to win. That night, Bruce and Harold declared they would never compete against each other again. Russ and Nancy realized the boys had grown to truly care about one another.

Through their high school years, one or the other would lose weight to ensure they didn't end up in the same wrestling weight class. Then they went out for different sports. Years later, Bruce said, "On the outside, Harold and I are very different. But on the inside, we think alike."

In her April–May 1969 prayer letter, the last one written by Nancy *Goehring*, she explained to her supporters, "We will live in Ventnor, New Jersey, for the coming school year. Russ will continue to carry out his responsibilities as missionary-at-large for the Far Eastern fields from the ABWE headquarters in Philadelphia. After our first year of adjusting and getting ready, we will go to live in Manila, where Russ will be better able to carry out his responsibilities."

The school year was finished, and it was time for the new Ebersole family to move to the Philippines.

In July 1970, the Ebersole family took a flight from Chicago's O'Hare airport to Manila. Russ and Nancy's hearts were torn as they said goodbye to Rusty. He was excited about beginning college, but Russ and Nancy thought he looked so young and alone waving farewell. Now the rest of the family would be half a world away from their oldest child and brother.

Russ introduced his new wife and family to the missionaries in Japan and Hong Kong on the way to the Philippines. The Ebersoles lived at the ABWE guesthouse in White Plains, a sub-division of Manila, for the first few months. While waiting for their shipment to arrive from the U.S. and for furniture to be made, they searched for a home. They needed at least four bed-rooms and a room for Russ' office. With their large family, a nice yard would be a plus. But that was almost unheard of in Manila.

God provided a home in the sub-division of Loyola Heights. It met their needs even beyond what they had asked God for. There was a fenced-in lot that came with the house, giving the children a place to play ball with their friends. Russ had room for his office, and the combined living-dining room afforded space for the many gatherings held there.

Hospitality became a large part of Nancy's ministry, as this letter testifies, "We've had a lot of company this past week, Steve Swartz' parents from Borneo; the New Tribes pilot, Monty Rasmussen, with his wife and four children; and Cathy Kendall and her parents. Last weekend, Loren Reno was with us for Sunday dinner. The Howards, Brannons, and Kathy Cartner were also here. The Hubbards and Salas were here last Saturday night, and so it goes."

For the first time in her life, Nancy lived in a huge megapo-lis—a great contrast to rural Indiana and Hebron. She was thank-ful for the home God provided, but found that the cement block fence, topped with broken glass, which surrounded it made her feel imprisoned rather than protected. Nancy had seldom driven in any city. Now she was facing some of the world's worst traffic snarls and tie-ups in their large suburban Carryall, which had no air conditioning.

Like mothers in the U.S., Nancy taxied the children to extracurricular activities and picked them up until they were old enough to take public transportation. On March 9, 1972, Russ wrote to Nancy's mother, "Our schedule, as usual, is quite full.

With seven children in six different grades at Faith Academy, all of them having their own special activities, it is almost a full-time job for Nancy to get them to and from everything. We are glad they all are happy and content at school."

Nancy also made many trips to the Manila Airport, taking Russ and picking him up. Besides that, she was able to have a discipleship ministry with women in Homesite Baptist Church, and worked with primary students at Faith Academy in a Pioneer Girls Club.

Russ' ministry took him all over the Philippines—speaking in churches and conferences, and helping both missionaries and nationals. Whenever he spoke within driving distance, the family went with him. He also traveled to Australia, Papua New Guinea, Japan, Hong Kong, and Bangladesh, where he had administrative responsibilities. Every summer he returned to the U.S. for ABWE's board meetings. There were no faxes or e-mails at that time, and phone service was extremely expensive—where it was even available. Russ arranged his schedule to be at home for almost all of the children's events at Faith Academy; he also found time to chair the board at that school.

Nancy's experiences in East Pakistan had all been positive. Her colleagues had rallied around her when she walked through her deepest valley. Her first few months in Manila were disillusioning to the 32-year-old woman still filled with idealism. Russ began dealing with some mind-boggling problems that she never dreamed could exist. In addition, the need for confidentiality meant the problems couldn't be shared with others. Nancy faced a spiritual battle and needed to learn to cast everything upon the Lord. She began to realize that Satan would go to any length to protect his strongholds. One of his strategies was to attack the missionaries wherever he could find a chink in their armor. She moved from disillusionment to anger. But, thankfully, she moved on to love and mercy as her response. She realized the great need for constant intercession for missionaries.

The children's adjustments also proved a challenge. Cheri, then a sophomore, came home from school those first few weeks in tears. Like most teenagers, Cheri found it traumatic to make the big move from the United States to another culture. It was difficult as a high-schooler to break into existing cliques. In a few months, however, she had made friends and was happy to be at Faith Academy.

Nancy was still getting to know the strengths and weaknesses of the family God had entrusted to her. She understood more and more her own lack of wisdom, and often fell on her face before God begging for wisdom. She had never struggled so with impatience as she did when the number of her children increased. She wrote to her mom:

> Mother, you used to talk about the fact that you stopped teaching school when you got to the point that you wanted to knock kids' heads together when they were naughty. I'm afraid I feel that way with our seven sometimes. But I can't quit. God has called me to this. Mother, how do you keep kids from bickering over things that don't even matter? For instance, one will say, "Volleyball is a sissy sport." Another will disagree and, before long, all are in a heated debate. How do you get across the fact that there are some areas that they can each hold their own opinion and neither side be either wrong or right?
>
> Really, in most areas they are pretty good kids, and we have a lot to be thankful for. It's just that being a constant referee gets to me so badly that I'm afraid I don't have the positive influence on them in other areas that I so desire. The two areas I feel I need to work with them the most are 1) teaching them to accept differences of opinion without taking it as a personal affront, and 2) helping them to see that they will be happiest if they are trying to think of ways to make others happy instead of working to get their own way. The determination these kids have will be wonderful if channeled in a way that pleases God and helps others. Maybe each one feels that

with so many of them, they must push for what they want.

Pray that the Lord will give me wisdom and strength. I seem like the most unlikely person by nature for this big task of training so many strong-willed, active, and noisy children. But the Lord has promised that "His strength is made perfect in weakness." Just pray hard for me, Mother.

Harold, still finding his place in the middle of a large family after being the eldest and only son, reeled under all the additional changes. He developed a cough that sounded much like whooping cough and would not go away. He missed many days of school his first few months at Faith Academy. Thankfully, after a few months the cough disappeared, and he began to enjoy school.

All the children adjusted to life in the Philippines before many months had passed. They entered wholeheartedly into their studies and activities at Faith Academy and developed lasting friendships. They formed their own family peer group, bringing many young friends into it. Cheryl enjoyed singing with the Madrigals and Guys and made the Honor Society. In time, Beth, Sue, and Joy all enjoyed being cheerleaders—cheering their brothers on in various sports. Bruce played basketball and volleyball; Harold ran cross-country; and both boys wrestled.

The kids were active in student government and represented their classes in student council. Several were class officers. Bruce was the family campaign manager. If any Ebersole ran for an office, the whole gang of Ebersole kids would be found working together on the living room floor to make the campaign posters. At school they would buttonhole their fellow students, asking for their votes. Bruce would station himself by the ballet box, saying to each student, "Vote for my sister!" The Ebersoles were told that the kids at school simply stated, "You don't run against an Ebersole." Others said you couldn't walk along the outdoor corridors without running into an Ebersole. They did have the advantage of numbers!

The Ebersole home always had many children in it, their own and many others. Russ and Nancy were thankful for the fine friends their children chose. They didn't worry about where their children were. They were most often at home—afraid they'd miss something if they weren't.

Determined that the children should learn responsibility and the value of hard work, Russ and Nancy assigned chores to each of the kids. Their Filipina helpers, needed because of their many guests, were never allowed to put the children's things away or to make their beds. When they invited their friends to stay overnight, which was often, it was the children's responsibility to be sure a place to sleep was ready for their guests and to help them with anything they needed. When the children volunteered to take food to a party or bake sale at school, they were responsible to make it.

Prior to any trip, Nancy gave each child a packing list of things they were to take. At first, Faith had to have her suitcase checked, but it wasn't long before she, too, could carry out this responsibility. The boys worked in the yard. The children washed the dogs and the cars, much to the amazement of their on-looking neighbors. Before they could go on school outings (favorites were sporting events at the U.S. Navy and Air Force bases), their rooms had to pass inspection.

Russ and Nancy worked hard at trying to treat all of the children impartially. They often had dinner guests from the United States who had not known their family before. When the children excused themselves, some guests would ask, "Okay, which children belong to which parent? During the whole dinner we've been trying to figure it out by watching the interaction at the table, and we haven't a clue." Russ and Nancy would then answer their question, inwardly rejoicing because this was one of their goals.

Since Russ was often gone, Nancy tried to carry on the family values while he was away. It was her ambition to keep all discipline current, so that the children would never hear, "You are really going to get it when your dad gets home." She wanted each child to look forward to Dad's return with the same joyous anticipation she felt. She also wanted Russ' return to be a happy occasion for him.

Cheryl was a pleaser and one of the easiest of the children to work with, but one day Nancy and Cheryl had a talk about a point of behavior needing improvement. After some discussion, Cheryl stated, "Mom, you expect us to be perfect." To which Nancy countered, "No, Cheryl, we don't ever expect you to be perfect. We know all too well that you have imperfect parents. But we do have a perfect standard given us by God. It is our responsibility as parents to point you to that perfect standard." Russ and Nancy's aim was to give their children guiding Scriptural principles on which to base their complete philosophy of life.

Three years after the Ebersoles' arrival in the Philippines, Cheryl graduated from Faith Academy and was ready for college. Now the family faced another "first." Most of Cheryl's things were packed into boxes for mailing. She would be flying with her father, who was returning to the United States for ABWE's board meetings and candidate classes. On the way they would stop in Thailand to see the Philippine Association of Baptists for World Evangelism (PABWE) missionaries. They would then go on to Bangladesh, where Russ would minister to ABWE's large missionary family. They would also have one day in Zurich, Switzerland, and two days in Amsterdam en route.

Cheryl was filled with excitement and anticipation of this special trip with her dad. Nancy and the rest of the children saw Russ and Cheryl off at the airport. Returning home, Nancy went to Cheryl's room. All of a sudden Nancy was overwhelmed with the finality a parent feels when a child moves halfway around the world. Nancy sat down on the floor and began crying. She thought, *Cheri can't come home from college for weekends. She won't be home for Thanksgiving or Christmas. I don't know when we will see her again. Oh, Lord, this is so hard. Please help me.* The empty loneliness was a constant reminder to pray for Cheri and Rusty in the United States.

# Chapter Twenty-eight

# Typhoon and Travel

Even before the Ebersoles were fully settled in their home, Russ became immersed in his responsibilities, but the family still had time for fun.

One memorable trip the Ebersole family made was to Pagsanjan Falls, a two-hour drive south of Manila. None of the Ebersoles had visited that popular tourist attraction, but Russ remembered Gene telling of the time her family rode the rapids when she was a girl.

After arriving at Pagsanjan Falls, the Ebersoles had to rent three large dugout-like canoes, each poled by two men. Susie, who disliked water and had not wanted to make the trip, insisted on riding with her dad. So, she and Faith were with Russ, Harold and Joy with Nancy, and Cheri, Beth, and Bruce were in the third boat.

The trip in the canoe up to the falls was against the current and took one and a half hours. Some of the many rapids are so large and rough that loaded boats cannot navigate. Passengers must hike over the rocks and meet the boats on the other side of the rapids. To add to the situation, heavy rains caused the river level to be very high.

On the return trip, running with the current, the boats "shoot" the rapids—that is the exciting part! Russ' boat was the last of the three to leave the base of the beautiful falls. He and the girls watched the other two boats "shoot the rapids" and come safely out the other side. Russ' boat was not so lucky! It was filling with water as they navigated the largest rapid and shot through it. The boat began to sink. Seeing this, the two other boats returned to help. Russ' boat men paddled furiously toward the bank, but just before they reached it, the boat capsized.

Between his cameras, wallet, and two little girls, Russ hardly knew what he was doing. The girls hung on to their overturned canoe, and soon were helped into one of the other boats. It all happened in about two minutes but was not forgotten for a long time.

As Russ and the two girls climbed back into their boat to proceed down the river, Susan said, "I sure was glad when that happened that I knew the Lord!"

Not all their outings were that exciting, but each gave Russ, Nancy, and the children a greater appreciation for the beauty of their adopted land and helped to bond the family even closer together.

After only a few months in their new home, typhoon Yoling crashed into Manila full force—with 140-mile-an-hour winds. Rain blew through their closed jalousie windows as if they were wide open. The whole family mopped frantically, using every towel in the house. Suddenly, the neighbors' big corrugated tin roof rolled up and flew into their yard with a loud crash. Their own tin roof kept up a rhythmic "whumping," sounding as though the next "whump" would carry it up and away. Then the deadly quiet, announcing the eye of the storm, settled over them, but only long enough for them to catch their breath and move to the other side of the house to mop up water. Their roof held tight. They were grateful they sustained no damage, and were too busy even to be afraid.

When the typhoon finally blew over, the Ebersoles jumped into their Chevy Carryall and headed for Faith Academy. The children's school sat high on a hill overlooking the valley in which Manila is located. Driving to the school, they saw electrical lines dangling like strands of spaghetti. Corrugated tin roofs were scattered all over the place; houses stood with rooms exposed to passersby. When the Ebersoles arrived at Faith Academy, they were amazed by the extensive damage. The gym no longer had a roof, one wall had collapsed, and the roof was gone from the library. The dorms, too, sustained damage, but no one suffered any serious injuries. Many of the boarding students needed a place to stay until their parents could come from provincial areas to pick them up. The Ebersoles took several children home with them to camp out.

When they arrived home with their big gang, Nancy discovered the two young women who worked in their house had taken everything from the freezer and laid it all out neatly on the counter. Using all the self-control she could muster, Nancy asked, "Why did you take all the food out of the freezer?" Their response was, "It was dripping, Ma'am!" The girls, fresh from the province, had no experience with freezers. Realizing this, Nancy simply said, "Don't ever, ever do that again without asking me." Their mistake meant every bit of meat from the freezer had to be cooked quickly or it would spoil. Their only means of cooking was an electric stove—and who knew when the electricity would be back on?

Russ quickly bought a tabletop gas stove and a tank of gas. With 15 hungry children, all that food was soon eaten up. The Ebersoles heard later that, when the dorm kids returned home, they told their parents, "The Ebersoles really eat 'high on the hog'!" It certainly was an all-you-can-eat menu so as not to waste the meat.

One of the most difficult and time-consuming of Russ' responsibilities during the initial years in the Philippines was to make arrangements for the transfer of ABWE's properties throughout the country to national entities. The Philippine government had ruled that all foreign-owned land would have to come under Filipino jurisdiction by the end of 1974. Since ABWE began its work in the Philippines in 1927 and had spread to many parts of the country, there were many properties that had to be transferred.

For months, Russ spent many hours with the mission's lawyer working on this tedious assignment. It also involved extra travel for Russ, although he tried to coincide such trips with his speaking schedule. It was with great relief and thanksgiving when the last properties were finally transferred.

In addition to missionary and administrative responsibilities and speaking in meetings in the Philippines, Russ also made overseas trips to the five other countries where ABWE worked in the Far East. He traveled alone for most of these, as Nancy had her hands full at home. However, on occasion, she was able to accompany Russ.

In October 1971, Russ and Nancy traveled to East Pakistan and Thailand. Nancy had not been back to East Pakistan since leaving after Harry's death in 1965. Naturally, she returned with mixed emotions, but the Lord gave her a wonderful visit with her former missionary colleagues and national friends.

Their trip took place during the brutal civil war between East and West Pakistan. The war began on March 26, 1971, and continued until December 16. A few nights before the Ebersoles arrived, East Pakistani guerillas had tried to bomb the Dhaka airport. The presence of the military was in evidence everywhere. The night before they arrived in Chittagong, a West Pakistani-owned gas station was bombed. The city throbbed with apprehension and tension.

In spite of the hostility, Russ wrote in their December 1971 Christmas letter, "Our hearts were encouraged to witness the high spirit of dedication in spite of heartbreaking tragedies and unknown tomorrows of our missionaries and national believers. Never before in the history of our mission's work in this country have we seen such response to the gospel as in the past six months. Fear and death stalk the land, but many are finding peace and eternal life in Christ Jesus!"

Russ continued, "The highlight of the visit for Nancy was the time with Ancherai, the faithful tribal evangelist with whom she and Harry worked in the Chittagong Hill Tracts. He came out of the hills to visit her, and I was amazed at how well she understood and spoke the Bengali language after an absence of six years."

Returning to Bangkok, Thailand, Russ and Nancy felt as if they had been released from bondage and now enjoyed liberty in comparison with the political conditions in Pakistan. It was a joy to spend several days with the eight Filipino missionaries serving under PABWE. Russ enjoyed ministering God's Word at the first missionary conference in the church established by his Filipino friends in Bangkok. Thai believers there pledged to give over $500 that year for missions.

# Chapter Twenty-nine

# Hijacked!

Russ had been invited to speak at a conference at the Bethel Baptist Hospital in Malaybalay, Bukidnon, in the Philippines, and at the dedication of a new surgical wing. Malaybalay was where his first wife, Gene, grew up. When Russ suggested Nancy accompany him, she was excited to visit Gene's former home.

There was another special surprise for Nancy. They would leave a day or two before the conference and have a "second honeymoon" in a lovely seaside hotel in Davao City. From there they would fly in the small mission plane to Malaybalay for the conference.

Russ and Nancy arranged for missionary colleagues Dave and Char Boehning to stay in their home to care for the children during the five days they would be away, and they made reservations at the Davao Insular Hotel for Monday, March 29, 1971. However, since their good friend Dr. Bill Stevenson was scheduled for brain surgery, the Ebersoles decided to stay with his wife, Marilyn, during the surgery.

They changed their tickets to March 30, a day that would be etched forever in their minds. Rising early, they drove to the international airport, boarded the Philippine Airlines BAC 1-11 jet, and departed on schedule at 6:00 a.m. for Davao City, a flight that normally takes an hour and a half.

Thirty minutes into the flight, they were leisurely eating breakfast thousands of feet above land when they heard a voice over the intercom demand, "Answer me in Maranaw (a Muslim dialect used on the island of Mindanao) or I'll blow this plane up!" *That sure isn't the pilot,* Russ thought. The flight attendant was standing in the aisle next to Russ. Russ asked, "What's going on?"

"Nothing, nothing, sir," the man stuttered. Just then, a young man, wearing the pilot's hat, a leather jacket, and dark glasses and wielding a gun, stepped out of the cockpit to announce, "This plane is being hijacked." Turning, Russ saw three other armed men in the middle and rear of the cabin—six hijackers in all.

Within minutes, the captain announced, "We are being hijacked. I am still in control of the plane. Please do whatever the hijackers tell you to do."

At first, Russ and Nancy thought they were imagining the whole thing; it seemed like some mystery thriller. But a few minutes later, when a pistol was placed at Russ' chest and one of the young men frisked him, he knew it was all too real.

Immediately the plane changed course. The Ebersoles wondered where they were going—and if they would ever get there! One of the hijackers said, "Please, everyone, just relax. If you need anything, raise your hand." One man asked for a blanket as he shivered uncontrollably. Another asked permission to use the toilet. The cabin was as silent as a tomb. Most of the fearful passengers looked like "zombies."

During the next hour, the same young hijacker placed his gun at Russ' chest several times. The first time he asked for identification; the second time he wanted to know Russ' nationality. He seemed pleased when Russ said, "American." One other American man sat a few rows ahead. Russ was sure the two of them would be held hostage.

Wanting to inject some humor into their dangerous situation, Nancy said, "You know, Russ, this is all your fault!" Startled, Russ asked what she meant. "Well, you remember every time a plane was hijacked to Cuba, you said you wanted to be on it? You said you'd have an overnight in Havana on Castro and return the next day! Now, you have your wish. We're being hijacked, but not to Cuba. I wonder where they will take us?"

On a more serious note, Nancy said, "We know for sure we are supposed to be on this plane. Remember, we changed our departure date because of Bill's surgery yesterday. For some reason, the Lord has placed us on this hijacked plane today." As Russ and Nancy pondered this, they had great peace in their hearts: *"And we know that all things work together for good to them that love God, to them who are the called according to his purpose"* (Romans 8:28). Even a hijacking!

Thirty minutes after they were scheduled to arrive in Davao City, Russ asked Nancy if she could see land. "No, just ocean," she said. She gave the same answer 15 minutes later. Russ wondered if the fuel would hold out. Just then, they heard the captain saying, "Fasten your seat belts. I'm hoping to land in Hong Kong in 20 minutes."

Kai Tak airport, in Hong Kong, was under tight security as the plane landed and came to an abrupt stop a quarter mile from the terminal. The runways at Kai Tak jut far out into the bay. Russ and Nancy could see police gunboats on either side of their runway.

For several hours they sat in the hot sun as the hijackers demanded the plane be refueled before they would release any passengers. Finally, the airport officials agreed and refueled the plane. Then the hijackers released only half of the passengers, including the children and most of the women. Russ stood in the aisle next to the young hijacker who had approached him several times. "Let my wife get off with those other women," he demanded.

The polite hijacker answered, "Sir, she is not getting off this plane."

By now, Russ was upset and insisted that his wife be released. "We have eight children. They need their mother. I'll go anywhere you want to go, but let my wife off now."

The hijacker turned to Russ, gun in hand, and in a firmer

tone said, "Sir, I told you she is *not* getting off this plane!"

It was obvious he meant what he said. The hijackers wanted to be sure all four Americans on that plane went into Communist China with them. Russ encouraged Nancy, "Just think, honey, you'll be the first American woman ever hijacked to Communist China!" Nancy quickly retorted she'd rather not have that distinction.

At 12:20 p.m. their plane landed at the White Cloud airport in Canton, the first plane ever hijacked to China. The plane, parked far from the terminal, was surrounded quickly by Red Army guards with bayonets. The crew and the hijackers were whisked away in separate cars. The 19 passengers were taken by bus to the terminal and seated in a clean, spacious transit lounge. Surrounding the room were large red placards in both English and Chinese, harshly denouncing the American "imperialists" and all their "running dogs." Tables were loaded with communist propaganda in a half-dozen languages, and passengers were invited to take copies of Chairman Mao's little "Red Book" which had become the Communist "bible." At the end of the long room was a huge, colored picture of Chairman Mao beaming down upon them. "Big brother" indeed had his eyes on them.

After about an hour, the passengers were escorted upstairs and served lunch. The soldiers made sure the four Americans were seated at the same table, and they guarded them closely. When the food came, Russ asked those at his table if they would mind if he thanked God for the food and committed their situation to the Lord. No objections!

During the afternoon, Russ and Nancy became better acquainted with their fellow passengers, especially the two Americans. One was an oilman who was a Mormon. The other, George Drysdale, was the president and CEO of Marsman, a large company doing business throughout the Philippines. George was a congenial fellow, and throughout the afternoon, Russ was able to explain his ministry to George and to share the gospel with him.

Periodically, throughout the afternoon and evening, several young Chinese girls served the passengers Chinese tea. They were dressed in the same baggy-looking uniforms worn by the Red Army soldiers. When they approached the Americans, they seemed terrified. Obviously, the anti-American propaganda that bombarded them had taken hold and influenced their opinions of Americans.

Midway through the afternoon, several officials approached the 19 passengers and asked them to fill out identification cards. One question was, "What is your profession?" Russ was reluctant to put down missionary. He thought for a while and wrote, "Clergy."

About an hour later, the official returned and approached Russ. Pointing to the word, the official asked, "What clergy?" Russ pondered what to say and finally responded, "Minister." Again, the official looked puzzled.

By this time, Nancy was beginning to grow concerned, and George was having a difficult time holding back his laughter. Russ tried again, "Preacher." Again, the puzzled look. Russ tried one more time: "Teacher." "Ahh," the official murmured. "You teacher? Good!" As he turned and left, Nancy breathed a huge sigh of relief.

The passengers were again taken to the second floor restaurant. As the food was placed before the Americans, the oilman began eating his soup. George quickly said, "Wait, Russ hasn't asked the blessing yet." By that time, everyone wondered what would happen to them; George sensed the need for divine blessing—and protection!

Back in the lounge, most of the passengers slept or rested on chairs and sofas. Chinese attendants brought blankets for each of the Filipino passengers, but none for the Americans. "Maybe they forgot us," Russ thought. So he walked down to the table, picked up four blankets and returned. The Americans would also keep warm.

Later that night, a group of uniformed men—they all wore the same type of uniforms, both men and women, and you couldn't tell a colonel from a private—called the passengers together. The leader spoke through an interpreter. "This is the first time in the history of the People's Republic of China that such an incident has happened. We did not expect this. The People's Republic of China looks with great disfavor on such incidents." Russ thought to himself, *So does the Ebersole family!*

The leader continued, "After considering this incident (Russ was sure the telephone lines between Canton and Peking burned all that afternoon), we have decided to let the plane and passengers depart at 10:00 a.m. tomorrow to return to Manila." What wonderful news—until he spoke the next words: "As for you Americans . . . " They held their breath! "We want you to know that the American imperialists are the worst enemies of the People's Republic of China. But individuals can be friends. Therefore, you also will depart with the plane tomorrow." The Americans hoped the communists would keep their word.

Around midnight, the passengers' luggage was searched. Then the officials said, "Now we will take you to a hotel so you can rest." That was a surprise, as the passengers had not been allowed to leave the transit lounge since arriving. They rode a bus about one mile to their "hotel." In the blackness of the night, it looked more like an army barracks, which it was. As Russ and Nancy stood up to get out, the guard said to Russ, "No, no, you and wife not together."

Then he marched Nancy and a Filipino woman off into the darkness. Russ and the two American businessmen were taken to a second floor room. The Filipino male passengers went to another section.

The room the men were in was spartan but clean, with four single beds against the walls and mosquito nets draped over them. Two bright lights hanging from the ceiling could not be switched off, so the three Americans slept under a spotlight.

At 6:00 a.m., they were awakened by the sound of reveille and a rendition of the Chinese national anthem read over a loud-speaker. Then a woman's voice quoted Chairman Mao's sayings in Chinese. This went on incessantly. It is no wonder the Chinese people had become brainwashed over the years.

Russ and his companions got up to dress and wash. They had been told the night before not to leave their room before 7:00 a.m. Seeing no guards around, they walked down the hall and started down the wide stairs. Just then, several Red Guards climbed toward them with bayonets. They beat a hasty retreat back to their room!

Soon another guard came and took the men to their waiting bus. There they met Nancy and the other passengers. As Russ kissed his wife, he said, "Some honeymoon, huh? You on the first floor and I on the second of a Red Army barracks in Canton!"

At the airport, the six hijackers were marched into the transit lounge to make a public apology to the passengers for what they had done. This was, however, a bit of political propaganda, as they explained they had done it to learn more about communism and how to impose that system on their own country.

Not wanting to hear this propaganda, Russ left the group and walked to the end of the hall. The young hijacker, who had placed his gun at Russ' chest several times the day before, followed him. He personally apologized to Russ. Russ asked, "Why did you do that? You jeopardized all our lives yesterday."

This hijacker, Glenn Rosauro, asked, "How long have you been in my country?" Russ told him for many years. Hearing this, Glenn said, "Then you should know why we did this. We've tried to change our government by ballots. Now, we'll do it by bullets!"

Russ tried to explain there was corruption in every government because of sin in the hearts of men. And the only way to change any government was for the hearts of individuals to be changed by Jesus Christ. Surprised, Glenn asked, "Are you a missionary?"

"Yes," Russ answered.

Glenn told Russ, "Do you know they hate missionaries here in China?"

"Yes, I do," said Russ.

"Do you know why?" Glenn asked. He answered his own question, "Because you are CIA agents."

Russ laughed and assured Glenn he wasn't a CIA agent. He took from his pocket a copy of Chairman Mao's little "Red Book." He told Glenn, "This is your little 'Red Book.' This is the political system and philosophy you are following. Its teaching is backed up by a gun." Then Russ took from his shirt pocket his little, leather-bound New Testament, which also happened to be red. "This is my little 'red book.' It contains my life's philosophy and is motivated by the love of God, not by the hatred and brutality of men." Then Russ shared the gospel briefly with Glenn.

Russ learned Glenn came from a well-educated family on the southern island of Mindanao, where his father was the dean of a liberal arts college at Mindanao State University. Russ told Glenn he didn't belong in China; he should be back with his family in the Philippines. Russ invited Glenn to return with the other passengers, but Glenn said going back would be a certain death warrant for him.

At 10:00 a.m., the passengers were driven out to their plane and took off for Hong Kong. At the Hong Kong airport, each passenger was thoroughly debriefed by members of the Hong Kong police, who wanted to learn all they could about the experience in Canton.

Russ was surprised to see two of his ABWE colleagues who served in Hong Kong, Bill Commons and Bob Paswaters, at the airport. They had been able to gain entrance to where the newly arrived passengers were. They jokingly remarked to Russ, "Russ, you're taking your responsibilities as Far East administrator much too seriously! Surveying Communist China is not a part of your job description, is it?"

A new crew had been sent to Hong Kong from the Philippines to fly the 19 passengers and the crew back to Manila on the same plane that had been hijacked. Captain Antonio Misa and his crew joined them in the cabin of the plane.

Captain Misa asked Russ, "Would you like to go to the cockpit with me and see just what happened yesterday?" Russ jumped up, and the two men entered the cockpit. Captain Misa explained how two hijackers entered the cockpit, one with a pistol at the back of Misa's head and the other with the plane's fire ax over the head of the co-pilot. Captain Misa remarked that he tried to keep cool, and then, with a grin, said, "When you have 12 children, nothing really bothers you!"

The captain also described how he flew his plane at the highest possible altitude to conserve fuel. Then he showed Russ his logbook. He explained that a few minutes before his scheduled departure the day before, one of his mechanics told him that they had overloaded the plane with 750 pounds of fuel. He asked Captain Misa, "Do you want me to defuel you?" The captain replied, "No, I can handle the extra weight; I want to leave on time."

Then the captain told Russ that when they landed in Hong Kong the day before, he had enough fuel for just five more minutes of flying time. He said, "See how lucky we were!" Russ quickly remarked, "Captain, we were not lucky. The Lord's good hand of protection was on all of us."

Arriving in Manila, the Ebersoles were engulfed in a loving reunion with their family and surrounded by members of the media who bombarded them with questions. As they walked away with their children and friends who had come to welcome them, Nancy said to Russ, "I wouldn't take one million dollars for this experience, but I wouldn't give a red cent to do it again!"

The sequels to their experience are equally exciting. Russ had many opportunities to testify to God's goodness and faithfulness throughout the Philippines in the months that followed the hijacking.

A few months later, Russ was speaking at a Bible conference in a rather isolated area in the mountains on Negros Island. An old couple came up to him after the meeting and said in the local dialect, "Mr. Ebersole, we were praying for you and your wife many times the day you were hijacked." Surprised, Russ asked them, "How did you know we were hijacked?" They smiled and said, "Transistor radio!"

The Ebersoles heard of people all over the world, many of whom they did not know, who also prayed for their protection, and God wonderfully answered.

Russ and Nancy came to know and love their fellow passenger George Drysdale. On several occasions, Russ visited his office in the Makati Business Center. Each time he had the opportunity to share God's Word with George.

Russ wrote to his family on March 13, 1973, "I had lunch today with George Drysdale, the businessman with whom we were hijacked. We saw him last Friday night at the International School gym, where the high school choral and band competitions were held. I talked to George after the program, and he invited his pastor and me for lunch. We had a good time at lunch, then we dropped the pastor off and went to George's office, where I had a fine opportunity to talk to him for about one hour concerning salvation. He seemed very open, and admitted that he guessed he did not know the Lord in a personal way. I enjoyed the day with George, and he suggested that we try to do this regularly. He even offered me the use of one of his very nice offices whenever I am in Makati and want to come up to study. Please pray for him."

Later in the year, on December 19, Russ again wrote to his family, "Remember George Drysdale said I could use one of his offices in Makati whenever I needed it. So I phoned him about this and to ask him out to lunch. The first thing he wanted to tell me was, 'Russ, I believe that I am a *real* Christian now.' I asked him how he knew. He said he had been thinking about our last conversation, and a man working with Young Life had also been witnessing to him, and he had been reading the Bible. He said, 'I realize now that my good life could never get me to heaven. I was putting the cart before the horse. Now I'm trusting Christ and what He has done for me.' You can imagine our joy and the fine time I had with him over lunch at the Manila Polo Club and in his office for about two and a half hours. I believe he was genuinely saved. Now he needs teaching."

That was many years ago. George has hosted a weekly Bible class in his home for businessmen for many of those years. He has often told Russ and Nancy how thankful he was to be hijacked with them.

Many years after the hijacking, Russ and Nancy were driving from Cagayan de Oro City, on the coast of Mindanao, to the Bethel Baptist Hospital, in Malaybalay. Riding with them was their friend Dan Asuncion, the hospital administrator. He asked Russ if he heard that one of their hijackers had been saved. "Which one?" Russ asked.

"Glenn Rosauro," Dan replied. "My cousin is a good friend of his. In fact, he had originally planned to join Glenn and the others in the hijacking. Glenn returned to the Philippines some time ago and recently told my cousin that he had accepted Christ as his Savior."

Russ remembered his brief conversation with Glenn in the transit lounge of the White Cloud airport, in Canton. He remembered the two little "red books" he held in his hands as he shared the gospel with Glenn. And Russ reminded himself of what God says in Isaiah 55:11, *"So shall my word be that goeth forth out of my mouth; it shall not return unto me void, but it shall accomplish that which I please, and it shall prosper in the thing whereto I sent it."*

Russ and Nancy's hijack experience was a more dramatic example of what was happening in the Philippines. Their six hijackers were radical students. The anti-establishment spirit that permeated American society in the 1960s was also very evident throughout the Philippines.

The prestigious University of the Philippines was one of the centers of this radical movement. Russ and Nancy's home in Loyola Heights, Quezon City, was just two miles from the university campus. With demonstrations increasing in number and intensity, people, especially foreigners, were warned not to drive through the campus.

Late one afternoon, Russ was driving home from the hospital where Nancy was staying with Bruce, who had gastroenteritis. Russ was not far from home when he encountered a flaming barricade across the road and a number of student demonstrators. He had to turn around and drive in a wide circle around the university campus. As he was driving by the rear gate of the school, several students threw a small homemade bomb at his car. Thankfully it did not explode, and he finally managed to reach home safely.

In late summer of 1972, Russ returned from the States, where he had met with the ABWE board and administration. Rusty, who had just finished his summer quarter at Wheaton College, accompanied his dad. The family welcomed both Russes with open arms. It was Rusty's first time to be with his family since they had left for the Philippines in July 1970. Rusty reveled at the opportunity to be home and fully entered into the school activities of his siblings. In fact, he was asked to substitute teach math for several days and to accompany one of the choirs on the piano.

On occasion, Rusty also traveled with his dad to different parts of the country. As a pre-med major, he was thrilled with the opportunities to view ABWE's medical-evangelistic work. On a three-day flying medical trip on the island of Palawan, he was taking blood pressures and assisting missionary Dr. Jim Entner. During his two weeks at the medical clinic in Malaybalay, he witnessed many surgical operations and deliveries. He saw so many of the latter that the doctors kidded him about soloing on the next one!

In September 1972, Rusty accompanied his dad to the town of Maasin, on the island of Leyte. Missionary De Payton was beginning a new church there and invited Russ to preach for several nights at evangelistic services he was conducting. One night, just before the service started, De and Russ were informed by town officials that President Ferdinand Marcos had just declared martial law, and the meetings would have to be canceled. Transportation came to a halt, and since all means of communication were shut down, Russ had no way to contact Nancy. It was several days before he and Rusty were able to return to Manila.

*Chapter Thirty*

# Adoring and the Archbishop

Beat-up trucks, buses, jeepneys, taxis, cars, and limousines all jockeyed for position as each one tried to claim a space and squeeze through any available spot. The size and condition of the vehicle, plus the nerves of the driver, determined right-of-way. In heavy Manila traffic, gridlock is common. The highways sometimes turn into one giant parking lot. Nancy was relieved that Saturday morning, as she took Susan and Joy to Makati for their SAT tests, that the traffic wasn't really so bad. Nancy had a pounding headache that aspirin hadn't touched. Bad traffic would add to her discomfort.

Nancy dropped the girls off and headed home. As she approached the area in front of the Mandaluyong market, the road was clear. Up ahead she saw an older woman beginning to cross the street. The next thing Nancy knew the woman had been thrown up onto the hood. Nancy braked, and the woman fell to the street in front of the car. Nancy jumped out to see if the woman was injured. A crowd quickly gathered. They began shouting, "Put her in your car! Take her to the hospital!" The people gathering were agitated and excited, but no one offered to help. Nancy was not a nurse, but she knew she could not and should not move the woman. Just at that moment, the unheard of happened. A police car with two officers pulled up from the opposite direction. They sensed the danger facing Nancy, a foreigner, and immediately put the injured woman in the back of their open car. They told Nancy to follow them to the nearest hospital. From the hospital she phoned Russ, who was working at home that morning. He immediately drove to meet Nancy. Although the woman, remarkably, only had bruises, the hospital admitted her for observation. Russ and Nancy went to her room and were relieved she was not seriously injured. They went home thanking God that He had protected the woman—and Nancy— in what could have been a dangerous situation. But the incident did not end there.

The next day, when Russ and Nancy went to the hospital to show their concern, they found the woman in animated conversation with her family. The moment she saw Russ and Nancy, she began moaning and groaning and fell back on her pillow. The Ebersoles suspected things might not go smoothly for them.

A few weeks later, Filipino friends Bart and Adoring Mendoza were eating dinner at the Ebersoles' home when a telegram arrived at the door. It was from an office in the Malacañan Palace, in downtown Manila. The cable was a legal summons for Nancy to appear in court. The family of the injured woman hoped to collect a large sum of money. Bart Mendoza, a retired Filipino army colonel, said, "Nancy, I'll take you there. I know the men in that office. I used to work there."

When the date arrived, Bart took Nancy to the specified office. Together they walked in, and Colonel Mendoza handed the official the cable the Ebersoles had received. Then he stated, "I believe these people are trying to get more money than they should because Mrs. Ebersole is an American. But we won't let that happen, will we?" He went into the next office and repeated the same statement to that officer. With that, they were finished, and Colonel Mendoza drove Nancy back home. That was the last they heard of the matter. The Ebersoles hadn't known Colonel Mendoza had once worked in that particular office, but God placed him at their table at the very hour the legal summons arrived. God timed everything perfectly.

Many years later, Mrs. Mendoza organized a different appointment in an official office. One morning Russ answered the phone and was delighted to hear the voice of Adoring Mendoza, who had just returned from a lengthy visit in the United States. Adoring and her husband, Colonel Bart Mendoza, came from Malaybalay, Bukidnon, and had known the DeVries family prior to World War II. Bart was a young officer in the Philippine army at the time, and Adoring's father was governor of Bukidnon Province.

During her visit in the States, Adoring had spent a week with Russ' parents in New Jersey. In accordance with Filipino custom, she wanted to reciprocate the warm hospitality the Ebersole parents had shown to her. Since she was Roman Catholic, Adoring thought one of the best ways to repay the hospitality was to arrange a special audience for the Ebersoles with Archbishop Jaime Sin, the highest Roman Catholic prelate in the Philippines. His palace and office were in the Mandaluyong section of Manila.

Adoring asked Russ, "Would you like to meet Archbishop Sin?" Although that was the farthest thing from his mind, Russ replied, "Oh, that would be nice," not believing it would ever happen.

"What day would be best for you this week?" Adoring inquired. Russ suggested Friday morning.

A few hours later, Adoring phoned back. "Russ, you have an audience with Archbishop Sin at 9:00 a.m. this Friday at his palace."

*Wow,* Russ thought, *she didn't waste any time!* He thanked her, turned from the phone, and said to Nancy, "Honey, you and I have an audience with Archbishop Sin this Friday morning!"

Nancy quickly replied, "Not me, Russ!"

"Oh, yes, Nancy, you don't want to miss this unusual opportunity."

As Russ and Nancy ate breakfast early Friday morning, Russ mentioned to the children the visit with Archbishop Sin. During their time of prayer, they asked the Lord to make that visit all God wanted it to be. Bruce remarked, "Dad, it's kinda strange that all the Roman Catholic people here are under a man named 'Sin.' "

Russ explained that the archbishop's father was a Chinese businessman with the rather common name "Sin." Russ also shared his excitement over the opportunity to meet this man who was such a powerful religious and political force in the Philippines. Russ didn't know it then, but the Pope would appoint this leader a cardinal just a few months later.

Russ and Nancy arrived at the palace promptly at 9:00 a.m. and were greeted cordially by an aide of the archbishop. The palace was a large, sprawling, old house, probably built during the Spanish rule in the Philippines.

The aide led them to a large stairway. At the top stood the smiling archbishop, a portly man with a cherubic face, wearing a long, white gown. He motioned the Ebersoles to come up, greeted them warmly, and led them into his office.

As they sat down, Russ noticed a copy of the Tagalog New Testament on the corner of the archbishop's desk and asked him about it. The archbishop replied, "I was reading from it at 4:30 this morning in my private chapel in the garden. Where were you at 4:30?"

Russ admitted, "I was sound asleep in bed."

Russ was sure that the archbishop had been informed who he was and what he was doing in the Philippines. The archbishop said with a smile, "I'm so glad you have come to talk to me about Jesus. You must be in favor of the growing ecumenical movement as I am."

Russ answered, "No, archbishop, I'm really not."

"Then, why have you come to visit me?" he asked. Russ explained Adoring's friendship, and how she had arranged the audience. Then he said, "Archbishop, although I could not work with your church, I really want to be your friend, and I want you to be my friend."

The Archbishop seemed to be pleased—and perplexed. He

wanted to know more. "But why could you not cooperate with my church?"

Russ stated that there were many reasons, but emphasized two. "Archbishop, I do not agree with your teaching on matters of authority and on the way of salvation." Intrigued, the archbishop asked Russ to explain.

Russ mentioned that his sole authority for faith and practice is the inspired Word of God, the Bible. He pointed to the Tagalog New Testament on the desk, and then presented the archbishop with a small, leather-bound pocket New Testament with his name inscribed on the cover. The archbishop was delighted to receive the gift. Russ continued, "Archbishop, you accept as authority not just the Bible but also the traditions of your church which have accumulated over the years, and the dogmas of the popes through the centuries."

Russ explained that when he conducted evangelistic meetings, he always used the Roman Catholic Bible. He said the major theological differences between himself and the archbishop did not stem from the Roman Catholic Bible, but rather from the traditions and dogmas which had been added to the Bible. He also pointed out that it appears when Scripture and tradition do not agree, tradition is honored above the Bible by the archbishop's church. The Lord Himself warned against this very thing when He challenged the Pharisees of His day, *"But he answered and said unto them, Why do ye also transgress the commandment of God by your tradition? . . . Thus have ye made the commandment of God of no effect by your tradition."* (Matthew 15:3, 6b)

The archbishop was listening graciously, so Russ continued, "The second reason I could not work with your church, Archbishop, is your teaching regarding salvation. This was at the very heart of the Protestant Reformation of the 16th century. I believe the Bible teaches that a man cannot be justified before God by anything he can do. At the heart of the teaching of your church are the sacraments which are a means of grace. Good works play an important part in your teaching on the means of salvation. Yet the Bible teaches, *'For by grace are ye saved through faith; and that not of yourselves, it is the gift of God—Not of works, lest any man should boast' "* (Ephesians 2:8, 9).

"Don't you believe in good works?" asked the archbishop.

Russ responded by using an illustration from life in the Philippines. "Yes, Archbishop, we do believe in good works. However, these good works do not help us to be saved; they follow salvation. It is like the horse and the *calesa* (a horse-drawn cart used in the Philippines). The *calesa* never comes before the horse. The horse always comes before the *calesa*."

At this point, Nancy quoted Ephesians 2:10: *"For we are his workmanship, created in Christ Jesus unto good works, which God hath before ordained that we should walk in them."* The archbishop requested, "Please repeat that verse." Nancy did.

Russ then continued to explain that when Jesus Christ died on Calvary's cross, He did everything for man's salvation. *"For then must he often have suffered since the foundation of the world. But now once, in the end of the ages, hath he appeared to put away sin by the sacrifice of himself"* (Hebrews 9:26). That is what He meant when He cried out from the cross, *"It is finished!"* (John 19:30).

The archbishop quickly responded, "But I also love Jesus!"

"I'm sure you do, Archbishop," Russ said, "but do you believe that Jesus is all you need for salvation? Is He alone sufficient to save you, or do you need something else?"

The archbishop did not answer, but obviously was thinking through these important matters. He had ordered coffee, tea, and cookies. As they continued to chat, the archbishop was fascinated to hear that Russ and Nancy had a family of eight children. He chuckled and said, "You sound like a good Roman Catholic family to me!"

Russ remarked that he and his wife had thoroughly enjoyed their time, and said, "We know, sir, your schedule must be full, and we appreciate so much the time you have given us."

The archbishop assured Russ and Nancy that it was a privilege to have met them, and thanked them for the informative time together. Then he said, "Thank you for the wonderful gift you gave me. I have something special for you." He went into an adjoining office and came back holding something in his hand.

"Six months ago I was in Rome with the holy Father. He blessed this medallion and several others for me. I would like you to have this. It has the current Pope's picture on the front and on the back the images of several other notable popes. I know you don't believe as I do in the pope, but I do want you to take it—it has a lot of real silver in it!"

Russ was sincerely thankful for the gift he received from Archbishop Sin and expressed his gratitude. Then he said with a smile, "Archbishop, I promise you I will never melt it down. It will always be a reminder of this special time with you." And it has been.

# Chapter Thirty-one

# The Short Furlough

The Ebersoles' furlough was due to fall during Beth's senior year at Faith Academy. Russ and Nancy realized that graduating with her classmates meant everything to Beth. They might consider extending their term an extra year, but the following year would be Bruce and Harold's senior year. If Russ and Nancy waited through that year, Susan would be a senior, and the following year Joy would graduate. All the children had close ties at the school, and each wanted to graduate from Faith. Russ and Nancy talked about a summer furlough, but it seemed impossible to visit all 39 supporting churches in such a short time.

One time when Russ was away, Nancy got out the list of supporters, a United States map, and a calendar. As someone who needs to visualize things, she listed each church by location and mapped out a possible furlough schedule, penciling in a date beside each church. When Russ returned, she showed him the schedule, and commented, "Perhaps it could be done." Russ, ever a man of action, decided the schedule looked good. He began writing supporting churches, giving them the dates Nancy selected. Amazingly, all but two supporting churches accepted those dates.

At that time, Faith Academy's school year was different than the school schedule in the U.S. In order to fit all the meetings in, the Ebersoles would have to leave school a month early. The children were all good students, so Russ and Nancy thought leaving early wouldn't pose a problem. The kids could do extra work and take their exams early. They already had the plan in action when they went to make arrangements at Faith Academy for the children to take early exams. There they hit a snag. The school could not pass students who missed more than a certain number of days in a semester. Taking their children out a month early would mean too many absentee days.

The superintendent gave three options: 1) leave the children in the Philippines with friends to finish out the year, (2) use an accredited correspondence course while they traveled, or (3) put the children in school in the States and send the records back to Faith Academy.

Russ and Nancy knew the first suggestion wouldn't work because they were scheduled to visit many relatives during the first month in the States. The second suggestion could not work with their extremely full roster of meetings. But the last suggestion might work. They were scheduled to be in Indiana during the last month of Mentone's school year, traveling to nearby churches. Russ wrote to the Mentone school to see if the children could be accommodated. Mentone school officials were more than willing to help. They fit six Ebersole children into their school system for that last month of the school year.

Nancy and Russ were again amazed at God's timing. Nancy had no idea when she pre-planned the schedule, and Russ had no idea when he contacted churches, that the children would need to be in school that month. The month in Indiana was the only time the family would spend that long in one place during the short furlough. Amazingly, it fell in the last month of the school year. Only God could have prearranged all of those circumstances!

Their short furlough from March to August 1974 kept the Ebersoles busy. Touching base with 37 of their 39 churches meant holding meetings in at least three churches each week: Sunday morning, Sunday evening, and mid-week. The entire family traveled together for most of the meetings. For the Florida stint, a good friend loaned the Ebersoles their motor home.

On one occasion, Faith took the seat by her dad and said,

"Dad, want me to preach your sermon?" Faith proceeded to go through the sermon with all the illustrations and vocal inflections. The whole family had the message memorized. Since they were in a different church every time, Russ had no need, and certainly no time, to prepare a new sermon for each meeting.

The Ebersoles had many good times sightseeing and visiting with family and friends during those busy days. Before they knew it, it was time to return to Manila so the children could begin school. Russ had to remain in the U.S. for a few weeks to attend ABWE's candidate classes and board meeting. Russ, ever the bargain hunter, found an excellent price on tickets, but they weren't exactly a direct flight. Those tickets scheduled them to fly to Brussels on Sabena Air. There, they would take a train to Amsterdam and fly from Amsterdam to Manila on KLM. On hearing of the arrangements, Nancy wondered how she would ever pull that one off with five Ebersoles and their niece, Pam DeVries. This was Nancy's first time traveling this far without an experienced traveler. She thought it was next to impossible, but if this was what God wanted, He would somehow help them make it through.

Russ drove the family to John F. Kennedy Airport, in New York City, said a tearful goodbye, and the family boarded their flight. They were a bit late pushing away from the gate and sat a long time on the runway. At last the captain's voice came over the intercom stating they were experiencing mechanical difficulties and would have to return to the terminal. The 747, upon its return, rammed the gate and popped out three windows. The plane would not fly anywhere that night!

Nancy went into the terminal and showed the agent her ticket, asking if there was any other flight that would allow the family to make their connection in Amsterdam. The agent said, "No." Nancy then went to the phone and called Russ, now back at his parents' home in North Caldwell, New Jersey. He returned to New York City and collected his family.

The next morning he started all over again to get tickets so that the children could make it to Manila for the beginning of their school year. He found a direct flight from Los Angeles to Manila on Philippines Airlines, leaving just a day or so later for only $50 more per ticket. Nancy and the children flew from New York to Los Angeles, then boarded their PAL flight to Manila. They were all settled in their seats when Nancy noticed a couple struggling up the narrow aisle with photographic equipment and all kinds of paraphernalia. She thought, *Hmm, what an interesting looking couple; not your usual travelers. I wonder if they are going to take pictures of some exotic place for* National Geographic.

The husband and wife sat down behind Beth. In a few moments, Beth bounced excitedly over to Nancy. "Guess what, Mom?" she said. "Those people sitting behind us are missionaries with ABWE. They're on their way to Bangladesh, but they're stopping in the Philippines to see ABWE's hospitals there. Their name is Bullock."

Nancy was delighted to be seated so near the Bullocks and refreshed by the adult companionship on that long journey. Who but God could have arranged to put Dr. John and Tense Bullock on that plane with Nancy and the kids? Who but God could have seated them near one another? God gave Nancy a wonderful reminder of His loving care as she began another busy term.

# Chapter Thirty-two

# "The Best-Laid Plans"

The Boy Scout motto, "Be Prepared," is a good one for every missionary, but often those well-laid plans have to be changed. Although he carefully arranged his schedule for months ahead, Russ' plans were often changed because of unforeseen events.

Back in Manila, in early November 1974, a long-distance telephone call from a deacon in a church in San Pablo City, several hours south of Manila, frantically announced that several young people had died while hiking in the mountains. One of the girls was a member of the Manila Baptist Church where Russ' colleague Dave Boehning was pastor. Russ and Dave left Manila as soon as possible. They were shocked to learn that three young women had drowned in a swollen river during a flash-flood. Two other young people miraculously had lived through the harrowing experience.

Two of the girls were from Iloilo City, where Russ had spent his first years of missionary service. Russ knew their families. One of the bodies had not yet been found and had probably been washed out to sea. Russ used his Carryall van as a hearse to bring one of the bodies to Manila, where it would be taken by ship to Iloilo for burial. Russ' heart went out to the father, who came to Manila to claim his daughter's body. While on the pier waiting to place the coffin on the ship, another ship arrived carrying the parents of the girl whose body had not yet been located. They, too, were good friends of Russ. The father was not a believer, and many prayed that God might use this tragic event to bring him to Christ.

Much of the world was engulfed by tragedy at this time because the Vietnam War was in progress. The two large American military installations in the Philippines, Subic Naval Base and Clark Air Force Base, were extremely active, with thousands of U.S. servicemen.

A ministry Russ enjoyed immensely was sharing God's Word with men at the Christian Servicemen's Centers on those bases and seeing some of them surrender their lives to Christ. Russ wrote his parents on December 20, 1974, "I drove from Clark Field to Subic Naval Base last Saturday afternoon and spoke there Saturday night and Sunday evening. The men were so eager for the preaching of the Word; five made decisions for the Lord Sunday evening, including a young pilot whose wife had accepted the Lord two weeks before."

Russ' brother-in-law and his wife, Bud and Ginny DeVries, served with ABWE on the island of Palawan. Bud had supervised the construction of the *Gospel Launch,* a seaworthy 45-foot-long boat, and was its skipper. On it, he traveled among the islands, holding evangelistic campaigns and ministering to the churches.

Bud was able to get a long-term lease on a small, picture-postcard, tropical island that he named Treasure Island. He built a group of simple, thatch-roofed buildings on it. Many youth camps were held there. Numerous Filipino young people, who were saved and challenged to God's service on that little island, serve the Lord throughout the Philippines and in other places of the world today.

Clark Air Force Base had an active youth program directed by the base chaplains. The program was known as the "God Squad." Bud got to know several of the chaplains, and encouraged them to send their youth to Camp Treasure Island for a week during summer vacation. The chaplains were thrilled with the opportunity to send their kids off the base and let them see what the "real" Philippines was like.

Bud invited Russ to speak at several of those camps. Russ

and Nancy and the 50 young people who attended will never forget one camp. Forty-five members of the "God Squad"—with five or six adult advisors, including the chaplain and his wife— flew from Manila to Puerto Princessa, the capital of the province of Palawan and the "port" of the *Gospel Launch*.

Careful, prayerful preparations had been made for months. Excitement reigned high among the young people from Clark Field, two DeVries kids, and five Ebersole kids as they boarded the *Gospel Launch* for Treasure Island.

The plan was to spend a day or so on Treasure Island, allowing the kids to become adjusted to life in Palawan Province during their first day of meetings. Then they would travel north in the *Gospel Launch* to the town of Roxas, a three-hour trip.

Russ and Nancy planned to drive the five or six hours from Puerto Princessa to Roxas in Bud's Jeep Carryall. Traveling with them were Dr. Phil and Ruth Young and their three children. Phil, a surgeon, and Ruth, a nurse, were the medical team at camp that week.

The plan was for everyone to rendezvous in the town of Roxas. The young people from Clark Field planned to paint the church there for one day, then travel back to Camp Treasure Island. The two nights they spent in Roxas involved evangelistic meetings—with the teens singing and giving testimonies and Russ preaching.

But, like the "best-laid plans of mice and men," things just didn't work out that way. Bud, with the teens and adult advisors, left Treasure Island in the launch to begin the trip to Roxas. Russ and his party used a *Boston Whaler* boat to cross from the island to Puerto Princessa, from where they would drive to Roxas.

Nothing in the local weather reports predicted any serious problems. The launch ran into heavy rain and rough seas en route to Roxas, but had no difficulty reaching its destination.

Although usually passable, the roads from Puerto Princessa to Roxas were always rough. As Russ and the others drove north, rain fell harder, and the roads grew increasingly muddy and extremely slippery.

Reaching the first river they had to cross, they noticed it was much higher than usual and running much more swiftly to the sea, just a short distance away.

The "ferry boat" used to cross the river was a simple raft made of logs, 55-gallon drums, and planks. Russ gingerly drove the Carryall over planks extended from the riverbank to the raft. The raft was pulled hand-over-hand by ropes fastened on each side of the river. They made it across and climbed the steep hill on the other side.

Arriving at the other river to be crossed en route to Roxas, the group found the bridge had completely washed out—and there was no possible way to cross. They decided to turn around and head back to Puerto Princessa, hoping the "ferry" was still running. When they arrived at the river, after sliding down that treacherous hill, they were told that the ferry could not cross; the river was too high, and the current was too swift. What were they to do? They were not between a rock and a hard place, but between a washed-out bridge and a non-functioning ferry!

Russ remembered that somewhere between the ferry and the river without a bridge, the Juan Catons, a Christian couple, owned a coconut plantation along the road. Knowing that darkness would soon fall, the whole group climbed the hill again and drove slowly, searching for the Catons' coconut plantation.

Russ spotted it on his left—a long, sandy road leading into the Catons' home. He drove slowly toward what he hoped would be a "refuge" from the storm, since the winds had picked up and the rain had become torrential.

Pulling up to the front of the house, Russ honked his horn and waited. The door opened and Mr. Caton peered out to see who was out in such a storm. Russ jumped out of the Carryall to greet him. Quickly explaining their plight, Russ said, "Brother Caton, we are trapped between the ferry and the washed-out bridge! Could we spend the night with you? There are seven of us."

Although Philippine hospitality is world-famous, Russ' request was asking Mr. Caton to go "the second mile."

"Of course you can," Mr. Caton answered. "Get in here where it is dry as quickly as possible. Mrs. Caton and I will be happy to take care of you as long as necessary."

The group spent two nights and two days with Mr. and Mrs. Caton. The house was not completely finished—most of the rooms, which were still quite bare of furniture, had no windows either.

Mrs. Caton went to work placing *banigs* (hand-woven mats) on the wooden floors of two bedrooms, and passing out light blankets for each person. At suppertime, she miraculously produced a delicious meal of fish, vegetables, and rice.

Meanwhile, the *Gospel Launch* had arrived in Roxas. The first night the teens and their leaders slept in the church. They, too, enjoyed great Filipino hospitality. The next day, as Russ and Nancy waited out the ferocious storm at the Catons' home, the teens painted the church. Early that evening, the believers served their guests a Filipino feast before their departure. The rain was heavy, but Bud's barometer did not indicate any serious problems. Bud wanted to get the kids back to Treasure Island as soon as possible. The youngsters thanked their Filipino hosts and waved goodbye.

The trip from Roxas to Treasure Island normally took three hours. That night, however, the *Gospel Launch* struggled for ten long, frightening hours as the rain pelted down and the sea raged. Bud later said it was the worst storm he had ever encountered on the South China Sea. He estimated some waves were 25- or 30-feet high.

Most of the teens stayed below in the cabin. Their delicious Filipino feast soon covered the floor, as most of them became deathly sick—and extremely afraid. Between the rough sea and the diesel fumes, conditions grew worse. Many of the teenagers began to wish that the boat would sink and bring an end to their misery.

Faith, then 12 years old, remembers that night clearly. She had gone below, but after seeing—and smelling—what was happening there, she quickly ran back up on deck and jumped on the roof of the cabin. There, she and her sister, Joy, were protected by the family's friend, Lieutenant Loren Reno, who sheltered both girls and covered them with a small tarp. Faith recalls, "I wasn't even afraid. Loren was taking care of us, and Loren was like Jesus to me!" (Loren, who has had an outstanding testimony through his years in the Air Force, is now a Brigadier General.)

The *Gospel Launch* finally bobbed its way to Treasure Island, where the seasick young people and adults were carefully helped off one by one. Grateful to still be alive, they all collapsed and fell into a sound sleep.

Back at the Catons, the storm still raged. All ears were bent to Mr. Caton's transistor radio, which gave periodic weather reports, none of them good! Several times Bud DeVries' *Gospel Launch* was mentioned. It had not been sighted since leaving Roxas the previous night. A few hours later, the announcer said that the DeVries' *Gospel Launch* had still not reached Puerta Princessa to pick up supplies. Then he asked if anyone had seen the launch.

Russ and Nancy prayed for the safety of their five children and all the others. Would they ever see them again? Late in the afternoon of their second full day at the Catons, a man ran to the house shouting, "The *Gospel Launch*! Mr. DeVries is here with the *Gospel Launch*!"

Everyone ran down to the shore. Bud waved, and in a few minutes, he and his boat boy came ashore in the *Boston Whaler*. He gave a quick report on his adventures of the past two days. But first, he assured his anxious audience that everyone reached Treasure Island safely.

Bud told Russ and Nancy and the Youngs to gather their

things and return to the beach; he wanted to leave for Treasure Island as soon as possible. When they reappeared as instructed, Russ and Nancy followed Bud's orders to get into the *Boston Whaler* so Bud could take them out to the *Gospel Launch* before returning for the Young family.

As Bud, Russ, Nancy, and the boat boy set out for the *Gospel Launch* in the *Boston Whaler*, the shearing pin on the motor snapped. Bud cut the engine. He, Russ, and the boat boy pushed the boat to the *Gospel Launch,* tied it up, and boarded. Bud immediately started the engine. He said it was too dangerous to ferry the Young family on the *Boston Whaler* with no engine. So the little party waved goodbye to Phil and Ruth and their children, and to the Catons, who had indeed proven a "shelter in the time of storm."

The night trip to Treasure Island was not easy, for they were forced to travel through dangerous, uncharted waters. They reached the island shortly before midnight.

As they jumped off the *Gospel Launch,* Bud shouted to Russ, "Get your Bible. The meeting starts in 15 minutes!" Russ looked at Bud in amazement, and shouted back, "You have to be crazy! It's almost midnight." Bud laughed and said, "Russ, you've missed two full days. We have to make up for lost time. The meeting begins in 15 minutes. Be there!"

Russ was there, and so were the teenagers, all of whom were thankful to be alive. Their hearts had been softened by all they had experienced. During the next few days, five of those young people accepted Christ as Savior, and others dedicated their lives to the Lord.

Before camp was over, the chaplain's wife told Nancy, "During that terrible storm, when we were traveling from Roxas to Treasure Island, I was talking to the Lord. I told Him that, if the launch went down, please let me die. I didn't want to have to face the Base Commander at Clark Field, whose twin sons were on board."

Chapter Thirty-three

# Back in the United States

In 1971, when Wendell W. Kempton became president of
ABWE, he made no changes in the administrative staff for the
first five years. He realized, however, that it was no longer possible for the president to handle all the missionary correspondence,
deal with the myriad office details, minister to the missionaries
and churches, and travel to the expanding world of ABWE. Dr.
Kempton saw the need to surround himself with veteran missionaries. With the approval of the ABWE board, he contacted
three men, one of whom was Russ Ebersole.

Russ was happy living in the Philippines, where he had close
contact with ABWE's missionaries in the Far East. He particularly enjoyed his frequent contacts with the Filipino Christians
throughout the country. Russ' natural inclination was to continue his ministry in the Philippines.

For three consecutive years, Dr. Kempton asked Russ to
become the executive administrator for the Far East. Nancy finally commented, "Russ, I don't think you have prayed much
about this. You really don't want to leave the Philippines, do you?
God may be directing you through Dr. Kempton's repeated invitation. Please pray about it." Both Russ and Nancy made this
important issue a matter of prayer. After several months, they had
God's peace about accepting Dr. Kempton's invitation.

Russ looked forward to serving with Dr. Kempton, despite
having to leave the Philippines. Several contacts with ABWE's
president had given Russ a real appreciation for this man. One
such contact occurred in 1965 when Russ was invited to speak

283

at the missionary conference of Baptist Bible College in Johnson City, New York. Russ roomed with a freshman student in one of the men's dorms where Wendell and Karolyn Kempton were houseparents.

After the first evening meeting, the Kemptons invited Russ to join them in their apartment for refreshments. That was the first time Russ had met the Kemptons. He was amazed when Wendell said, "Karolyn and I have heard so much about your wife, Gene. We never had the privilege of meeting her. Would you tell us about her, how you met, and what your ministries were in the Philippines."

Talking about Gene was the one thing Russ most wanted to do, but even his closest friends seemed to avoid the topic, probably not knowing what to say. Yet here was a complete stranger allowing Russ to bare his heart about his beloved wife.

A few nights later, the Kemptons again invited Russ to join them after the meeting. At their request, the conversation again centered on Gene. Russ probably shared more about Gene during those two evenings than he had since Gene's death the previous year. Russ knew from those two evenings with Wendell and Karolyn that the Lord had given Wendell Kempton a big, caring heart for people.

Russ and Nancy had the privilege of entertaining Dr. and Mrs. Kempton and two of their children, Stan and Wendy, when the Kempton family visited the Philippines for a month in 1974. The Ebersoles hosted the Kemptons in their home and also traveled with them as they visited missionaries throughout the country. Those informal times endeared Wendell Kempton to Russ and confirmed in his heart what he had experienced with Wendell when he first met him years before.

Making the decision to return to the States had many ramifications. One of Russ and Nancy's concerns was Joy's schooling. Along with all her siblings, she had a great desire to graduate from Faith Academy. Now she would be leaving the Philippines just before her senior year. It so happened that Joy had taken heavier class loads during her first years of high school at Faith Academy. In checking with the administration, Russ and Nancy learned it would be possible for Joy to accelerate and graduate a year ahead of her class. This meant she would graduate with her sister Susan, just prior to the family's departure for the States.

The job of packing for such a move was monumental. This was especially true since Russ' responsibilities kept him away from home until just two weeks before their departure. Before leaving the Philippines, Russ and Nancy wanted the family to see their dear friend Quita Arquesola, who had been Russ and Gene's faithful helper and was a real part of the family. Russ invited Quita and her husband, Joling, to spend a few days with them in Manila—special days of fellowship and reminiscing.

With much hard work and perspiration, everything fell into place for their departure from the Philippines. After many difficult goodbyes, Nancy and Russ and their three teenage daughters, Susan, Joy, and Faith, left the land and people they loved.

Russ and Nancy, knowing this would be their last opportunity to travel with the girls, had planned several special stops en route to the States. One was in the beautiful country of Switzerland. Russ and Gene had met Walter and Leisl Lutz during their years in Bacolod City. Walter managed a number of large sugar plantations on Negros Island, and he and his wife had lived many years in the Philippines. Now Walter and Leisl Lutz had a lovely home in an Alpine village. They invited the Ebersole family to spend several days with them. Their home and quaint village were picture-postcard Switzerland. The girls especially looked forward each afternoon to seeing the old cow herder, with the long white beard like Santa Claus, drive the cows home after a day in the pastures. Each cow knew where she belonged and would automatically turn off into her stable.

The most interesting stop, however, was in Israel. Their personal guide was George Janvier, a young man whom the Ebersoles had met in Manila. George had been traveling around the world with a friend, working wherever they could to pay their way. While in Australia, George met an ABWE missionary who led him to the Lord. After that, George spent time with ABWE missionaries in Papua New Guinea and in the Philippines, and studied for a semester in ABWE's China Baptist Theological College in Hong Kong.

George then went to Israel to study. He had traveled throughout Israel and was familiar with many biblical sites which were not usually seen by the average tourist.

Susan, Joy, and Faith will never forget the times when the family and George would crowd into their small rental car to visit a fascinating biblical site. At each stop, George would open his Bible and read the biblical accounts of the events surrounding that site. His joy and excitement made the Israel trip unforgettable.

In 1976, America's bicentennial year, ABWE opened a new field—the United States—with the goal of planting churches in growing suburban areas throughout the country.

Russ and Nancy were delighted to hear that one of ABWE's first church-planting projects would be in Indian Mills, New Jersey, just 15 miles east of Cherry Hill, where ABWE's International Headquarters was located. The missionary pastor was Bob Dyer, who had served faithfully under Russ' administration in Papua New Guinea.

The Ebersoles wanted to be part of this new ministry, which was called Shawnee Baptist Church. That desire led them to purchase a home which adjoined the ten acres of land the church owned and on which the sanctuary would be built. Their relationship with Shawnee Baptist Church over the years has been a very special one for Russ and Nancy.

In 1977, Russ joined the administrative staff in Cherry Hill. Some people wondered what an executive administrator does.

Of course, no two days were alike, but the job description included the following:

- Communicating with the missionaries and visiting the fields regularly.
- Encouraging and counseling the missionaries and assisting in crisis situations.
- Guiding the fields in evaluating and formulating strategy for more effective ministry.
- Ministering in schools, churches, and missionary conferences throughout North America.
- Promoting the ministries and projects in the region for which he was responsible and recruiting new missionaries.
- Teaching in Candidate Seminar, Field Preparation Seminar, and other training programs.
- Serving on President's Advisory and the Missionary Administrators Committees.

As administrator of the Far East, Russ traveled frequently to other parts of the world. Emergency trips to meet special needs were also part of his job description.

In a wistful statement written to her mother, Nancy said, "Russ has been gone now for five days. That leaves about 58 to go. Somehow it always seems longer when I know I can't telephone and give him a buzz or get one from him late some evening."

Some of Russ' responsibilities led him to "Far-away places with strange-sounding names."

# Chapter Thirty-four

# China Revisited

The People's Republic of China first opened its doors to foreign visitors in 1979. Ever since he and Nancy were hijacked in the spring of 1971, Russ had wanted to return to China. Much had happened in the intervening years. The Cultural Revolution caused seismographic changes in the lives of China's one billion people.

In 1980, Russ learned he might be able both to visit and to carry Bibles into China. He contacted a knowledgeable organization in Hong Kong for initial information and strategy. They explained that to get into China, he would have to join a tour group. Russ then got in touch with a travel agency in New York City. The agency told Russ they preferred groups of 30 and asked him if he could locate half of that number.

Russ quickly sent out word, and during the next month recruited ten people. Among them were Rev. Jaymes and Dorothy Morgan, veteran ABWE missionaries to South China and Hong Kong, both of them fluent in the Cantonese language.

Russ explained to all in his group that they would be carrying Bibles and other Christian literature to contacts in the city of Xian, one of the stops on their tour.

Russ and Nancy met up with the rest of the tour group, which included 15 people they had not met before.

While in Hong Kong for a few days, the group was given explicit instructions on handling the Bibles and literature they would carry into China. Back in their hotel, Russ and the others divided the literature throughout their suitcases and shoulder bags. The team traveled from Hong Kong by hydrofoil (a boat that skims the water's surface) to Canton, their first stop.

Everyone wondered what might happen during the Canton customs formalities, which often included luggage searches. Different inspectors examined the tour members. A young woman was the inspector for Russ, whose suitcase was half-filled with Bibles. She asked, "What do you have in your suitcase?" Russ replied, "Oh, just everything I need for this trip." She waved him on without opening his bag. As he walked out of the inspection room, Russ turned and saw that his friend Jerry Horne was having a much tougher time with his inspector.

Waiting in the next room for Jerry was his very anxious wife, Dee. She said to Nancy, "If I were a drinking woman, I'd have to have one right now!"

Finally, Jerry joined the others. Wearing his cowboy hat, Jerry looked much taller than his six feet four inches. He turned to Russ and said, "Wow, you're the guy who organized this thing and got through clean as a whistle, and I'm the one in trouble. What a way to start!"

Jerry's inspector had opened his shoulder bag and counted every single piece of literature—all 158 of them. The inspector ordered Jerry to bring back that exact number when he left China. Thankfully, the Bibles he was carrying were in his suitcase.

Russ left most of his clothes in Hong Kong in order to make room for Bibles in his suitcase. Arriving at their hotel in Canton, he was slightly embarrassed when the small Chinese bellboy tried to pick up his suitcase. He probably thought, *These Americans sure wear heavy clothes!*

In Canton, the group met their guide, Mrs. Woo. She, like all the official guides, had been chosen carefully by the communist government. Her job was to make sure the tourists saw only those sights the government selected. She was also to give them the "party line" on conditions in China. Mrs. Woo seemed to have eyes in back of her head; she didn't miss a thing!

She outlined the trip, giving general information about each city on the itinerary. She explained that the schedule would be full, but they would have a rest period each day after lunch. And she emphasized that the group must always keep together. No stragglers allowed.

After seeing some of the major sights in Canton and the surrounding countryside, the group flew to Shanghai, a bustling city with throngs of people. Most of them—both men and women—wore the baggy suits favored by Mao and the communist leaders. The roads were jammed with bicycles, but very few cars or trucks.

Early one afternoon, after lunch, Russ decided to go out on his own to see some of the sights not on the official itinerary. He walked at a brisk pace along the streets, observing the thousands of people who filled them.

All of a sudden, he heard a woman's voice behind him calling, "Mr. Ebersole, Mr. Ebersole, what are you doing here?" He couldn't believe his eyes—there was Mrs. Woo! Running up to Russ, she said breathlessly, "Mr. Ebersole, don't you know you should not be here?" Russ replied, "Don't worry, Mrs. Woo, I just wanted to get some fresh air and exercise."

From Shanghai, the group flew to Beijing, the capital of China. Just before take-off in an old plane, the flight attendant announced, "Please fasten your seatbelts." Russ and Nancy looked down to discover they didn't have any!

One highlight of the Beijing tour was walking along the "Great Wall" of China, which the tourists learned was not a single, continuous structure. Rather, it consists of a network of walls and towers. Another favorite was the "Forbidden City," which stands in the center of Beijing. It is protected by high walls and a moat on all four sides, and consists of dozens of halls and courtyards. The visitors wondered how the rulers of the Ming and the Ching dynasties ever found their way around the maze of buildings.

Everyone in the group looked forward to their next stop—
the city of Xian—but for different reasons. This was where Russ'
recruits would deliver the Bibles. The closer they came to Xian,
the more excited—and perhaps fearful—they became.

However, on the morning of departure, Mrs. Woo and several other officials said their flight had been canceled, and they
would miss Xian altogether. That news fell like a bombshell and
created an immediate furor among the passengers, especially from
two Jewish lawyers from Cleveland, and Russ.

The lawyers angrily complained that they had paid good
money for this tour, which included Xian. In fact, for them, Xian
was the most important stop on the itinerary! They wanted to see
the 8,000 life-size, fully armed terra cotta warriors that had been
excavated in 1974. They intended to see this world-famous sight.

For another reason, Russ loudly voiced his defiance at the
sudden cancellation, although, of course, he didn't mention the
Bibles. The heated discussion lasted a long time. Several other
officials were called in to explain that "bad weather" in Xian
made it impossible to fly there. This reason was neither accepted
nor believed.

Finally, after a number of hours, during which every member
of the group stood his ground, the officials offered a compromise.
They would put the group on an overnight sleeper train which
would leave that evening on the long journey to Xian. This
would give the group one less day in Xian, but it was better than
not going at all. The compromise was accepted, and they boarded
the train late in the afternoon.

Tourists, along with Mrs. Woo and another guide, were
placed in their own sleeper car. Each compartment held four
bunk beds, two upper and two lower. The two lower ones turned
into comfortable seats with a table between them. The cabin even
had lace window curtains.

The tourists soon found out that their sleeping car was locked
at each end so they could not move into any of the other cars,

except when Mrs. Woo led them to the dining car.

Whenever the train stopped, they were allowed to get out of the car but were not allowed to walk away. Russ climbed off at each stop to stroll along the train, trying to see everything that was going on. Again, that shrill voice called out, "Mr. Ebersole, Mr. Ebersole, please come back. The train is leaving!"

Throughout the next day, Russ and Nancy enjoyed the view of rural China as the train rumbled on. Nothing seemed to be mechanized. They were amazed to see men and women pulling heavily loaded wagons by hand.

Their compartment mates were Jerry and Shirley Day, who had been fellow students with Nancy and Harry at Bryan College. Jerry was the pastor of a thriving Bible church in Columbus, Indiana.

In the afternoon, the train finally reached the city of Xian. Russ was concerned. His instructions had been to meet their contact early in the morning on their first day in Xian. They had missed that first day because of the plane cancellation. Had their primary purpose for this trip been foiled? Or would God somehow enable them to deliver the Bibles?

Very early the morning after their arrival, Russ and Jay Morgan slipped out of the hotel, carrying as many Bibles as they could. Their contact was to meet them along the road, several blocks from the hotel, and signal them with a whistle. Russ and Jay came to the meeting place unable to see anyone in the semi-darkness. They walked on, stopped, and then walked back. They did this several times, with no response. Then they returned to the hotel, dejected.

The next morning would be their last day in Xian. Jay and Russ were determined to try again. The others in their group were all praying. Russ realized there were more Bibles than he and Jay could handle. So Russ asked Jerry to join him and Jay the next morning to help deliver all the Bibles. Dee was not at all happy about her husband's involvement in this "cloak and dagger" plan. She said, "My husband is twice as big as these people. He's the one everyone will notice. I want to take him home with me!"

Jerry thought for a few moments and said, "Yes, I'll help you, but I sure hope we all get back safe and sound!"

Before dawn the next morning, the three men, loaded down with Bibles, left the hotel. They slowly walked to their rendezvous point. They were walking single file with Russ in the lead when they heard a sharp whistle. Russ turned and saw a man dressed in black slip out from behind a bush. The stranger quickly said his name. That was the name Russ had been told. This was the contact man! He had a bicycle with a large basket. A friend with a similar bicycle joined him, and the Bibles were transferred to the baskets. No one else seemed to be in the vicinity. The young men explained that the Bibles would be distributed immediately to pastors in the hills, none of whom had Bibles. Then the two men bicycled off into the darkness.

Later in the day, as the group walked through a park, that same young man, with several young friends, walked past. He gave no indication at all that he knew the three men who had delivered Bibles to him earlier that morning.

Years later, Russ heard this man had come to the United States to study in a Bible school. Russ was able to write him several times. His plan was to return to his country and to serve the Lord there.

The group was able to see the incredible terra cotta army and view some of the ancient walls and other wonders in the fascinating city of Xian. But, by far, the greatest thrill was seeing how God wonderfully enabled them to provide Chinese pastors with His Word.

From Xian, the tour group flew back to Canton, their last stop before returning to Hong Kong. Russ and the Morgans had a special reason for revisiting Canton. Jay and Dorothy Morgan had worked as independent missionaries to South China. In

1946, they joined Victor and Margaret Barnett as ABWE missionaries. They learned the Cantonese language and, along with the Barnetts, continued church planting in Chek Hom. They worked there until August 1949, when the Communist Revolution forced the Morgans to leave China. Jay and Dorothy went on to serve the Lord in Hong Kong, the Philippines, and Japan.

Pastor Chen, the Chinese pastor with whom they had worked in South China prior to the war, continued the ministry after Jay and Dorothy were unable to remain in China. The Morgans had not seen Pastor Chen for over 30 years. His daughter worked with the Morgans in Hong Kong and wrote to the Morgans about her elderly father. The Morgans arranged to meet Pastor and Mrs. Chen in one of the large parks in Canton on the last Sunday of the Morgans' visit to China—if everything went according to schedule.

When the tour group arrived in Canton, Russ asked Mrs. Woo if he and the Morgans could visit the only Protestant church open in the city of Canton on Sunday. She hesitated, explaining that they were to leave for Hong Kong that afternoon. Russ assured Mrs. Woo they would return to the hotel in time. She finally gave permission but asked, "Do you know how to find the church?" Russ answered that the Morgans had been there before and knew the way.

The church was not far from the park where they were to meet Pastor Chen. The Morgans and Russ took a cab to the church, a large, old structure. They were surprised to see a great number of people entering. Once inside, they walked up into the balcony to find seats. Soon, the entire church was full. Contrary to what they had been told, many young people were present.

The choir walked to the platform, followed by the two Chinese pastors. Jay excitedly said, "I know those men! I met them before the war. They were faithful servants of God!"

What a joy to hear that large congregation singing praises to God so enthusiastically, and to listen to the professional-sounding choir, realizing this was taking place in Communist China. As one of the pastors started preaching in Cantonese, Jay interpreted for Russ. After about 15 minutes, Jay whispered, "He is preaching a fine sermon, faithful to the Word of God!"

After the service, the Americans mingled with the throngs of people leaving the church. Jay made a beeline for the pastors who remembered him. What a reunion they had!

They also spoke to an elderly lady and asked if she knew the Savior. Her wrinkled face broke into an angelic smile as she explained how she had walked with the Lord Jesus for more than 50 years.

They had to get to the park, a brief cab ride away. Arriving at the entrance, the Morgans and Russ decided to go separate ways in order not to attract attention. They had the impression they were being followed—and most of the time they were!

The pastor's daughter had told Jay approximately where the pastor would be sitting in the park. After a few minutes, Jay spotted him and his wife and quickened his pace. They embraced one another for a long time before reminiscing about their days of ministry in South China so many years earlier.

Jay brought a tape recorder to preserve those special moments. He asked Pastor Chen to give his testimony of his days under the communist regime, for he had suffered much. Jay also had a large-print Bible in Chinese script. When he presented it to the old pastor, tears ran down the pastor's face. He clasped the precious book to his chest. For many years he had not seen a new Bible, and his old one was badly tattered.

The Americans could not stay long; their presence could mean trouble for that faithful old pastor. After prayer and another fond embrace, they bid farewell.

The Morgans and Russ caught a cab back to their hotel. Mrs. Woo was relieved to see them. If she knew what they had been doing that morning, her anxiety would have escalated tenfold. In an hour or so, the entire group left for the train station.

After a short ride, they crossed the border and entered Hong Kong. Nancy breathed a sigh of relief. She felt as if she had just been released from prison.

# Chapter Thirty-five

# Into Burma

Russ and Nancy looked around dubiously at the condition of the plane they had just boarded. They wondered if the engines were in as poor condition as the cabin! They were about to take off from Bangkok, Thailand, and fly to Rangoon, Burma, on March 16, 1981.

ABWE's president, Dr. Wendell Kempton, often said, "The strength of ABWE is its board." One of these board members, Dr. Joseph Stowell, Sr., started as an advisory board member in 1940. He was elected to the full board and Executive Committee in 1950, and served as both vice-president and representative for ABWE.

It was Joseph Stowell who initiated this trip into Burma. In 1981, Dr. Stowell served as representative of the General Association of Regular Baptist Churches. In that capacity, he received communications from national leaders around the world. One such letter came from Rev. Go Za Kham, in Rangoon, Burma (now Myanmar). At that time, as is still true today, the country was poverty stricken and ruled by despots. It had also been closed to foreign missionaries since 1965.

Rev. Kham invited Dr. Stowell to visit him in Rangoon. He wanted to show what God was doing, in spite of much opposition, among the group of Baptist churches with which he was affiliated. Rev. Kham's hope was that like-minded churches in the United States might help and encourage the Burmese believers.

Because of other responsibilities, Dr. Stowell was not able to accept the invitation. He was, however, interested in discovering more about what God was doing in Burma. Knowing Russ and Nancy would soon be making another of their extended Asian trips to ABWE's fields, Dr. Stowell asked Russ to try to arrange a meeting with Go Za Kham.

Russ wrote to Rev. Kham, who responded with a warm invitation. Russ and Nancy included a three-day visit to Rangoon during their three-and-a-half-month trip. Russ was excited about making the first contact for ABWE in Burma. Their flight was not long, but it was so rough and frightening that Nancy renamed the Burma National Airline the "Burma Scareline."

The Ebersoles underwent a thorough luggage inspection at customs. The officer even wrote down the serial number of Russ' camera to be sure he did not sell it on the black market in Rangoon.

Russ was relieved to hear his name called by a man standing in the dimly lit waiting room. He wore a *longie* (a long, skirt-like piece of cloth, wrapped around the waist and extended to the ankles) and introduced himself as Rev. Go Za Kham. He and his teenage son hoisted the Ebersoles' suitcases above their heads and walked out to their waiting taxi. Russ and Nancy had never seen such an ancient-looking vehicle that was still running.

Russ asked the driver, "How old is your cab?" He proudly announced, "The engine is from 1970." He didn't really know how old the chassis was.

They were driven to the President Hotel, where they would spend the next few nights. It had no frills but was clean and adequate. Go Za Kham, after telling them he would meet them the next morning after breakfast, said goodnight and left. Russ and Nancy took a walk along one of the city's main streets. It was dimly lighted, and everything in sight seemed to be in a state of disrepair.

After a good rest and breakfast, Go Za took them to the home of one of the believers, where a group of seven or eight young men had gathered. These men were all from the same tribal group as Go Za Kham, the Chin tribe, and were involved in Christian ministries. Several of them were in charge of Christian village schools.

Russ asked each one to give his personal testimony and some background about his work. The Ebersoles heard how God reached into each life, and felt a kinship with the men from their very first meeting. After several hours, the Ebersoles took them to lunch at a quaint roadside restaurant.

Later in the day, David Mo picked up Russ and Nancy at the hotel. As they had done with the other men earlier, Russ asked David to share his testimony of how he had been converted. David's father was a well-to-do official of the Burma Railroad System, working with the British prior to World War II. As a young man, David became involved in drugs, and his health greatly deteriorated. He was finally hospitalized and was not expected to live. At that time, a member of his family brought him a Burmese Bible. David was extremely weak and knew he might not live. He picked up the Bible and began reading. Before long, the Spirit of God convicted him, and there in his hospital bed, David invited Jesus Christ to be his Savior. From that time, not only was his life transformed, but his health began to improve as well.

David's burden was for young people trapped by drugs, as he had been. Eventually, he was able to set up a Christian Center where those with drug problems could receive loving care and counseling, and hear about the One who alone could give them true freedom. David also established a small Bible school where young men and women studied the Word of God.

The Ebersoles went with David to one of his evening meetings at the center, housed in a large, two-story home on the outskirts of Rangoon. Russ and Nancy were not prepared for the "Christian rock" band at the front of the auditorium, with all their electronic equipment, that provided a loud and lively prelude to the service.

David explained to Russ that foreigners were not permitted to speak at public gatherings. So he suggested that Russ simply give "greetings" to the large audience that filled the room, and then just keep talking. David would interpret. Russ gave the longest "greeting" ever.

After the meeting, David's wife served a delicious native meal to the guests. She had been born in Burma to Filipino parents. After dinner, she excused herself to go to bed. She had to rise at dawn the next day to cook for the Bible school students.

A midnight curfew was in effect in Rangoon. After enjoying the meal and talking with many of the young people, Russ mentioned the late hour to David. He did not seem as concerned as Russ, but finally he and the Ebersoles jumped into his World War II–era Jeep to head back to the hotel.

Before they started, David lifted up the driver's seat, opened the cap to the gas tank underneath, and placed a measuring stick inside. "We are really low on gas," he said. "I don't think we have enough to get back to the hotel."

Russ replied, "What do we do now? There are no gas stations open at this hour." (It was now after 11:00 p.m.)

David smiled, "Don't worry! I know where we can get some gas."

He jumped in next to Russ, Nancy sat in back, and they drove off into the darkness. After a few miles, David turned off the main road onto a narrow, crowded street past a number of small shops and houses. There were no lights on in any of them. David stopped and turned off his headlights, so they were in pitch darkness.

A few young men were sitting on a bench in the darkness. David jumped out of the Jeep and approached them. "What kind of bike do you ride?" he asked, giving the "password" for buying gas. They quickly ran to a motorcycle nearby and began to siphon gas into David's tank. He paid them and roared off for the hotel, arriving just before midnight. As they parted, Russ told David, "I sure hope you make it back home on time!"

The next day, Go Za Kham showed the Ebersoles a few of the sights in Rangoon. The highlight was their visit to the Shwe Dagon (the Golden Pagoda), which Nancy had visited on her long journey to East Pakistan in 1963.

To Burmese Buddhists, the Pagoda is the most holy place in their country. Following the prescribed custom of removing their shoes before entering, Go Za and the Ebersoles walked around the huge base of the Pagoda. They passed many altars to Buddha, before which men and women placed their offerings of food, flowers, and burning incense. Russ and Nancy's hearts were heavy as they thought of the Burmese people living in spiritual darkness, under the control of Satan.

David Mo and two former drug addicts, who had been converted, joined Go Za and the Ebersoles for lunch. Russ and Nancy enjoyed being with these Burmese men whose lives had been *"turned from darkness to light and from the power of Satan to God"* (Acts 26:18).

Later that afternoon, Russ and Nancy were driven to the airport to fly back to Bangkok. They shook Go Za Kham's hand warmly and thanked him for all his help. Much to Nancy's relief, their return trip was on a Thai Airline plane. As they boarded the plane, they rejoiced at the way God's hand had gone before them and opened up this new door of ministry in Burma!

That was the first of several visits Russ and Nancy made to Burma. Since then, several unusual doors of opportunity have opened to ABWE. Its GAP (Global Access Partnerships) ministry, under the direction of George Collins, is assisting the fine ministry of Faith Baptist Bible College, in Tiddim, in the Chin state, under the capable leadership of Rev. Do Suan Mung.

For several years, students in Burma have participated in GRBSEP (Grand Rapids Baptist Seminary Extension Program).

Teaching modules have been held in the city of Rangoon, and a number of men and women have received theological education. Various ABWE missionaries teach the modules under the direction of ABWE missionary Dr. Norm Barnard.

# Chapter Thirty-six

# Full Circle

One Sunday in 1982, as the Ebersole family gathered around the dinner table, Russ mentioned the need for a high school teacher in Chittagong, Bangladesh. Russ turned to Harold and asked, "Do you think you could go to Chittagong for a year or so to teach?" Harold had graduated with a teaching degree in secondary science and had taught for a year in a Christian school in Colorado. He had fulfilled his contract and planned to return to the East Coast for the summer. Harold promised to pray about it, and within weeks decided to go.

During Harold's short-term service in Bangladesh teaching MKs from August 1982 to December 1983, he also experienced many other facets of missionary life, this time as an adult. A special place he liked to go to think and pray was at his father's (Harry Goehring's) grave. Because the grave site was located at Memorial Christian Hospital, a three-hour drive from the school in Chittagong, it was only on special occasions that Harold was able to make the trip. The verses his mother had inscribed on Harry's gravestone impressed Harold greatly. *"Whosoever will come after me, let him deny himself, and take up his cross, and follow me. For whosoever would save his life shall lose it; but whosoever shall lose his life for my sake and the gospel's, the same shall save it"* (Mark 8:34b, 35).

Harold thought of his father, who had given his life for the gospel's sake so many years before. Harold determined that he, too, would take up his cross and follow the Lord. He decided to return to Bangladesh to give his own life in the ministry of translation and evangelism that his father laid down when God called him to heaven.

During Harold's first day at home after returning from Bangladesh, he told Russ and Nancy he thought God was calling him to serve in Bangladesh. Nancy immediately asked, "What ministry in Bangladesh do you feel God is leading you to?" Harold responded that he believed God was directing him to the same ministry his father had been in. Only then did Nancy tell Harold that, from the time of Harry's death, she had prayed that, if it was God's will, He would call their only son back to the ministry Harry had. She never told Harold this, because she knew how important it was for the call to come from God, not from family pressure.

Years later, Nancy received a letter. She had not known until that day that another prayer warrior was lifting the same request as hers to God. At the time this friend wrote the letter, she was dying of cancer.

December 8, 1988

Dear Nancy,

As I was paging through one of my journals the other day, I came across something I decided to share with you. It has always been most interesting to me how the Lord gives certain prayer burdens to His children—ones that somehow remain strong throughout years, and only He knows how He will accomplish His will, and just what that will is. Your Harold was one of those "specials" for me. Hardly a day has passed since you returned as a widow from East Pakistan that I haven't prayed for him, and for you and your family before and after you became Russ' wife. I rejoice to know Harold and Shawne are in Dhaka learning the language—another step on God's path for them. I'm so thankful for God's provision of Shawne for Harold and vice-versa.

It was in the fall of 1965 that I first talked to the Lord about thrusting a certain young man, Harold Goehring, into His harvest field. Not just any part of the harvest field—East Pakistan (now Bangladesh) in particular.

Harold was seven years old and had returned to Mentone with his widowed mother, Nancy Goodman Goehring, and two little sisters, Joy and Faith. Nancy moved in with her mother, Mildred Goodman, and enrolled Harold in second grade at the Mentone School. That is where I watched and prayed as a little boy so tender in heart and desirous to please, worked his way through the loss of his beloved father, Harry Goehring, ABWE linguist in the land of East Pakistan. Often I'd glance in Harold's direction and find him looking up towards the trees and the sky via the two high windows. Usually I just left him to his thoughts, for I knew where he was. The few times I touched his shoulder as I passed through the aisles, he'd softly reply, "Sorry, Mrs. McDugle. I was think-ing about Pakistan and remembering."

I knew how it was. I, too, grew up without an earthly father. Time goes on, but the heart thinks and remembers. Harold needed time to do that. It's part of healing. Oh, it's not the morbid "Why did you let it happen, dear God?" Just a heart that loved much and was learning to face the real sting of death—separation for a season from a loved one.

The years passed by; Nancy, in God's providence and kindness, married Russ Ebersole, and between the two of them now there were eight children. Off they went to the Philippines, then back to live in New Jersey and work in a new area for ABWE. Daily I prayed for them and in particu-lar for Harold, that the Lord would keep his heart seeking eternal things, keep it always free from bitterness, and someday send him back to go on with the work his father began years ago. God is to be praised for that becoming a reality! To God be the glory, great things He hath done!"

Jan McDugle

God's good hand moved two women to pray the same prayer and allowed them each to praise His name for God's answer.

Harold has been involved in teaching, Bible translation, and field administration. In addition to teaching their boys, Caleb and

Luke, Shawne has taught women's Bible studies, and adult literacy. In the fall of 1999, Harold Ebersole wrote this prayer letter:

"Oh! The places you'll go." Those immortal words of Dr. Seuss run through my mind as I think over our amazing trip into the hills far above Ruma for the Sangu Area Bible Conference last week. It was an opportunity I have hoped and prayed for since coming to Bangladesh.

In our last letter we asked you to pray that God would allow us to travel into the Chittagong Hill Tracts. During the past couple of months that prayer has been answered. I was able to visit two villages where my father preached the gospel in the early 1960s. In my father's time there were only a few converts and a handful of village churches.

Last week 1,000 tribal people from 41 village churches gathered in Mrakhyang village to attend the Sangu Area Bible Conference. Some had walked as much as three days to be there. This was a village my father visited in 1963, along with Jay Walsh, Vic Olsen, and Gene Gurganus. ABWE missionary Joyce Wingo lived there alone for two years.

A drumbeat echoed over the rugged hills as one of my father's companions, retired evangelist Robichondro Tripura and his wife, Pastor Guni Jon Tripura, nurse Nancie Della-ganna, and I approached the Tripura village. When we got close we heard the sound of singing. In the past the drum had been used for funerals, but now Christians use it to accompany their songs of worship and praise. We entered the village and saw hundreds of people lining the path to welcome us. This was the first time in over 30 years foreigners had been given permission to stay in remote villages.

To get to Mrakhyang, we rode a boat upriver over sandbars to Ruma. We then walked for a full day on a winding, one-lane "road" over the Chembuk mountain range from Bandarban to the end of the line. We then trekked across rocky rivers and streams; through canyons, bamboo forests, jungle, and fields of cotton, peppers, and squash; along slippery muddy trails, straight up and down the sides of mountains. The paths we used were certainly not trails as we know them. Perhaps game trails would be the closest comparison. There were places we could not handle without help, yet the tribal people do it carrying 50–80 pounds on their backs!

The scenery was amazing. Rugged mountains, rocky streams, cascades and waterfalls, deep canyons, mountain-top lakes, ridge-top villages, hillsides covered with crops, stars rising and moon setting over the hills.

We stayed in bamboo homes perched on stilts with huge tree trunks for beams and rafters. (How did they get those beams up trails we could hardly climb?) Ten to a room, we slept on the bamboo floor wrapped in blankets hand-loomed from cotton grown on nearby hills. We also ate, sat, relaxed on the floor—there is no furniture in the homes.

We ate all sorts of delicacies made from newly harvested crops seasoned with either dried fish or fish paste. We drank warm buffalo milk. We sampled boiled banana stalks, banana heart, rosella leaves, and many other unidentified leaves, stems, and plant parts.

We dined on fried pig intestines, and pork fat, boiled pigs' feet, grilled liver, dried shark, and even dried elephant meat.

It's no wonder I got sick the last night of our stay. Several of the tribal leaders prayed for me, and my fever broke just an hour or two before we were scheduled to leave. God gave the strength needed to walk out as planned.

We swam in spring-fed Boga Lake on top of a tall mountain, and bathed in mountain streams surrounded by people. (Not to mention changing clothes, also surrounded by people.)

What an experience to see a roughly hewn stone proclaiming, "The Gospel was first preached in this village by Chala Lushai in 1958." Now, the believers listened to God's Word, watched the Jesus film, and sang worship songs the young people had written themselves—all night long, night after night.

At the end of the conference, plans were made to preach

and show the Jesus film in new villages. Pastor Guni Jon Tripura would like to begin a mobile Bible school in the area next year. It is crucial that these people who are so open to the Spirit's leading be given solid biblical teaching.

God has worked mightily in Mrakhyang village and has given amazing fruit for their efforts. That one village is the home of the tribal leaders who have been most used by God for the past 40 years: Ancherai, Robichondro, Guni, Ashai, and Shattaram, the head evangelist in the Sangu area. And my father was in on the beginning.

# Chapter Thirty-seven

# Visit to Romania

During a meeting in 1983, the administrators of ABWE established a series of ten-year goals. Among them was the goal of establishing a specific ministry in the restricted access countries of the world where missionaries may not freely enter. At that time, Russ didn't know how this would happen, but he trusted God to work this out.

Three years later, Russ was preaching at the First Baptist Church, in Wheaton, Illinois. After the Sunday morning service, Elizabeth Tson, wife of Dr. Josef Tson, president of the Romanian Missionary Society, chatted with him. The Tsons were good friends of Russ' sister and her husband, Bill and Doris Waldrop.

Mrs. Tson mentioned she was sorry her husband had not been present for the service. He was speaking elsewhere that day. She said, "I'm sure my husband would like to have you preach in Second Baptist Church, in Oradea, Romania. He will be in his office tomorrow. Please call him before you leave."

Russ phoned Dr. Tson, who said he would be happy to arrange a visit for Russ to preach in several of the churches in Romania. Would Russ contact him about an acceptable time?

Later that week, Russ mentioned this invitation to Wendell Kempton. He said, "Russ, that's great! Boy, I wish I'd been invited." Russ replied, "Wendell, you're the president! Of course they would want you to go."

In 1986 Romania was under the ruthless communistic dictatorship of Nicolae Ceausescu. Conditions there were as poor as in any of the communist-dominated countries in Central and

Eastern Europe. Its people lived in fear. Christians were persecuted, pastors were imprisoned, and churches were closed.

But God had kept the doors of the Second Baptist Church
open, along with many other churches. In fact, the Spirit of
God did a great work under its courageous pastors, Dr. Nick
Gheorghita and Paul Negrut. The church was filled at every service, and many came to know Christ as Savior. Knowing this,
Wendell and Russ anticipated an exciting trip and ministry. They
were not disappointed.

The men carried Christian books and a substantial amount
of money for the pastors in Romania. In Frankfurt, as they waited
for their transfer to Bucharest, they exchanged most of their
money into the currency of Romania. They did not know that
Romanian authorities did not permit this. Wendell had two
"money socks," which he and Russ placed on their legs.

Arriving in Bucharest, they lined up to go through security,
which included a scanning machine. Russ watched as the people
ahead of him went through the machine and then were also
thoroughly frisked from head to toe. He turned to Wendell and
said, "They're going to find our money."

"That's okay," Wendell replied. "I'm sure it's no problem to
take it in."

Russ went through the machine first and then a soldier gave
him the most thorough "frisking" of his life. The soldier felt the
wad and asked what it was. Russ answered, "It's money." The soldier was not happy. He told Russ all foreign currency had to be
exchanged in Romania (where the exchange rate was much
lower than elsewhere).

By then, Wendell stood next to Russ and was undergoing his
frisking. He had the same experience. The officials counted the
money and gave each man a receipt for the exact amount. They
thought they would be given the same amount back on their
departure from the country. Not so. That money became the
property of the government—or some of its officials.

Then their suitcases were opened and searched. Russ was first. In his suitcases were seven or eight books to give to the pastors. "Why do you have so many books?" the soldier asked.

"I like to read on long trips," Russ replied.

Wendell's suitcase was then opened, and the soldier saw a number of books. He asked the same question. Wendell gave the same reply. The soldier, with a smirk on his face, said, "But all your books are the same!" They then led Dr. Kempton into a small room where he was thoroughly body searched.

Over an hour had passed, and both men wondered if they would ever get out of the airport. Finally, they were released, caught a taxi, and drove into the city to the hotel where Russ had reserved a room. The hotel was old and shabby, with dim lighting. They sat on their beds and wondered where to go from there. They did not know a single person in Bucharest, and they were really heading for Oradea.

All they had was the phone number of one of the pastors in Bucharest whom Josef Tson knew. Russ and Wendell had been warned to be careful what they said on the phone, as all phones were tapped. Deciding to wait until early the next morning to phone, they both fell into a fitful sleep.

Dr. Tson had made arrangements for the pastor to pick the men up at the hotel and take them to the domestic airport for their plane to Oradea. Early the next morning, Russ left the hotel to find a phone. A man at the other end of the line answered in Romanian. Russ tried to explain in English that he and Wendell had arrived. The man gave a grunt and hung up. Did Russ have the wrong number? He tried again, with the same result. On the third try, the man answered Russ in English. It was indeed the pastor, but he wanted to be sure he was talking to Russ. Soon he drove up to the hotel and took the men to the airport. Staying in his car, the pastor explained how to get their tickets. Then he drove away. He was not eager to be seen with two foreigners.

Finally, tickets in hand, the two men boarded an old plane of the national airlines, Taron. They were thankful to be met in Oradea by the smiling faces of pastors Nick Gheorghita and Paul Negrut, who drove them to their hotel. The Americans were warned to be careful what they said in the room; it was bugged. Also, the Romanians told the Americans they would probably be followed wherever they went. They were right. In fact, a soldier had been placed in the hotel room next to theirs.

The week in Romania was an eye-opening experience for Wendell and Russ. Each preached in the Second Baptist Church, as well as in several smaller churches in rural areas and in two city churches in Bucharest. Each of the churches was crowded with men, women, and young people who gave their full attention to the preaching of God's Word.

Russ was asked to preach at the Friday evening prayer meeting at the Second Baptist Church, in Oradea. He was thrilled to see so many present. However, after the service, Pastor Nick apologized. "I'm sorry, Russ," he said. "We usually have over 2,000 for our prayer meetings, but tonight there were less than 1,900!" With a grin, Russ replied, "That's okay, Nick. I usually don't preach to more than 1,900 at prayer meetings in the States."

The Romanians love music. Each church has its own choir; many of them even have orchestras. They are especially fond of brass musical instruments. The visitors had never heard such enthusiastic singing and playing.

In spite of many ironclad restrictions, constant police surveillance, and much poverty, the Romanian believers were among the most vibrant and happy Wendell and Russ had ever met. It was both challenging and convicting to be with them.

One day, riding through Oradea with Pastor Nick, the two Americans saw a man with a knife in his hand pursuing another man. As the two Romanians ran along a trolley track, Nick stopped the car. Wendell shouted, "Go get him, Russ!"

The boss had spoken, so Russ jumped out of the back seat, sprinted across the street, and chased the man with the knife. Realizing Russ was catching up on him, the man threw his knife in the bushes but kept running. As the man came upon a stopped trolley, Russ closed the gap between them, made a flying tackle, and knocked the man to the ground. The Romanian was terrified and obviously had been drinking, for the smell was overwhelming. Russ stood the man on his feet and wrapped his arms around him.

Pastor Nick yelled to Russ to bring the man to the car. Russ wrestled him across the street and put him in the back seat, hopping in beside him. By this time, the man was crying and begging Nick, in Romanian, to let him go.

Nick drove through the streets looking for a police officer or a soldier, but none was in sight. He said, "Can you believe it? They are constantly following us and harassing us wherever we go, but when you need one, you can't find him!"

Finally, they saw an officer leading several of his men along the sidewalk. Nick stopped and explained the situation. The officer replied, "Sorry, this section of the city is not under my jurisdiction!" Nick threw up his hands and, tired of hearing the crying and pleading of the drunken assailant, let him go.

Russ' clothes were a mess, and he smelled of alcohol. Wendell said, "Beautiful tackle, Russ!" *All in the line of duty,* Russ thought.

Before leaving Oradea, pastors Nick and Paul extended an invitation to Wendell and Russ to return to hold a week of evangelistic services in the Second Baptist Church. They didn't know it at that time, but Russ and Wendell's visit to Romania was God's way of helping ABWE fulfill the ten-year goal of having an effective ministry in restricted access countries.

The next year, Dr. Kempton returned for that evangelistic campaign. With him was a music team, including Michael and JoBeth Loftis. In January of 1988, Russ and Nancy were part of a weeklong campaign with a different music team.

Hundreds of people received Jesus Christ as their Savior during those campaigns. And, while in Romania in 1987, Michael and JoBeth Loftis were challenged to give their lives for missionary service with ABWE in Eastern and Central Europe. In 1990, as ABWE missionaries, they pioneered that new ministry. In the 12 years of their leadership, more than 100 missionaries were appointed to serve in Hungary, Romania, Ukraine, Slovakia, Croatia, Bosnia and Herzegovina, and Russia. On March 1, 2001, Dr. Michael Loftis became ABWE's fourth president.

# Chapter Thirty-eight

# Family Reunion

It was Christmas at the family home in Shamong, New Jersey, and the Ebersoles were playing a game. Son-in-law, Dr. Dennis Costerisan, asked the question, "If you could be anywhere in the world right now, where would that be?" Each one wrote his answer on a paper napkin. When Dennis collected the responses, everyone had written the same place: Baguio, the summer capital of the Philippines. Baguio is located 150 miles north of Manila and is nearly one mile in elevation.

This did not surprise any of the players, for most of them had enjoyed wonderful vacations in Baguio during their years in the Philippines.

ABWE owns a lovely facility in Baguio, consisting of six apartments (each with its own fireplace) and a recreation hall. The grounds include a basketball practice court and a children's play area. Mrs. Marguerite Doane, a generous benefactor of the mission, purchased the property prior to World War II. She wished to provide a place for rest, relaxation, and rejuvenation. The complex was named Doane Rest in her honor. Doane Rest became the favorite vacation spot for missionaries—if space was available. Missionary families throughout the Philippines and other parts of Southeast Asia treasured happy memories of days spent at Doane Rest.

When Russ and Nancy heard the word "Baguio," they both smiled knowingly. They had long dreamed of holding a family reunion at this place they all loved. But could that dream ever become reality?

Russ and Nancy realized that five of their eight children would be in Asia the following year: Harold and Shawne would be in Bangladesh; Bruce and Sharon, and their small daughter, Christine, would soon transfer as short-term ABWE missionaries from Port Moresby in Papua New Guinea to Baguio itself, to direct the student center there.

Then there were the three doctors: *Russ,* Melody, and their three children were stationed north of Manila at Subic Naval Base, where he was a pediatrician at the Cubi Point Hospital. *Dennis* Costerisan, Cheri, and their three children, were located on the tiny island of Yap, in Micronesia. Dennis was serving four years with the Public Health Service, paying back his medical education. And *John* Briggs, Susan, and their two children were on the island of Saipan, where John was paying off his medical school debts.

On their 1989 Asia ministry trip, Russ and Nancy briefly touched base with each of the children. They asked what would be the best time for a family reunion. The consensus was January 25 to February 5, 1990.

Russ phoned Doane Rest and talked to their good friends Priscilla Bailey and Millie Crouch, then the guesthouse hostesses. He asked, "Do you have any vacancies next year for January 25 to February 5?" Amazingly, they responded, "Yes, the whole compound is free. Why?"

Russ replied, "We'd like to have a family reunion there at that time." Millie, always a comedian, chuckled, "I'm not sure even the whole compound is adequate for your family, Russ. But it's available, and we'd love to have your gang here."

Immediately, Russ and Nancy contacted the family and began to think through the tremendous logistical challenges they faced.

They learned that Russ and Melody were expecting their fourth child on January 25, the first day of their planned reunion at Doane Rest.

Russ and Nancy were also concerned because Harold and Shawne would need a visa to allow them to leave and return to Bangladesh—not a simple matter to obtain.

Because of limited resources, Beth told her parents that her family could not afford to go to the Philippines. And even if they did somehow find the money, Bob probably could not get that time off from teaching and coaching at Northside Christian School, in St. Petersburg, Florida. When the brothers and sisters heard about this, they said, "It won't be a family reunion without Bob and Beth!"

Joy, the only Ebersole unmarried at that time, was engaged to John McQuade. She hoped he would be able to join her to meet her family members who would not be able to attend their wedding.

Faith's passport got lost in the mail a few days before their departure.

Then Russ and Nancy watched as God caused all the details to fall into place:

- Russ and Melody's baby, Stephen, made an early appearance.
- Harold and Shawne's visa was granted in time.
- The Ebersole siblings chipped in to provide the needed airfare for Bob and Beth, and Bob's school allowed him the time off.
- Faith was able to get her passport replaced before the flight.

Over a two-day period, and from various directions, the Ebersole family descended on the Manila International Airport. By the early morning of January 26, all travelers had arrived.

Bruce arranged for a small tour bus to take the family around Manila that same morning. Their first stop was their home in Loyola Heights, where the family lived for seven years. The Ebersole children wanted their spouses to see where they spent many happy days while they were growing up.

Russ first went next door to say hello to his friend Ruben Asedillo, an attorney. Ruben was surprised to see Russ, and asked, "How is the family?" Russ grinned and said, "They're all outside in a bus, Ruben. Come on out and see for yourself!"

As Ruben walked out and saw the bus filled with Ebersole children and grandchildren, he said, "Russ, this is unbelievable!" He then explained that the Ebersole's old home next door was now occupied by a Filipino family who had moved in just the week before.

The lady of that home was out front working in the yard. Russ looked over the gate and greeted her. He explained that his family had spent seven years in that house and had returned for a family reunion. They would love to see the house again, if she would allow it. She was startled to see how big the family actually was but, being a true Filipina, she graciously invited them all inside.

The next stop, a half hour or so ride away, was Faith Academy, the largest MK school in the world. All eight Ebersole children attended there; six of them graduated from the school. The kids were excited to see many of their former teachers. They also visited one of the dorms where Nita, the family's former cook and dear friend, now worked. They found her busy in the kitchen. Quietly, Bruce walked up behind her and lifted her into the air. Astonished, she swung around and said, "Bruce, I didn't know you were in the Philippines. Only you would do a thing like this!"

Their next stop was the beautiful American cemetery, located in perhaps the quietest place in all Manila. Reverently, they looked out on the hundreds of white markers stretched across the grass carpet, reminding them of the high price paid to liberate the Philippines, their adopted country, from Japanese invaders in World War II.

Long before they arrived in Manila, Russ and Nancy had

written to Mrs. Enriqueta Arquesola. Quita, as she was called, had been a beloved member of the Ebersole family. She began working with them in 1954, when Gene and Russ first arrived in the Philippines. Ten years later, she accompanied the family to the States when Gene was so ill with cancer. Quita was a great help to the Ebersole family during the weeks before and after Gene's death until she returned to the Philippines.

Quita married a fine Christian man, Joling Arquesola, a foreman in a copper mine in the mountains of south Negros. She had two grown children. It would not be a family reunion without Quita! In Manila, when she saw Beth with her baby girl, Emily, Quita squealed, "She is just like you were, Beth. She is a 'little Beth.'" Quita took the baby into her arms and, for most of the reunion, that's exactly where Emily stayed.

The next day the Ebersole clan boarded a bus for Baguio, filling it with bodies and baggage. The five-hour trip from Manila is challenging, especially when the bus begins to snake around the many hairpin curves in the mountains leading to Baguio City. Bob constantly leaned out a front window to take pictures with his video camera, shouting, "What a fantastic ride!"

Arriving in Baguio, the Ebersoles settled into their apartments at Doane Rest. Since Bruce and Sharon were living at Doane Rest while they worked at the Student Center, they assumed much of the responsibility for organizing such a large group.

Plans called for one or two families in rotation to care for cooking the meals, which they all ate together in the recreation hall. Each day, one of the men led devotions. The Ebersoles also took advantage of as many of Baguio's attractions as possible.

For many years, Camp John Hay had been an American R&R base. While it primarily served military personnel, Filipino and American civilians could also use most of the base's facilities, including a beautiful golf course, tennis courts, a bowling alley, and playgrounds, as well as several good restaurants.

Baguio offered horse and pony rides, which the grandchildren loved. A small downtown lake sported several kinds of boats for rent. And the Baguio market is famous for its great selection of vegetables, fruits, and beautiful flowers. Baguio is the center for the famous Filipino woodcarvings and other fine native handicrafts—a wonderful place to shop!

The Ebersole family postponed Christmas celebrations until the reunion in Baguio. Their friends Don and Polly Taber, at that time the hosts at Doane Rest, loaned them a small artificial Christmas tree. After dinner one night, the grandchildren decorated the tree with typical Filipino ornaments and hung up their stockings.

The next morning, Cheri organized a family Christmas buffet breakfast after the stockings were opened. Shawne read the Christmas story. Then everyone opened the gifts brought from the States.

One evening, babysitters made it possible for the adults, including Quita, to enjoy an engagement dinner for John and Joy at the Forest House. A beautiful, wooden teacart was their engagement gift from the family.

On both Sundays in Baguio, the family divided up to attend several area churches; Bruce spoke at one of them. Some of his siblings and Quita went to hear him preach. After the service, Quita ran up to him and, with tears in her eyes, said, "Oh, Brucie, you were such a naughty little boy and now you are preaching!"

Bruce replied with a laugh, "Quita, now I'm a naughty big boy!"

The entire family went to the Hyatt for the hotel's special buffet breakfast. Some months later, a powerful earthquake hit Baguio City; it destroyed many buildings including the Hyatt Hotel. In the very place where the Ebersoles enjoyed that buffet breakfast, several people were killed.

After one Sunday morning service in a new church in Trinidad Valley, the pastor, Carlos Salinas, invited the family to lunch at a Chinese restaurant. Russ asked him, "Brother Salinas, do you realize how many are in our family?" Pastor Salinas, a businessman, assured Russ that he did.

Pastor and Mrs. Salinas were greatly used by God to start a number of churches in mountain provinces. They also financially assisted many other churches and Christian ministries. Some years later, Russ and Nancy were saddened to hear that Carlos had died on an operating table in Texas, where he had gone for heart surgery. His wife and children continue to serve the Lord faithfully in various parts of the Philippines.

All good things must come to an end, including the Ebersole's Baguio family reunion. As they left the "City of Pines" by planes and buses, each of the party thanked the Lord for making the dream a reality.

# Chapter Thirty-nine

# Overcoming the Wrath of Man

Missionary work and especially foreign travel are greatly influenced by world events. War clouds hung over the Middle East, and just as it was time for the Ebersoles to leave on their Far Eastern trip in 1991, Iraq invaded Kuwait, and tensions in the Gulf began. Americans were warned not to travel to many destinations, several of which were on the Ebersoles' itinerary. Acts of terrorism were expected at airports and many other places. News reports told daily of escalating events as Saddam Hussein carried out his mad schemes. Nancy remembered the hijacking of many years earlier and, having served in a Muslim country, decided that ignorance would have been bliss. She didn't have the luxury of ignorance.

The Ebersoles were scheduled to fly through London. Normally the flight would continue over the Middle East, so Nancy asked Russ if they could change their tickets and fly from the West Coast. But their tickets were non-refundable. Nancy suggested postponing their trip until things settled down. But Russ felt keenly that some of the people they were responsible for were in difficult circumstances, and they should not flinch. He felt it was just the time they should be on hand to encourage people.

On the Sunday before their proposed departure, Nancy suddenly said to Russ as they walked home from church, "I can't leave on this trip with you unless God gives me peace." Russ hardly knew how to respond. They both began to pray fervently that God would give Nancy the needed peace. Russ made several phone calls. One of them was to their friend Loren Reno, then serving at the Pentagon. Colonel Reno gave some precautions to follow, but assured Russ that if God was leading them to go, they could rest in His hands.

On Wednesday morning, just a few days before they were to leave, Nancy was reading in Deuteronomy during her devotions. The verses she read seemed to have been written just for her. She read, *"The beloved of the Lord shall dwell in safety by him; and the Lord shall cover him all the day long, and he shall dwell between his shoulders"* (Deuteronomy 33:12). As she read that, she thought, *I am beloved of the Lord and can rest in Him. He will shield me. I can rest as secure in Him as our grandchildren do in us when they lay their heads on our shoulders.* She read on. Deuteronomy 33:26 seemed to jump from the page straight into her heart. *"There is none like unto the God of Jeshurun, who rideth upon the heaven in thy help, and in his excellency on the sky."*

Nancy and Russ would spend hours in the heavens on long flights. Why should she be afraid? Then she read on to the familiar verse, reassuring her that God would be their refuge: *"The eternal God is thy refuge, and underneath are the everlasting arms"* (Deuteronomy 33:27a).

An overwhelming sense of peace swept over her. She went directly to phone Russ, who was working at the ABWE office. She said, "I'm all right now, honey. God has given me complete peace." Then she shared with him the verses God had used. They left on the trip, sensing God's protective hand in a special way.

During a later Far Eastern trip in February 1995, Russ and Nancy stayed at the Christian and Missionary Alliance (C&MA) Guest Home in Bangkok, one of their favorite oases. One morning at breakfast, they met a gracious Cambodian woman who worked for the Far East Broadcasting Company. She had a great burden for her country which she shared in detail with the Ebersoles.

The same day at the CM&A guest home, Russ and Nancy

met the J. D. Crowleys, a young couple working among tribal people in the northeast section of Cambodia. Mrs. Crowley was expecting a child, and they had come to Bangkok for her delivery. J. D. loved Cambodia and its people. Their new Cambodian friend and the Crowleys encouraged the Ebersoles to investigate the possibility of ABWE starting a ministry there.

That same afternoon, Russ and Nancy met with Somboone Agunsri and Pastor Kiatisak Sirapanadorn. These men were the first Thai converts of PABWE's ministry. PABWE had sent its first missionaries, the Roberto Gequillanas, to Thailand in 1964. Somboone and Pastor Kiatisak attended PABWE's first young people's camp and were saved at the same service. Pastor Kiatisak later studied at the Doane Baptist Bible Seminary, in Iloilo City, where he trained to be a pastor. For many years he has pastored the Grace Baptist Church in Bangkok. Somboone, after college, began working for Thai International Airlines. He was now one of the airline's pursers and a faithful layman at Grace Baptist.

Russ told about the discussions he and Nancy had earlier in the day, and mentioned how much he would like to visit Cambodia. He was interested to see if the doors of Cambodia might open up for ABWE ministry.

Somboone asked about Russ' schedule. It was tight, but there were two days the following week when, if possible, Russ could fly to Cambodia. Somboone was on the phone immediately, calling a friend at Thai Airlines. "Could Russ get tickets for those two days?" Somboone asked. The answer was, "It will be difficult because those flights are booked, but I will try." The man was as good as his word. Within half an hour he called back saying he had the reservations.

Pastor Kiatisak then told Russ that he had a close friend in Phnom Penh, Cambodia's capital. "I'll phone him right away," Kiatisak said. Within a few minutes, he arranged for his friend to meet Russ at the airport, and to provide Russ with a car and a driver during his stay.

The next day, Russ and Nancy spent more time with their new Cambodian friend and the Crowleys. J. D. dictated a letter to the minister of religious affairs in Phnom Penh. The Cambodian woman took this dictation and wrote the letter in the Khmer language. Pieces were falling into place for Russ' brief visit the next week.

Russ and Nancy ministered in Sakhon Nakon, in northeast Thailand, just before Russ left for Cambodia. PABWE missionaries Art and Phoebe Inion had worked there for a number of years and established a church in that large town. Art had been a member of the young people's group in Bacolod City, in the Philippines, years before when Gene was the advisor. God had wonderfully worked in Art's life during that time and called him into the ministry. Russ was looking forward to their time together.

After a busy weekend in Sakhon Nakon, the Ebersoles flew back to Bangkok on Monday, and on Tuesday morning Russ flew into Cambodia. He was met at the airport by Pastor Chua, Pastor Kiatisak's friend, and a young Cambodian pastor visiting from the United States. They had made hotel reservations and dropped Russ off so he could get settled.

The young pastor later returned with a car and driver, making it possible for Russ to cover a lot of ground during his brief stay. Stopping at the Bureau of Religious Affairs, Russ was not able to see the director. However, he had a lengthy discussion with the assistant, a friendly woman who gave Russ helpful information on how his organization might enter Cambodia.

Russ visited the C&MA office. The mission ran CAMA, a fine handicraft project, in the country. They were cooperative and gave further information. Russ also visited a small, independent Bible school in the center of Phnom Penh.

One stop that will forever be etched on Russ' mind was Tuol Sleng, the prison which had been a school building before the Khmer Rouge. The school became a brutal torture prison where thousands of people were executed. The public was now able to view the cells and instruments of torture. The last of the gruesome exhibits was a room with a large map of Cambodia made of hundreds of skulls of people who had been killed in that place.

During his visit, Russ learned much about Cambodia. Between 1975 and 1979, the fanatical Khmer Rouge government of Pol Pot brutally murdered over two million Cambodians, between one-quarter and one-third of the entire population. The forced evacuation of all cities and towns to concentration camps, the savage killing of former military and civilian leaders, as well as those who were wealthy or educated and religious leaders of all kinds, left the country in a degraded, primitive state. The vast majority of Christians were cruelly killed in an effort to "purify" the Khmer people from religious influence.

A quarter century of war and genocide left a horrible mark on this once outwardly placid country. Today, Cambodia has one of the poorest economies in the world. Many who survived the horror of Pol Pot's camps have permanent emotional scars, and the nation is still in spiritual bondage to the terror and violence, with demonic overtones, that have rent the nation asunder.

Although Christianity was nearly wiped out by the Khmer Rouge during the late 1970s, the devastation of war and genocide brought an openness to the gospel. In the refugee camps of Thailand during the terrible 1970s, large numbers of despairing Cambodians turned to Christ. Since that time, some have returned to their home country to share their faith. There continues to be a great openness to the gospel at the present time, both in Phnom Penh and, even more so, in the provinces.

In 1980 there were only approximately 600 Christians in the entire country. As few as ten small house churches existed at that time in the nation. In 1990 Cambodia accorded legal status to the Christian community. By 1995, estimates of the number of Christians in Cambodia varied from 5,000 to 30,000! Estimates of the numbers of churches/congregations varied from 30 to

300. This growth is attributed to the fact that the gospel brings hope to a country where social norms disintegrated during the political chaos of recent decades.

The people of Cambodia had suffered much. Many of God's servants lost their lives during the Khmer Rouge's bloody regime. Sobered by what he had seen and learned, Russ boarded his plane for Bangkok. How grateful he felt that the hand of his loving God was still at work among Cambodia's suffering people. Russ prayed, "Lord, may it be your will to open the door of this land to ABWE!"

On that same trip, the Ebersoles spent time with experienced ABWE missionaries Jim and Shirlie Moore. The Moores had served as church planters and in other capacities in the Philippines. They had been involved in moving the Grand Rapids Baptist Seminary Extension Program (GRBSEP) from Manila to Singapore. During 1995, when Russ and Nancy visited, Jim was in charge of the ABWE business office in Manila. Russ shared his burden for Cambodia and challenged the Moores to consider working in that country.

In April 1996, the ABWE board voted unanimously to approve the opening of Cambodia as a new ABWE field. Jim and Shirlie Moore participated in a survey of Cambodia in September 1996. They were so concerned by what they saw that they determined God was leading them to spearhead ABWE's work in Phnom Penh.

Within a couple of years, others joined them, including Robert and Kristi Cady, Angela Atwell, and Dr. Barry and Katherine White, who transferred from Togo.

Through Bible studies and personal contacts, groups of new believers and interested inquirers are forming. Reaching out to the thousands of street children whose lives are often in danger has won many children and their families for Christ, resulting in a growing congregation of adult believers.

Vietnam was another country in Southeast Asia that had

closed its doors to missionaries in 1975. It was as well known to Americans as any country in that part of the world, thanks to the divisive Vietnam War. Russ hoped to visit Vietnam, if possible. On a visit to Bangkok, Thailand, in 1995, Russ was given the name of an American working with an NGO (non-government organization) in Vietnam. His agency helped rural communities in a variety of ways and had contacts with the underground church. Russ was given his telephone number in Ho Chi Minh City (formerly Saigon), but was unable to reach him.

After a full Sunday morning ministering in one of the Bangkok churches, Russ and Nancy returned to the C&MA Guest Home for a brief rest. That evening, Russ was scheduled to speak at another church in the city. They still had not been able to talk with their contact in Ho Chi Minh City, and were to fly to Vietnam the next day.

Just before they went to their room, they met a young man who knew their contact man in Ho Chi Minh City and told them he had a new telephone number. No wonder Russ had been unable to reach him! The young man, who had grown up as an MK in Vietnam, also gave Russ helpful information about Ho Chi Minh City and explained the current religious atmosphere in the country.

The next morning, the Ebersoles were pleasantly surprised at the hassle-free customs formalities in Ho Chi Minh City. They took a cab and drove into the city to their hotel.

Russ phoned his contact immediately. The man planned to leave the city for a visit in an outlying province the next morning, but agreed to see the Ebersoles that evening.

Russ and Nancy ate an early dinner, then walked the streets of Ho Chi Minh City. They were amazed by the new construction and refurbishing going on throughout the city.

Their contact joined them at the hotel later in the evening. He described the government's attitude toward religious groups and explained that it was possible to set up non-government organizations if a mission had experienced personnel and professionals the government felt could provide services the country wanted. He also shared some of the exciting things God was doing in Vietnam. How grateful the Ebersoles were that the Lord had provided his telephone number and arranged for him to be in Ho Chi Minh City that night.

By the end of the 1990s, ABWE had a gateway to enter and stay in Vietnam through teaching English as a Second Language. Contacts had also been made with indigenous pastors and small house churches.

ABWE's first career missionary couple for Vietnam began evaluating and developing ministry opportunities there in 1998. Later, in 1999, the board voted officially to open Vietnam as an ABWE field.

# Chapter Forty

# Finishing the Race

The cover of this book shows an intricate design hand woven by Igorot tribal women living in the mountains on the island of Luzon in the Philippines.

Just as weavers planned and produced their beautiful cloth, the Master Weaver continues to create the fabric of Russ and Nancy's lives. Many colorful threads have been divinely woven through unusual and exciting events.

But, as is true in each life, the muted colors of daily experiences, including difficult times of responsibility and testing, have played a vital part in the pattern God has designed.

**Grateful Caregiving**

For ten years, much of Nancy's time and energy revolved around the care of both her own and Russ's mother. Nancy was thankful for siblings, children, and friends who shared this responsibility.

Nancy never forgot the agony of the day she had to tell her mother she could no longer live alone in the little Indiana farmhouse which had been her home for over 50 years. Each of them shed tears as they discussed her future.

The decision was made that her mother, Mrs. Goodman, would spend time with each of her four children in turn. This allowed Nancy to travel with Russ on his ministry trips. However, within a few years, both Nancy's younger sister, Shirley, and only brother, Roger, died of cancer. Nancy ached for her mother because of these grievous losses.

After these deaths, Mrs. Goodman spent half of the year with Nancy and the other half with her older sister, Marilyn Miller, in Florida. Nancy's ministry with Russ was greatly curtailed as she daily gave full care to her mother. Yet she believed this was an equally important ministry before God. She daily prayed that God would be glorified through it.

When Mrs. Goodman became ill with pneumonia and was hospitalized, Russ and Nancy realized that Nancy did not have the strength to continue caring for her mother at home. Nancy and her sister had to make a decision which Nancy had said in her younger years she would never make: to move her mother to a place where she could receive round-the-clock care.

Several years before this, Russ' mother had expressed the desire to be in a Christian retirement center. She had lived for five years with Russ and Nancy in a lovely little apartment attached to their home. While living there, she made many wonderful friends at Shawnee Baptist Church, which adjoined the Ebersoles' property.

Russ and his sister, Doris Waldrop, investigated and decided on a fine Christian full-care facility in Quarryville, Pennsylvania. This was also where Mildred Goodman spent her last months. She lived until she was 96. Russ' mother, Sue, enjoyed her five years in the unassisted living section of the same facility, making many friends and having a bright testimony. A few months after the homegoing of Mrs. Goodman, Mrs. Ebersole fell and broke her hip. From that time until her death the following March, at the age of 99½, her health failed.

During the traumatic losses of Russ' and Nancy's first mates years before, Nancy's mother and Russ' parents had provided homes and loving care for Russ and Nancy and their children over a period of years. The care that Russ and Nancy were able to provide for their elderly mothers was a small token of their deep gratitude.

## Passing the Baton

Years ago while at Wheaton College, Russ ran on the mile relay team. He passed many batons to his teammates. In 1995, Russ passed another baton, that of administering ABWE's Far East fields, to a beloved colleague, Bill Commons, who ran his leg of the race with distinction. In January 2002, Bill presented the baton to ABWE missionary to the Philippines, Kent Craig, as Kent became the regional administrator for the Far East. Bill Commons was appointed the vice president for strategic initiative and research.

The ABWE board appointed Russ as vice-president of missionary ministries in 1995. In that role, he and Nancy are involved in care giving. One of their major responsibilities is directing the ministry of "debriefing." Along with other mission personnel, Russ and Nancy conduct lengthy interviews with each furloughing missionary, allowing the returnees to air the highs and lows of their terms of service.

Russ's speaking schedule in North America remains full and fruitful. The Ebersoles also continue their overseas travel, seeking to encourage and share God's Word with missionaries and nationals throughout ABWE's world.

During ABWE's 75th anniversary in 2002, Russ was asked to chair the planning committee for a number of anniversary banquets. The first was held on January 31, in Iloilo City, Philippines, where ABWE started in 1927 and where Russ and Gene began their missionary careers.

In February 2002, Russ wrote,

> Greetings from Iloilo City. I want you to know the Lord has answered our prayers in giving us a wonderful 75th anniversary banquet on January 31, with 220 people attending from all parts of the Philippines. What a thrill to see so many with whom I served and fellowshipped over the years.
>
> I was especially blessed by the presence of Alejandro Caspe, a 94-year-old pastor from the far island of Palawan. To

my knowledge he is the only living pastor who knew the founder of our mission, Dr. Raphael C. Thomas, in the 1920s. I interviewed him as part of the banquet; his sense of humor is still sharp and he still preaches once a month!

On February 1, we had an outdoor rally at Doane Baptist Bible College and Seminary, with over 800 attending. I wish you could have heard the 75-voice choir singing "A Mighty Fortress Is Our God!" Martin Luther's heart must have been rejoicing. We were thankful to have ABWE's former president, Dr. Wendell Kempton, speak at both meetings. An unexpected finale the night of the rally was a large 75th anniversary logo in fireworks high above the crowd and then an explosion of fireworks.

The Lord has given Russ and Nancy rich and exciting lives in which they have continually experienced the great faithfulness and the good hand of God. They have a deep desire to finish well. They echo Paul's words in Acts 20:24, *"But none of these things move me, neither count I my life dear unto myself, so that I might finish my course with joy, and the ministry, which I have received of the Lord Jesus, to testify the gospel of the grace of God."*

### The Interwoven Family

Russ and Nancy thank God for His grace at work in the lives of their eight children who are walking with the Lord. Along with their believing mates, they are seeking to rear their children for God's glory.

When asked how it is that all of their children are walking with the Lord, Russ and Nancy say, "It is God's grace. We certainly didn't have all the answers and often fell on our knees seeking God's guidance. We pointed them to Scriptural principles."

One of the great advantages their children have had is the prayers of God's people. Many were especially burdened to pray because of their loss of a parent.

Shortly after Gene went to be with the Lord, Russ was preaching in her home church in Grand Rapids, Michigan. After the service, a dear friend, Gladys Meyer, approached Russ and asked if she could pray for a special need of his children. Six-year-old Bruce was having an especially difficult time adjusting to his mother's death. Gladys promised to pray for him.

Many years later, Russ was preaching at the same church during a missionary conference. He was amazed to see Gladys come in with her daughter, for he knew that she was having severe health problems. At the close of the service, she told him that she seldom was able to attend church but wanted to see and hear Russ. And, she wanted to know about Bruce. How thrilled she was to know that he was having a fruitful ministry as a youth pastor in New Jersey—a wonderful answer to her daily prayers of over 30 years!

*A special prayer request of Russ and Nancy to all readers of this book would be that you pray for their children and their families:*

### Russ and Melody Ebersole

Russ married his college sweetheart, Melody, a music major, a year after they graduated from college. After medical school, Russ served as a medical officer in the U.S. Navy, including a tour at the Subic Naval Base in the Philippines. Resigning his commission, he entered private practice as a pediatrician. When God challenged Russ and Melody to foreign missions, Russ left his practice and they applied to ABWE. They were appointed in 1998 for missionary service in Togo, West Africa, where they will serve at the Karolyn Kempton Memorial Hospital. Russ and Melody have five children, four of whom will accompany them to Africa.

### Dennis and Cheryl Costerisan

Dennis and Cheryl were high school classmates at Faith Academy in Manila, Philippines. In college, Cheryl trained to be a nurse. After college graduation and marriage, Dennis attended medical school with a public health scholarship. After graduating, he was assigned to the small island of Yap, in Micronesia, for four years as he fulfilled his medical training obligations. He is now a busy family physician in Mount Zion, Illinois. Dennis and Cheryl actively serve the Lord in their local church. They have four children.

### Bob and Beth Dare

Bob and Beth were classmates at Bible college. Since their marriage, they have served the Lord for many years in St. Petersburg, Florida, at the Northside Christian Schools, where Bob is the athletic director and football coach. Beth teaches Bible to middle-schoolers and is the school photographer. They have four children.

### Harold and Shawne Ebersole

Harold was trained as a high school science teacher and taught in several Christian high schools. As a short-term teacher in Bangladesh, God challenged him to missions, after which he took seminary training. God led him and Shawne, an elementary teacher, together when she was an ABWE appointee. They have served the Lord in Bangladesh since 1988. Harold, a Bible translator, is also chairman of the large field council, and Shawne teaches MKs. They have two children.

### Bruce and Sharon Ebersole

After graduating from Bible college, Bruce and Sharon, a nurse, were married. After 11 fruitful years in the youth pastorate, Bruce, with a number of young couples, started a new church in Denville, New Jersey. They are excited about what God is doing there. Bruce and Sharon have five children.

### John and Susan Briggs

John and Susan met in college. After graduation, they married and John studied medicine. In order to pay back his medical debts, he served on the island of Saipan for four years. John and Susan live in Fremont, Michigan, where John is a busy family physician. They are serving the Lord in their local church. They have five children.

### John and Joy McQuade

Joy graduated with a B.S. in nursing. She worked several years before she met her husband, John, at the college and career group at their church. John graduated from college after they were married. He is the materials coordinator of Safe Masters in Barrington, New Jersey, where they live. They are active in their local church and have six children.

### Scott and Faith Parker

Scott and Faith met at their church's college and career group. Faith is a nurse. Scott works on the Philadelphia Stock Exchange. They live in Shamong, New Jersey, just a few minutes from Russ and Nancy. They serve in their church and have five children.

How grateful Russ and Nancy are to the Lord for His faithful leadership in the lives of their children and grandchildren (all 36 of them!). They rejoice in seeing how the Lord is also weaving into their lives the pattern of His design.

> *"Behold, children are a heritage from the Lord,*
> *The fruit of the womb is a reward.*
> *Like arrows in the hand of a warrior,*
> *So are children of one's youth.*
> *Happy is the man who has his quiver full of them."*
> (Psalm 127:3, 4)

> *"I have no greater joy than to hear that my children*
> *walk in truth."*
> (3 John, verse 4)

The authors and the publisher of this book
invite you to correspond if you wish to know more
about Christ and the Christian life.

ABWE
P.O. Box 8585
Harrisburg, PA 17105-8585

For more information regarding ABWE or books
by ABWE Publishing, visit our website:
www.abwe.org or phone toll free 1-877-959-2293.